Ordinary Men, Extraordinary Lives: Defining Moments

Compiled and Edited by
Jim Sharon, Ed.D.

Published by Energy for Life
Centennial, Colorado

First printing 2011

ISBN: 9780983649205

LCCN: 2011933290

This book is dedicated to people everywhere who actively devote themselves to fostering genuine love, peace, and well-being on our precious planet.

Acknowledgments

First, I want to thank Lisa Shultz and Andrea Costantine, who compiled *Speaking Your Truth: Courageous Stories from Inspiring Women,* for paving the way for me to consider compiling this book. Witnessing the popularity of their women's anthology gave me confidence that a men's anthology could be a viable undertaking. Also, Andrea offered strong encouragement and clear writing guidelines during an orientation seminar for contributing authors and, months later, followed up by volunteering to edit several men's manuscript drafts.

Aside from serving as "midwife" for our book by gently suggesting I might want to develop a male counterpart to *Speaking Your Truth,* my wife Ruth Sharon offered me tremendous support and encouragement throughout the project. Consistent with her attentive, serving nature, Ruth often affirmed that this was the "perfect" project for me, reminded me to pace myself, and assisted by editing several stories and responding to my periodic questions about word choice or grammar. She also did an exceptional job proofreading half of the anthology. I am especially appreciative of Ruth's vision, clarity, and inspiration regarding the book and Whole Man Expo, an outgrowth of the anthology project.

Obviously, without the contributions of the anthology authors, this book would not have come to fruition. I am extremely grateful to each of them for perceiving the value of collective male transparency as a much-needed and wanted service to people (not just men) worldwide. These very caring men deeply touched my heart with their dedication and rigor, as well as their trust in me to edit and publish our book. Many guys graciously offered various forms of support during our synergistic work together and I am indebted to them for standing by my side. I strengthened some friendships, including several long-term ones, and made new friends in the course of working closely with these awesome men.

Sue Collier of Self-Publishing Resources continually demonstrated that I made a great choice in selecting her among the many publishing coaches I interviewed to shepherd the book through every stage. Knowledgeable in all aspects of self-publishing, Sue pleased me with direct, clear answers to my barrage of questions at each meeting. Her warm and easygoing personality was icing on the cake.

Kate Deubert, a member of Sue Collier's team, was also an absolute pleasure to work with, and proved to be an excellent copy-editing. The authors and I had considerable confidence in Kate's work.

I am very grateful to Kyle Durlam of Durlam Design for efficiently and elegantly designing the book cover and doing page layout. Kyle regularly accommodated my schedule and generously discounted his services. He and I got along famously throughout our work together.

My son Michael Sharon of Future Films did a masterful job filming and editing a YouTube project introduction and the author's orientation seminar. He will also be the main videographer and film editor for Whole Man Expo.

Many thanks to Bill Green and Nathan Hindman from Sagen Media for designing the anthology booksite and to my daughter Alaina Green for frequently providing outstanding professional marketing assistance.

I am really enjoying and valuing my relatively new relationship with the staff of Lightning Source, who have eased the way for me in their printing and distribution of our anthology.

True to form, my good friend Maury Cohen of Editrix generously volunteered to substantively edit a few of our manuscripts, including my own; her contributions markedly enhanced the stories she edited.

I extend deep appreciation to the renowned professionals who contributed strong endorsements of this book (see the back cover). Each of them took time from their busy schedule to review the book and craft their comments. I am especially grateful to Roy Baumeister, Ph.D., who humbly accepted edits of his Foreword draft and was willing to promptly rework it, providing an evocative dimension to this anthology.

Finally, I want to extend my appreciation to family members and friends who graciously made monetary contributions during the incipient stages of this project: Dana Cain, Chris and Sylvia Ebersberg, Paulette Dittemore, Richard Eidlin and Heather Shannon, Alaina and Bill Green, Rob Hamilton, Eliot and Eileen Lowey, John and Sue Mariner, Miriam Sharon, Margie Tyler, and Eileen and Joel Yager.

With deep gratitude,
Jim Sharon

Table of Contents

Foreword

by Roy Baumeister, Ph.D.

What is it like to be a man? Ironically, these days the answers come mostly from women. The scholarly work on gender is primarily written by women, indeed often by feminists. It is rare to hear what men have to say about being men. The present book is a very welcome exception, with men telling their own stories about their lives.

One solid scientific fact about gender is that men are more different from each other than women are from one another. What researchers call "male variability" has been documented in many different contexts. It affects even simple things such as height: There are wider variations in how tall men are than in how tall women are. Intelligence is another, more important example. When Lawrence Summers, then president of Harvard, ignited a firestorm of controversy by suggesting there are more men with super-high IQs than women, he was actually standing on solid scientific ground. People thought he was saying men are smarter than women, but in fact there are more men at both extremes. There is absolutely no question there are more retarded boys than girls.

Behaviorally too, men go to extremes more than women, and this book will illuminate the wide range of male experience. One point of departure for my book, *Is There Anything Good About Men?*, was a flaw in the feminist critique of society. Feminists correctly looked up to the top stratum of societies all over the world and saw mainly men: There are far more male than female presidents, senators, corporate CEOs, and the like. Seeing all this, feminists quite reasonably concluded that society is set up to favor men: It must be great to be a man. The mistake in that way of thinking is the failure to look at the bottom rungs of society—prisoners, junkies, homeless persons, "losers"—who are also disproportionately male. Men find their way to the extremes. You will hear some of their voices in this book.

Men's penchant to take risks and end up at either the top or the bottom of society is one of the driving engines of social progress. And that brings us to one of the great things about men one hears very little about these days. It was men who created culture and progress. Art, literature, theology, philosophy, technology, science, medicine, government, economic trade—all these things and more developed from the way men related to each other. It is not because of any innate superior capacity that men have, nor is it because of any inherent evil traits that made men conspire together to defraud and oppress women. It stems simply from the way men organize and relate to each other. While women specialize in creating wonderfully intimate pair bonds, men tend to create large networks of shallow relationships. These are not as satisfying or nurturing as women's intimate relationships. But they are a fertile basis for establishing systems to share information and accomplish tasks. Ultimately, that is why human culture emerged mainly from men's relationships, fostering the problem of gender inequality that bedevils the modern world. Men generated wealth, knowledge, and power. Women's very real contributions have mostly lain elsewhere.

The fact that men created wealth, knowledge, and power propelled men to the dominant position in society, and women have suffered as a result. Yet men have suffered too. Creating human civilization was not a straight and pleasant path. Groups of men competed against other groups, and many men lost these competitions, suffering all manner of misfortune. Even today, men continue to bear the stresses, setbacks, and other pains of their role. Our society has rightly become sensitive to the problems and woes that fall upon women. Yet men have plenty of problems and woes as well.

Both men and women need to increase their understanding of how difficult it can be to be a man. In this book, you will hear men's voices describing their struggles. These are not recitations of how great it is to enjoy the privileged role of man. Rather, they explain how individual men have sought to cope with the stresses and pressures of their roles, and to find a way to be human beings within the demanding context of manhood.

One focus of my book was male expendability. Contrary to the feminist assertion that society values men more than women, most societies (including our own) treat women as precious and men as expendable. When the *Titanic* sank, there were too few lifeboats for the passengers, so the men had to die while the women lived. The richest men had a lower survival rate than the poorest women (though the recent movie depicted things differently). In countless other ways, male expendability is a fact of life. Although almost as many women as men have jobs (recent news stories documented that during the economic downturn, actually more women than men had jobs), the unpleasant and dangerous ones go overwhelmingly to men. United

States Bureau of Labor Statistics report each year that about 93 to 95 percent of deaths on the job are male. Our society needs somebody to do the dangerous jobs, and it gets men rather than women to do them.

This topic of male expendability symbolizes two major themes. One is that the male role is inherently risky. This is built into our biological heritage. Today's human population is descended from twice as many men as women (a statistic that my book labels "the most underappreciated fact" about gender differences). Most men who ever lived did not reproduce, whereas most women who ever lived did reproduce. When cultures compete, they prefer to risk their men and safeguard their women, partly because the size of their population depends on their women. A society that loses half its men can be back to full strength in the next generation, but a society that loses half its women will have a shortfall of births. When cultures compete, the one with the larger population has a big edge, so cultures tend to favor values and practices that maximize their population. That means treating women as precious and men as expendable.

The other theme is that men and women have somewhat different ways of being social. It has become conventional wisdom in psychology to say that women are the relationship experts. Marriage counselors and researchers advise husbands to listen to their wives, because women have a better understanding of and capacity for intimacy. Perhaps they are right. But that reflects how women specialize in close, intimate, one-on-one relationships. Larger networks of shallower relationships are created much more by men than women. Men form large groups and networks: teams, corporations, military units, scientific institutes. It is difficult to list any large group activity that appeals to women more than men.

To be sure, the close, intimate relationships (favored by women) are in many ways more important to individuals than the large networks of shallow relationships men tend to create. But those large networks are more important to culture and society. The advantages of systems (such as sharing information, division of labor, and trade or exchange) are more fully realized in large groups than in pair bonds. As a simple example, thirty people who share information will get farther than two people who share information: They will accumulate much more to share. Ultimately, that is why culture grew out of the men's social sphere, not the women's sphere. Literature, science, religion, economic trade, military organization, government, technology, and other cultural achievements depend on the interactions of many people, which is how men relate to each other—and so all those things were created by men.

The things we dislike about men, such as competitiveness and egotism, are linked to what is great about men, such as their creation of culture and progress. It is time to stop thinking of men and women as enemies and instead view them as partners. A fresh and unbiased effort to understand men would be a vital step in this direction. This wonderful book is a great start. Read it with an open mind.

Introduction

by Jim Sharon, Ed.D.

While I reclined on my couch late in the evening of July 30, 2010, my wife Ruth suggested I might consider compiling a men's anthology. During the preceding months I had witnessed the mounting enthusiasm displayed by Ruth, my youngest daughter Alyssa, and several other contributing authors as they approached the launch party for the women's anthology *Speaking Your Truth*, compiled by Lisa Shultz and Andrea Costantine. Despite enjoying the women's excitement and being involved in men's "work" for nearly four decades, my initial response to Ruth's query was a casual, halfhearted "maybe." However, that seed literally germinated overnight. The next morning, a business-coach colleague assisted me in mapping a preliminary plan for bringing this book to fruition.

By early October, I had gathered most of the authors, selected a self-publishing coach to shepherd the process, and developed a clear production timeline. During those incipient months, I garnered a strong calling and excitement for the project. I was pleased that most of the contributing authors who attended a lengthy December orientation expressed eagerness to reflect on and depict their defining moments.

Throughout the project, I maintained regular email and telephone contact with the authors. During 2011 many of the men gathered socially and collaborated with fellow writers in a peer-support and editing process prior to submitting their stories to me and to my editing assistants.

The contributors selected the title of our anthology via a consensual vote. These various experiences created a bonding that further energized and synergized the authors.

Much to my delight, virtually all of the authors proved extremely diligent in each phase of the writing and refining process. Surprisingly, many of the men marveled at how much healing they encountered in the aftermath of submitting their stories.

Early on, I had promised the men that our anthology would set the stage for further projects to foster men's overall well-being. The first such major project organically began in March 2011 as I founded Whole Man Expo to "honor men striving for (the ideal of) balance, and the women who support them." Slated to be held in September 2011 at a Denver area hotel, this inaugural event will feature diverse topics and activities that promote men's development and public awareness of key men's issues. *Ordinary Men, Extraordinary Lives: Defining Moments* will be officially launched at the Expo. Many of the authors will participate in the event as speakers, panelists, sponsors, or volunteers.

My strong desire is for this anthology to serve its readers as a model of male transparency, and as a source of encouragement to seek support and to persevere in the face of difficulties. I once heard it said, "Adversity is the canvas upon which you paint your greatness." May our book inspire ordinary people internationally to create authentic, extraordinary lives replete with love, beauty, and purposefulness. Furthermore, may men attain greatness by developing themselves on all levels and by collaborating with women in diligently serving to evolve humanity.

Part One: Fathers and Fatherood

Ending the Family Cycle

by Steve Jones

I love reading about the underdog and how people have overcome challenges in life. When we read these stories, we often say to ourselves, "My situation is not all that bad; I, too, can be everything God intends me to be." As I write this about my life, it is almost as though I am writing a fictional story, because at the time we rarely realize just how tough life can be.

I was raised in a middle-class home with four older siblings. We all had the same mom, but I was my dad's only child. On the outside of our quiet Bellingham, Washington street all seemed ordinary, but on the inside of our house, life was far from normal.

My father, who was a World War II Navy vet, and his older brother Glen, were raised by their grandmother. A few months before my dad was born, his father died of an illness. His mother, who was studying to be a nurse, soon remarried. Her new husband was not fond of children; he fished in Canada and wanted to take her with him and leave the children with family. Being a very loyal mother, she would not leave her two- and four-year-old boys behind. So her husband shot her to death and then shot himself.

Thus, the two boys were instantly orphaned. Four-year-old Glen made sure he and his toddler brother (my dad) ate crackers and had water. A neighbor heard the baby crying a lot and observed Glen dressed oddly while playing in the yard, which led her to discover the tragedy.

I relate all of this because I now know how my dad turned out the way he did, and without help, good people can repeat generations of pain and dysfunction.

As far back as I can remember, my dad drank every day except Sunday. The family came to accept his drinking as normal. He came home from work as a senior draftsman for a power company every day about 4:45 p.m. On Mondays and Tuesdays, he would sit on the couch, read the evening paper, smoke cigars, and drink five Rainier beers before dinner. At 6:00 p.m., like clockwork, Mom would bring him his dinner in the living room. Dad would scoot his ashtray over and eat at the coffee table while he watched news, sports, etc., on the television. Then he would lie down on the couch and continue watching TV until going to bed around 9:00 p.m. On Wednesday, Thursday, and Friday nights, he would drink his usual five beers before dinner, then after dinner he would drink another ten or twenty beers and smoke quite a few William Penn Perfecto cigars. Saturday, he would get up at about 8:00 a.m. and drink all day and night. He rested all day on Sunday to recover for work the next day and repeated the week all over again.

Dad made brief trips to the store to get more … (you guessed it) beer and cigars. But what my dad never compromised on was attending every game in which I played. Whether I had a game after Dad's workday or on Saturday, he was there. Dad loved sports and he was proud to watch me play. I felt I was important to him because he seldom missed one of my games.

Dad had a foul mouth; he loved to cuss out my mom and all of us kids. At times, he resorted to smacking us boys around, punching wherever he could, pulling us down from the top bunk—never a dull moment.

I dealt with Dad by taking control of certain situations. When Dad started drinking, I knew the "crap was going to hit the fan." So, at about eight years old, I would start some chaos to get him stirred up. For example, I might talk loudly to Mom or walk in front of the TV, which would tick him off. Thus, instead of waiting for Dad to act up, I would start something on my own terms. My strategy worked. He would chase me outside. I could get one up on him in the yard because I was quick. I would trip him, take his legs out from under him, and get on top of him. Since Dad was strong, I had to make sure he didn't get ahold of me, since he would do some damage when he did.

After a while he gave up chasing me and would just throw things at me from his couch position. One day when I was either eight or nine, Dad was ticked off at me for some reason. I moved quickly to get out of the living room because he picked up a salad dressing bottle to throw at me. As I ran for the doorway, it hit me in the back of the head. I saw stars. Mom called the police. It seemed like a half-dozen police cars came. The lead officer examined the marks on my body. The officers told my dad what he did was wrong and that they intended to arrest him for domestic violence. But Mom had to agree to press charges in order to have him arrested. A "spike" went through my heart with my mom's next words: "No, I couldn't do that." At that point, it became cemented in my mind that neither of my parents cared enough about me to protect me.

I decided to stay away from home as much as possible. I would go to the doctor's house up the street and shoot hoops alone. In school, I was always in trouble, fighting, causing problems for my teachers and classmates. That is how I worked out my pain.

I loved my mom, but she had a lot going on. At the time, I felt that all that was good and pure in my life were my nephew Tommy and my niece Tammy. These toddlers were so precious. When I made them laugh, all my problems seemed to disappear. I loved them with all my heart. One horrible October day, my sister's stove blew up. She carried badly burned Tammy, age two, out of the house and went back for Tommy. Suddenly, the house blew up and four-year-old Tommy was gone. Tammy died two months later from her severe burns.

At that time, nothing else mattered to me; I was a broken, angry ten-year-old with nobody. I could have lived or died. Our family didn't really like to talk about the loss. When I would bring it up or cry, I was told to quit because I would upset everyone. So I stuffed down a lot of grief and emotion. Since I couldn't talk about my pain and bring it into the light, I often numbed myself with alcohol, drugs, and sex.

When I was in seventh grade, Dad was just getting worse. He stopped the physical abuse, since he could no longer easily scrap with me. I loved to fight and was good at it. When Dad threw shoes at me from the couch, I caught them and threw them back even harder. Involved with girls, drinking, pot smoking, and police encounters, I was spinning out of control during my middle-school years. I continued playing sports, but didn't have my heart in them. All the extracurricular activities were taking a toll on me.

In March of my ninth-grade year, my mom filed for divorce and left my dad. I chose to stay with Dad; my older sister Karen went with my mom. Since Dad never cooked, we often ate out. I observed that his will to move on was beginning to dwindle. He had a deadly disease, but didn't want to admit it. All he wanted was for Mom to come back. He went to counseling just so she would see him trying, but he never wanted to address his health issue.

One day after school and practice, I told Dad I was going to stay at Mom's that night for the first time and for one night only. For two months I had stayed with Dad. Despite his flaws, I loved him very much and at times found him to be kind. I could never have left him. I was all he had and at the time, he was all I had. I began to feel really sorry for him.

Since I was going to stay with Mom that night, Dad suggested we get dinner first. While we ate we discussed the same things as usual, mainly how he wanted Mom back. I said, "Mom isn't coming back until you quit drinking." Dad replied, "I want to make you a promise. You will never see me drink again." Quite surprised, I said, "You promise?" He repeated, "I promise." As we pulled up to Mom's house, Dad leaned over, hugged and kissed me, and told me he loved me. At that moment, I felt hope in my heart that our family would be restored.

After school the next day, I came home to eat and rest up for my game early that evening. While I was watching cartoons, my sister Karen entered the house. Suddenly she started crying and screaming. She read me a note on the fridge, where Dad had placed his watch and ring, which he never took off: "Steve, I am sorry for doing this. I don't want a funeral; I want to be cremated. Take care of Mom and be a good boy. I love you, Dad."

We immediately informed Mom, who proceeded to call the police. Karen drove us to Mom's house. Dad was in the garage. He had committed suicide by way of carbon monoxide poisoning. I fell apart.

I had a lot of mixed emotions. Part of me felt so bad that my dad was alone inside of himself and that his only relief was to take his life. Part of me was furious, especially because of the hope he had given me the previous night. Suicide is what he had in mind to fulfill his promise. Part of me also felt guilty, thinking that if only I hadn't stayed at Mom's house that night, Dad would still be alive.

That summer after my dad's passing, I had a chance to live with my sister and work in an orchard. I had a lot of time to contemplate my life and where I was headed. I thought about my dad's legacy and how I would remember him. It became as clear as a bell that I had to change my ways. I had seen a lot of tragedy from poor choices; my mom's heart had been broken enough. Deep down, I wanted my life to count for something.

When school resumed in the fall, a handful of coaches reached out to me. One of those men was Coach West, the head football coach, who was big and gruff. Listening to my grief, he showed me that he had a heart. I can't express what that meant to me. Also about that time, I started dating Laurie, a schoolmate since seventh grade. She was beautiful and athletic; she could throw like a dude, but she was all lady. She knew my background, but she liked me anyway. I had previously been around girls who were big party hounds and played mind games. For me, Laurie was a dream come true, so I worked very hard not to blow my opportunity. She had parents who loved each other. Laurie's mom heard that

I came from "rough stuff," but she still accepted me into her home. Along with the football coach, Laurie's dad became a father figure to me. I felt so grateful that they all believed in me.

I knew I had to change friends; my association with all the pot smokers and drinkers had to end. So I did, because I wanted so badly to "become someone." During the next two years, my junior and senior year of high school, I began to turn myself around. I elevated a 2.0 grade point average my freshman and sophomore years to a 3.4 GPA my final two years. In sports, I became a "training animal," training instead of partying, and a successful high school athlete in three sports, then had a great college career playing two sports.

I married Laurie when we were both twenty-one. We started a family right away and have three great sons today. I began working in the corporate world and eventually developed a home-based business that allowed me to become a full-time dad at age twenty-nine. Today I have the privilege to work with and mentor kids in prison. I have volunteered for years in a center for children grieving from the loss of a loved one. Furthermore, I have had the immense pleasure of speaking all around the country, sharing my story of hope. I also coach high school football and baseball because I know firsthand how important that influence is on the life of a young man.

During my youth, I never imagined amounting to much of anything. I have often wondered how we make it through craziness and tragic events. For me, first, I give thanks and the glory to my Heavenly Father, who gave me the strength I lacked. Second, I had a mom who loved me, believed in me, and unceasingly prayed for me. Third, I put myself in the company of good people. My wife Laurie is clearly the best thing that has ever happened to me, and her family has been a godsend. I got into an awesome business and associated with people who were going places in life. They taught me how to live a balanced life, set goals, read good personal development books, and listen to CDs about success. Finally, I became determined to build a life that really mattered. I began caring about how I was going to be remembered. The hardest question I ever had to answer was from my son Keenan. While discussing how my dad passed away, he asked, "How come Grandpa gave up?"

When we go to meet our Maker, He will not care about how much money we made, our golf prowess, or anything of the sort. I believe one of the questions we all will get is, "Did you make a positive difference in the life of a kid?" A few great people did for me and for many years it has been my turn to reciprocate.

Tombstones tell our birth and death dates. The crucial part is the dash in between—what we made of our lives. The question I often ask myself and others is, "How are you going to be remembered?"

Steve Jones *resides in Portland, Oregon, with his wife and three sons. Steve has built a successful business that has allowed him to create the life of his dreams. He speaks publicly throughout North America on success principles and winning in life. He loves seeing people overcome negative thinking and adversity to make great things happen in their lives. Steve feels very privileged to be able to work with youth in his community as a baseball and football coach. Coaching has given him the opportunity to invest in young men and to pass on the many lessons he has learned from his own life experience. Steve wants to communicate that, "where you come from in life does not dictate your future." Contact him at stevejones@wealthtips.com.*

Full-Circle Fatherhood

How I Lost My Mother and Became the Grateful Dad

by Doug Gertner

Here's what I remember about the day my mother died. There was an odd hush and hustle in our home that morning, just days after I turned seven. "What's Dr. Karr doing here?" I wondered, "And why do he and my father seem so concerned?" Hurrying around, holding pill bottles. All the while, my mother lay listless on her side of the bed. I recall my sister Toni, a toddler of two, wandering about, unaware of the silent barrier that prevented me from venturing into our parent's bedroom.

The ensuing days were a whirlwind, swept off to a cousin's house, my father's tearful explanation of my mom's death, the strange, confusing experience of the Jewish *shiva* ritual that filled our home with family, friends, food, and the sight of my grandmother wailing with the grief of losing her eldest daughter.

Here's what I remember about the year after my mother's death. We soon settled in as a family of three, plus a housekeeper hired to fill the maternal role and permit my father to work long hours as a young up-and-coming attorney. Even as I was reeling from the loss and adapting to my new identity as a "mother-less child," this was a magical time for me with my father. Rather than sit in the same seat at the table every meal, our silly routine was to swap seats between each breakfast and dinner. Some nights I would sleep in my dad's king-size bed, and I'll never forget the morning we were awakened by the blast of a popular song after I left the clock radio turned up loud while listening the night before.

During this year, I watched my father struggle to stay connected and care for me and my sister, his own grief, loss, and confusion hidden by the need to present a strong façade. His work was his refuge, and I felt the distance growing, even as I was the regular recipient of his attention. My earliest impressions of fatherhood were formed in these days: absence, emotional distance, strength and silence, sadness and loneliness. This was how I learned to be a man.

Here's what it taught me about being a father. Another lesson followed, soon after: A man needs a woman to complete him. It was only a matter of months before my father began seeing Bette, his legal secretary. The first time she came to our house, I did not recognize her until she uttered the greeting that I heard anytime I called my dad's law office. "Furman, Gertner, and Britz," she chirped in a cheery tone, and I immediately knew who she was. Soon after, I was introduced to Bette's daughters, and we spent time at their cramped apartment and in our larger home.

Despite their intention, these frequent social occasions failed to prepare me for that day, sitting in the passenger seat of the car in our driveway, when my father turned to me and said, "I am going to marry Bette. You and Toni need a mom." My body tensed with those words, knowing deep inside that this would change everything. My reply belied the fear, confusion, and anger I was feeling, "Okay, Dad, that's fine with me … "

A stepmother and an absent father. This all felt very fast, so sudden, because it truly was. Within eight months, I had lost my mother and gained a step-mother. "Who is this woman living in my house who I'm supposed to call *Mom*?" I wondered, "And why are she and my dad spending so much time behind closed doors?" Living with newlyweds and stepsisters in what was supposed to be *my* house, and with no mention ever of my real mother, gave me a sense of disappear-ing. I felt lost, alone, ignored, and neglected.

Like the story of Cinderella, my stepmom clearly favored her own daughters, and I was vilified and singled out as the source of many of the problems that arose in our home. I began having problems at school as well, and I even remember my stepmother telling me, "Mark my words, you will end up in jail one day." My heart sank, along with my self-concept, and I really felt like, and identified as, a "bad kid." I told this to the school principal during one of my many meetings with him, and to the shrink I was sent to for help. Never do I recall my father coming to my defense or even lending words of support or encouragement. Where was my dad? Where was the nice guy who had let me sleep in his big empty bed, who had played musical chairs around the dining table at every meal?

My father neither stepped up nor stepped in when I was a senior in high school and my stepmother said she could not live under the same roof as me. He gave me a suitcase, some cash, and drove me to the home of my fictive aunt, with whom I lived until leaving for college.

My own path to fatherhood took me through much soul searching. It was never easy for me to get close to women or to men. I made lots of friends, dated plenty, and still never felt whole or complete. In college, I found my way to a women's studies class called Philosophical Issues in Feminism taught by a male professor who had been a classmate of my father's at Harvard. Doors opened, lights went on, the class really got me thinking, and the notion of gender justice and equality was liberating. For the first time since my mother died, I was able to feel open-hearted and alive, knowing men and women in new ways and seeing a complete picture of human potential.

Personal growth and development emerged as central and important in my life, balanced with fun and recreation that also brought me peak experiences. My passion for live music found me enjoying dozens of diverse concerts every year. My love of nature and the outdoors brought me to Colorado where I finally felt at home. And while working on college campuses, I became active in teaching and learning about men and masculinity from a feminist perspective. By exploring new and different ways to be a man in society, I was freeing myself from the path that had been my father's, and I was becoming healed and whole as my own person.

While working on a university campus, I met my soul mate, a woman who shares and supports my beliefs and approach to the world of gender equality, as well as my taste in music and fondness for the natural world. Upon our first meeting I had an immediate vision of us spending our lives together. We became friends first and then more, and together we planned an egalitarian Jewish wedding and set out toward our life together. And even as our careers moved forward, we maintained a balance that values each of our roles both profession-ally and personally. We actually took turns being unemployed—she worked while I finished my doctoral dissertation, and I held a new job while my wife sought employment after leaving a bad situation.

We built a foundation based on equality and mutual respect, which was quite different from what I saw modeled growing up. Our strong foundation paved the way for the next big step we took together, becoming parents.

This is how I became The Grateful Dad. I became a father later than many. Later than my own father, who was twenty-seven when I was born. Later than most of my friends, who are now becoming empty nesters as I prepare to parent a teen. I was thirty-nine when my son was born. Although my partner was, at age thirty-five, considered in medical parlance an "advanced-age pregnancy," there is no similar distinction made for men. Whatever age we become dads seems just right, or at least not particularly noteworthy.

When we decided to become parents, there were obvious roles that could not be shared. But when our son was born, I was intent on walking the talk of involved fatherhood and being a full and active participant in every aspect of his life. I changed his first diaper and many more after that, and I fed, comforted, and bathed him as often as, and oftentimes along with, his mother. We both worked full-time outside the home, beginning soon after the birth, and we each took a half-day off when our son needed to stay home sick from daycare. An early indicator of our interchangeability in his life was demonstrated when our young son would call out in the night for comfort using the name "mommydaddy" as a single sort of parent he sought. And as he grows toward being a young man and continues to develop an awareness of gender differences, the parents he knows remain essentially interchangeable, even as he notes that one of us tends to play and watch baseball with him a bit more, while the other prefers to read books and paint with watercolors more often.

When our son was born, I took off all the time I had coming to me, less than three weeks, then returned part-time until scheduling and finances necessitated my decision to go back to work full-time. My wife was slightly longer away from her job before returning. The toughest part of every day was dropping him at daycare and being away from my child for more than eight hours; the highpoint of every workday was picking up my son and being together. I ached when we were apart and felt ecstatic when reunited.

One morning in the shower—the only place it seemed that I had time to think—it occurred to me that since I was expected to spend at least forty hours per week at work, that left only about thirty waking hours with my son, and slightly more with my partner, that is if we could manage to stay awake after our son went down. Rather than accept this, or let it get me down, I resolved to make my life more father-friendly.

I changed jobs, hoping that a progressive, high-tech company could somehow provide a more family-friendly work environment. And when that company laid me off after just ten months, I took the small severance package and started a consulting business with a focus on men's issues and fatherhood.

Although my wife and I both still work full-time and our son spends his days in a school he enjoys and where we are active with the parent association, my work in the fatherhood arena has provided new balance and joy in our lives.

Most days, we are able to go together to drop off our son at school and to pick him up. It is so significant to be active in his life, to enjoy this time together, talking, connecting. Even when my fatherhood work takes me away for an early morning training session or an overnight conference or speech, I have their support and the assurance that the approach to involved fatherhood that I am sharing with others is also helping me return to my family as a better dad each time. Life is good and full and rich and varied and satisfying.

Fatherhood comes full circle. My life changed again on the day I realized that my own father needed my help. It was a Sunday afternoon in June and I had not heard from my dad. Typically, he called on Sunday morning, usually too early on a day designated for rest, so I picked up the phone to call him. The voice I heard on the other end of the telephone sounded a million miles away, so distant and confused, nothing like the voice of the man I'd known for over forty years.

It soon became clear that my father's physical and cognitive health were in swift decline, that he could no longer manage his affairs, and that I would need to assume the role of his caregiver. Without giving it a second thought, I took responsibility for the life of the man who had given me life, and who had done his best to provide the support for me to grow into the man and father I have become. I felt deep compassion for my father as never before and could finally say, "I love you, Dad," and hear him say the same to me.

Now I have the gift of living in the same city as my father for the first time since I left for college, and my son has his Papa nearby, which brings joy to them both. Even as it is very painful to see a man whose mind was his greatest strength lose his ability to keep track of even simple details, I now have some sense of the pressure that my dad felt when he took on a new role as a young father. And my son sees me honor my own dad with the same sort of patience and attention he may one day need to offer me.

Being a son, and having a son, has amounted to quite a journey. I am truly a grateful dad.

Doug Gertner, Ph.D., *is founder and Big Bird (Principal) of Emu Consulting in Denver, Colorado. His work is dedicated to both organizational and employee development, and to involving fathers and enriching families through programs and services for staff and parents. Doug's alter ego,* The Grateful Dad, *brings a laid-back, rock-and-roll wisdom to his entertaining keynote speeches and lively workshops, including his top tips, quick quips, skills, stories, ideas, exercises, and activities to reflect on our own dads and bring father-friendliness to every situation. Learn more at www.thegratefuldad.org. And let him hear from you at doug@thegratefuldad.org.*

My Father's Gift

by Pierre Brunschwig

The sound of Dad's fist hitting my older brother's face sickened me. The fleshy crunch of the impact ran through my body. It made my head buzz and my heart pound. Why was my brother so hostile to Dad? Since my father's psychotic break four years ago, Dad was unpredictable and paranoid, his anger seething just under his skin. His chaotic flights of anger sprung from his voice, searing, cruel, paranoid. He had never hit one of us kids before, but I was still terrified of him. I had stopped wondering why he hated us so. He was clearly "broken." I just wanted to stay out of his way. I desperately wanted something in my teenage life to be normal. Shit! This could get worse. Would I have to get between them? My mother was yelling for them to stop. I was shaking, terrified, and immobile. My brother held his face. I wanted peace. I wouldn't get it, at least not until I left for college.

I received a message to go see my psychiatric rotation preceptor. She let me know that my father had died and to call my mother. My grandmother had found him unconscious on the bathroom floor and called 911. The paramedics could not revive him. No one in my family saw this coming. We might have. Dad had inhaled the cigars he smoked, often ate fast foods, and never exercised. Despite all this, I thought that he'd live a long life and that I deserved to be tethered to his dark world for its duration. I had imagined getting quite different calls about Dad, such as that Dad was being held by the police after a stranger had set him off and he'd hurt him or killed him. Less often, I thought he'd have a run-in with a cop who would observe how insane he was and his arrest would finally get him the antipsychotic treatment he had refused. These were the kinds of calls I waited to receive.

The news of my father's death made me giddy, like I had been unexpectedly freed from prison. I was aware that I must seem odd to my fellow doctors in training. After all, my father had just died. Where was my sadness? What was I going to miss of my father? Hadn't I lost him when I was much younger? I had a handful of fond memories of my father's graciousness before his madness moved in. Over time, however, the grief of losing my dad had slowly leached from me. For more than fifteen years, it was as if he had been imprisoned and I could no longer reach him. I could only contact his ghoulish guards, who kept my real father from me. I'd lost hope of knowing him ever again. Now we were both set free.

After high school, I went to college in Colorado, two thousand miles to the west. I had fled. I knew I couldn't stay. I was so swamped with the emotional overload of my dad's mental illness that I hardly knew who I was. Being away from my dad's madness gave me hope, even joy. I loved learning and I loved being able to sense myself, separated from my dad's rage and agony. My sense of freedom was limited, however. Sometimes I had sudden violent urges, with rage-filled images to strike out or even kill. These mental scenes were mercifully rare, but they linked me to my father's madness. They reminded me that I had not gotten away clean from the hereditary burden of madness. I shared some of his neurology. I tried to tell myself everyone has these urges. I told no one about this.

At my father's funeral, I held my younger brother Joe's hands over our father's corpse and led him in what I thought was our last words, our goodbyes. Dad's story had ended. I would move on without the burden of his suffering. We all would.

I went on to finish medical school and started my residency training in family medicine. I was still loving the learning and now there was the added richness the patients brought. I had been supplementing my medical education with generous portions of all things holistic. I often would steal away to attend conferences led by holistic physicians. I wanted this larger perspective of healing. It put soul back into the practice of medicine.

I'd traveled to Oregon to participate in another holistic conference. I had chosen a workshop that was run by a warm and intuitive physician. He had started a healing circle for students and residents. I had volunteered to assist another resident who would be the focus of the circle. As we sat together in the center of the circle, she described what she felt. It was uncanny how her description of a relationship matched my own with my dad. When she said she did not recognize the people she was seeing, I began to suspect she was unknowingly describing my relationship with my father. Gradually, it became clear to me that my experience had invaded her process and she was in fact talking about Dad.

Dad had been buried for over a year now. Was there something unsaid? We agreed to switch places. The group leader asked us all to focus on me and to be silent. I closed my eyes; there was Dad, clearly speaking to me. "Don't bury me so quickly!" His madness was gone and his voice was lucid and sweet. In that instant

I was filled with love for him. I wept, joyfully. Madness had robbed us of this kind of connection while he was alive. I had buried my father, suspecting that our opportunity to feel each other's hearts was over. I'd been wrong. Fresh waves of sobbing convulsed my body.

The last few years of my dad's life, his paranoia had abated. His stories had become more and more fictional. I had felt less afraid of him. I had let myself feel compassion for him. I had let myself feel his suffering. But I had never felt his love.

After the healing circle, I became accustomed to closing my eyes and seeing my father in my mind's eye. Mostly we would look at each other in silence. Though I tried from time to time to ask for guidance, I'd get only a sense of joyfulness and a reassuring gaze. I could feel his love.

"Don't resist it, Pierre," my counselor said. I spoke the words more forcefully. "I am gay. I am a gay man." The words terrified me. I had no idea what it meant to live a gay lifestyle. This would change everything. How could this be true? The openhearted, meditative place I had reached together with my therapist now made me shake. Had I lived a lie? I didn't know what it meant, really to be gay. Everything in my life would have to change if this were true. What would happen to my marriage? What about my daughter? How would I explain this to my family? I could not believe it myself. I was scared. My life had been a lie. I tried imaging leaving this office and starting to date men. I cringed, "Can I do this?" Though it seemed I was letting go of a lie, I did not feel release. I was simply frightened, not liberated. Something was wrong. I continued with my session.

As I lay there I felt something on my face; I moved to remove it. A mask? What was this doing on my face? I pulled it off. It felt thick and wooden. In my mind's eye, I could see a wooden mask and it felt as if it had been on my face for a long time. I could also sense that it was not mine. Its story was pouring from it. It had been my father's. His story was now rushing into my mind. He had been gay and this mask was his way of hiding his gayness from us and the rest of the world. He hid his sexuality with this mask. This was his secret. Shame had driven him to wear it. Over time, it had crushed him, driven him mad, living the lie of a gay man with a heterosexual mask. This broke his spirit: four kids, a wife, a stellar academic career, a research position at Boeing, all done while living a lie. I had seen his pain and misery, but I had not known his story. I had wanted to relieve his pain those years before he died. And somehow he had needed to pass on the secret—the thing that had crushed him. Was that my job to take his lie into the light? Why would he offer me such a difficult gift? It seemed I had not refused it. When and how had this happened? How many other men in my lineage had done something similar?

All the years since his death I hadn't noticed that I was wearing *his* mask. With openness and courage, I let my father's mask lead me through a web of discovery in its own time. On my father's face the heterosexual side of the mask faced outward, covering his gay nature. My gay side faced out, obscuring my heterosexual nature underneath. On me, this outward-facing gay facade had made it difficult to read clearly my real sexual nature. I could see how it had frustrated my relationships with other women and men; how I had struggled to date and how difficult it had been for my wife to really trust my sexuality. There had been something there between us all along. This would explain a lot.

This also threw me into a fresh new set of questions about my sexuality. How did I know that this wasn't an elaborate way for my subconscious to hide my own hidden homosexuality? I could still be gay after all. Perhaps I was just as much in denial of my real sexual nature as my father, and just as ashamed. This would surely require some sorting out. I began scouring my memories of making love to women. Had I always wanted to be with a man? Perhaps I wanted to be with both men and women. Certainly I was scared. I had never questioned my straight nature. My sexuality, which I had considered immutable, was now on the dissection table. If that was subject to change, what else might I have to call into question? Was I also mad? Dad had left me with a real mess.

For months afterward, I'd revisit the question of being gay. I would get the same answer, "No, I'm not gay." I began to trust my answer. But I was uncomfortable with my "feminine" traits. I couldn't separate the experience of my feminine side with the idea that it was a sign that I was gay after all. This made me furious at times. I wanted to rip the whole mess out of me and burn it. I felt contaminated. I imagined this is what drove my father mad, my questions in reverse. How uncomfortable it must have been for him to deal with his masculine nature as it obscured his feminine. Slowly, I began to realize how we both abandoned ourselves through buying into the contemporary notion of being a man. There was no place for the feminine, other than being gay, which our culture finds shameful. We had both been taught to fear our feminine nature and to belittle it in other men. By fearing and hiding from our feminine nature we were fractured men. In my dad's case this schism proved fatal.

I became determined that this suffering would end with me. I stopped equating my receptive, caregiving tendencies, desire to wear pastels, willingness to cry in the presence of others, even my openheartedness, with a lack of masculinity. I stopped judging my feminine qualities. I also stopped speculating that I have an unconscious desire to sleep with men. I began making room for her, my feminine nature. She began to settle in next to my masculine side. They no longer threatened each other. The fight was over.

More than two years have passed since I removed my father's mask. Since, I have sought help to get my house in order. This help has been indispensable. Large legs of the journey I made solo. I have strived to become transparent. I've told my story and that of my dad to many people and to my family, sometimes to get their impressions, other times to simply let the story do what it might for the listener. The shame of my father and my own are part of my story, but that previous shame is no longer informing my sexual energy. The story of my dad's chaotic and abusive nature now sits in my mind well lit, whole and knowable. I even feel fortunate. These last two years have been a journey of forgiveness, forgiving myself and my father. Nothing I have done has required me to face my fears and summon my courage more than this journey. Nothing has required me to open my heart more fully. I greatly appreciate my father's gift.

Pierre Brunschwig, M.D., is a family physician of twenty years, specializing in integrative medicine. He practices in Boulder, Colorado. He is married to Teresa Bradford. They have a nine-year-old daughter, Annabelle. The three love being together and enjoy the outdoors, traveling, and dancing.

Dudes Don't Yoga

by Samuel Nanfito

Midnight was upon us and the snaky line wound around and disappeared through the doors into the late night venue. Word had spread that the DJ playing there threw down an amazing set the night before and everyone wanted to see what it was all about. Pushing, elbowing, and close proximity persisted for the next half hour. The loudest complaints about the fiasco came from the mountain of a shoulder that I was pressed against—Kenny's.

"Man, this line would move a lot faster if all these yoga people weren't so laid back." We were at Wanderlust, a yoga and music festival in Lake Tahoe. Yoga practitioners spent the better part of the day twisted in unique positions called "asanas." Then at night, the general public descended upon the resort to share in the musical festivities. The dynamic, with such different energies converging, could become a bit muddled. "And y'all need to eat some steak. You're all too skinny. Quit stretching and eat some cows." Kenny was definitely the proverbial man's man. But seriously funny, too.

"We'll see what you have to say when all us yoga people can still stand in line when we're seventy and you're hobbling around with a big ol' belly," I offered.

"Seventy? Dude, I'm cashing out by like fifty. And I don't care if I can touch my toes or not. Linebackers only need to be able to tackle and I can tackle any of you yoga people." He had a point. Then, in his machine-gun delivery, he made another: "And anyway, yoga is for the ladies. Dudes don't yoga."

When my journey with yoga started more than a decade ago, Kenny's statement was practically true; it was pretty much me and the ladies. Soon after friends in San Francisco introduced me to hatha yoga (the physical branch of yoga the Western world thinks of when they hear the word "yoga"), I walked into my first official class at a big corporate gym in my not-so-progressive hometown of Omaha, Nebraska, and noticed something immediately: dudes didn't yoga.

Unsure footsteps carried me into the room. Conversations ceased and curious eyes followed me in the mirrors. Every student suddenly had a mat that needed adjusting or a dry throat that needed water. "Welcome … Have you practiced yoga here before?" the instructor asked me, trying too obviously not to bring attention to the obvious. The silent room answered the question for me, but to affirm its answer I said, "Nope. First-timer." "Okay, great. Well, grab a mat and we'll start in *balasana*." (Balasana? Huh?!)

"Inhale … Exhale … Become aware of the breath … Link the movement of your body with the movement of your breath … Become aware of any tension in the body and breathe into those places. Let it go … Create space with the breath … Inhale … Exhale."

Foreign phrases that I hadn't been expecting flowed from her. Awareness? Breath? Creating space? Somebody actually telling me when and how to breathe? It was a far cry from my days of weightlifting, having some sweaty friend leaning over the bench and yelling, "Go! Push! C'mon, Sam! Don't be a—," and so forth.

And I, of course, approached this yoga class similar to weightlifting, like most athletes new to the practice do, as if I were achieving something, trying to win something. Grunts and gasps and sighs of frustration issued forth while I overstretched my body in exotic ways and pushed myself beyond any healthy limit. I was going to be the best. I was going to be an expert even though it was my first time. I just had to look stronger than all these women. I, I, I …

Awareness of this false "I" and the revelation and realization of the true self is the true attainment in the practice of yoga, and any spiritual practice for that matter. Being surrounded by only women in that room unnerved me at first. The false self, much like Kenny, asserted itself very quickly, making judgments about the girlyness of yoga. Hours and hours in that room, however, showed me that surrender, rather than acting out some society-standard machismo, was how the true self would be realized. To attain the rewards that yoga could offer me, I had to break through the walls of programmed masculinity as taught by Hollywood, television, popular music, and American society in general.

I persisted, continuing to go to class and grow in my practice. I told few people of this new endeavor in the beginning and definitely endured some ribs once I started talking more about yoga: "Dude, you're starting to look like Jane Fonda" or "Can you do the splits, man?" Other guys didn't understand it, and honestly, I didn't totally understand it either, but I had an intuition to keep on the path. Walking through the gym where I used to pump iron and into the yoga studio wasn't always the easiest journey. I realized a new, different strength was emerging though, and trusted I would become a more whole man.

I remember one day after class, a woman I practiced with for a couple months stopped me and told me how much she appreciated my being in the class. "There's a balance in the room that wasn't there before." This statement was a true lift, and I remember it bringing on another thought in me: this same balance was starting to occur inside of me. Like the perfectly balanced shape of the yin and yang in Chinese culture, I was learning that, as a balance to my masculinity, there was value to understanding the femininity of my nature, as well. In addition to being strong and aggressive, I could be receptive, gentle, nurturing. The regulars started to bring other men to class to try out this unfamiliar science.

Almost ten years after the commencement of my yoga journey, I became aware that another journey, far more common to men than yoga, was about to begin: fatherhood. A yelp issued from my wife, Griselda, and echoed out of the bathroom on a cold December morning. "What? Do you have a zit?" I remember asking, sincerely, from bed. "No, I'm pregnant," my wife replied. Silence in the bedroom. This announcement came as a huge surprise and I wasn't ready for it. My yoga instructor's voice came to me: "Inhale ... Exhale ... Become aware of any tension in the body. Breathe into those spaces ... "

Our son, Kingsley, was born nine months later in a beautiful home birth in our Denver apartment. Shortly after, we relocated to Los Angeles for a job opportunity for Griselda. We weighed our options for childcare and how we could optimize our family situation. In the end, we decided that I would stay home with our baby boy. The decision wasn't so hard. Logistically, it made a lot of sense for me to stay home, rather than paying for someone else to raise our child while we both worked. What was hard was that this shift in identity hit me like a ton of bricks.

Crying and bottles and diapers and burps became my days, and though these monotonous activities were accompanied by Kingsley's incredibly innocent eyes and undeniable smiles, I found myself wondering what exactly I was becoming. I didn't have the comfort of identification with any profession or a standard measure of success, was being supported by my wife, and had a nonexistent social life. The traditional role of the man making a living and supporting his family was still deeply engrained in my psyche, and I was finding just how hard that programming was to contend with. I could hear Kenny loud and clear, "Dudes don't daycare."

"Oh, but they do, Kenny," I'd answer him in my head. "And you'd know it, too, if you could see me cruising around the neighborhoods and beaches of Long Beach with our stroller. Changing diapers on the fly on the beach. Busting out the formula and making a mean six-ounce bottle." The looks we would get were classic. Heads would rubberneck around in cars, the passenger pointing us out to the driver; I could hear them, "Was that a guy with dreadlocks pushing a baby stroller?" We would pass other parents (translation: moms) with strollers during our walks and they would give me that knowing smile, and oftentimes invite me to a "Mommy and Me … errr, parenting group."

Growing fully into my role as a stay-at-home dad was facilitated enormously by yoga. Much like walking into that yoga studio full of women, walking on the streets with my son strapped to my chest ("Yo, man, that looks like baby Carlos from *The Hangover*.") or feeding him a bottle at a coffee shop seemingly posed a certain challenge to my manhood, but on a far more encompassing level. I found that being present—a cue often heard in yoga class—and truly enjoying my time with my son pushed out concerns of judgment or mockery. A difficult yoga pose— like a headstand or crow pose—teaches you to relax and breathe deeply while in an uncomfortable position, and I took this practice to the streets with Kingsley.

One thing I knew for sure was that my appreciation for the stay-at-home mothers of the world was growing daily. When you're caring for an infant, the days have this way of slipping away, with nothing very tangible to show for it (like a clean kitchen or clean laundry or a gourmet meal). And yet at the end of the day it felt like I had run a marathon and the fatigue set in, despite the lack of defining achievement. Some days I felt like he never stopped crying. And the crying had a way of gnawing at my nerves.

One day Kingsley's screaming kept coming. It just wouldn't stop. At first I tried to reason with him, "Listen, there's nothing that can possibly be wrong. We just changed your diaper. You've eaten. You're not too hot or cold. And you just burped twice. You have nothing to complain about." He didn't care what my logic was; he wasn't having it. And the screaming went on … and on. My world swirled and dimmed. Walls closed in on me and light seemed lost in the world. It was loud and I felt helpless. My blood started to boil. I held him out in front of me. "Stop crying!" I yelled at him. "*Stop!*"

Was I losing my mind? How could this tiny creature be driving me to the edge of my sanity? How could I be yelling at a being so full of innocence? I plopped him in his bed and walked away, sitting on the couch with a million-mile stare. Maybe Kenny's right. Maybe dude's shouldn't daycare. I'm trying my hardest and yet I feel trapped in this baby world. I want my old life back.

Much like a yoga practice, the practice of parenthood has its amazing days and its really defeating days. You continue on, though. You become. You keep returning to your mat. You keep returning to your child. Just as the breath is the cornerstone of the practice of yoga, it is also one of the keys to successful parenting.

Weeks later, during a gnarly bout of teething, Kingsley cried out in frustration, grabbed my beard, and yanked it as hard as he could (inhale). I held him loosely and with unwavering love, pulled him to me and landed a kiss on his big cheek (exhale). "I love you, Kingsley." He grunted and pushed my face away (inhale). Another cry and a squirm of frustration followed (exhale). Another round of gentle cradling and kisses and affirmations of love followed (inhale). Surrendering to the goodness of this comforting, he slumped against my chest and closed his eyes (exhale). At that moment, I understood why parenting is the richest human endeavor. It gives insight into the mind of God and unconditional love.

I also understood why yoga had to be a part of my path. It allowed me to get past traditional stereotypes about masculine and feminine roles, helped me develop some of the more feminine characteristics that would make me a great caretaker to my son, and it gave me the strength to take on the challenge of changing my life to be a stay-at-home dad. Every day Kingsley cracks me up with something he's doing or learning. He looks me in the eye and says "Dada" and then yanks my beard again. I, in turn, thank him for the blessings he's brought to my life and for slowing me down to appreciate another of its phases. How much I would have missed out on if I had believed Kenny that dudes don't daycare and dudes don't yoga.

 **Samuel Nanfito** *is a creator and artist. He creates as a father, husband, friend, guitarist, painter, meditator, yogi and yoga instructor, hiker, bartender, engineer, and a growing human being. His latest incarnation as a stay-at-home father has shaped his life in unexpected, challenging, and beautiful ways. He and his son, Kingsley, stroll the neighborhoods of Los Angeles in search of adventure and inspiration.*

A Fifty-Year Journey of Fathering and Self-Development

by Rick Tidrick

Some twenty years ago my oldest daughter asked, "How did you become the father of nine motherless children?" This story is about abandoned children, death and rebirth, awareness and choice, personal growth, and my journey in becoming that father.

My nine children, five girls and four boys, represent three blended generations. They include four children from my first marriage, three who came with my second marriage, and two we home birthed and parented together. Today their ages range from twenty-four to fifty-one.

This story begins in 1966, when I was asked to resign my position of one year as the Assistant Director of the Denver Zoological Park (now, Denver Zoo). This was a self-esteem busting event. I was simply too brash at the time; being fired humbled me. In the same month, my mother collapsed from alcoholism, losing her New Mexico cattle ranch in the process. Thus began an emerging financial codependency, as I spent the next five years dealing with Mom's severe health, legal, and financial problems. This chronic stress initiated the gradual "losing of my soul" and eventually, my wife and children. These two simultaneous events changed forever the direction of my life, as I began to fail as a son, a parent, and a husband. Lacking in emotional intelligence (i.e., skills for processing my feelings), I was unable to acknowledge my failure and express my shame and guilt. My mother passed away from a forty-year bout with alcoholism at age sixty-nine in 1983.

My first wife was a beautiful, charming, passionate, educated, humorous, gifted, and loving woman of Native American heritage. I basically lost control of my life with the birth of our fourth child, following a birth-control loop being removed without my knowledge in 1969, and the loss of our fifth child, born prematurely in 1971, as a result of my wife's severe uterine infection from a birth-control loop left in place. When I recently sat with my oldest son in his therapy session, we suspected that my wife may have sought more children as a means of saving our marriage. A number of factors led to our drifting apart emotionally and finding ourselves spiritually bankrupt. Some of these involved her near-death experience from the infection, her mounting addiction to pain-killing drugs, and her increasing use of alcohol. I was emotionally frozen with feelings of failure as a husband and father and immobilized for several years with a fear of committing to the many newly-offered opportunities I received in the zoo profession.

My wife and I chose to leave the therapist's couch by 1972 to follow our own hearts for the next few years until our divorce six years later in 1978. Neither of us possessed the skills for processing our personal traumas. During those years, we each began exploring the new sexual freedom and the "me generation" of the '70s. My wife became a very successful "super volunteer" on the local and national scenes, which involved frequent travel. Two years before our official divorce, she had begun a new relationship. This resulted in less of her attention to our children, as they were often left to fend for themselves. My oldest daughter so much resented her surrogate mother role at age twelve that she never desired children of her own. My first wife died from alcoholism, some forty years in the making, in 2009 at the age of seventy-one, despite a thirty-day rehabilitation and another thirty-day intervention.

Emotionally divorcing my mother, a long-suffering alcoholic, and legally divorcing my evolving-alcoholic wife, I endeavored to "grow myself up." During this time, I gradually abandoned the children as well. I began following a different path, which included joining the human potential movement in 1972; my return to college full-time between 1972 and 1978; and completing a doctorate in Holistic Health, Psychology, and Counseling.

I began serving others by working for the Colorado Outward Bound School, along with my internship with five Colorado High School Senior Seminars in fulfillment of my master's degree program in Experiential Education. These were highlights in my journey of self-development. Also, through reengaging with the natural world—organizing many rafting trips as a small business in the 1970s, along with canoeing, climbing, hiking, and backpacking trips—I reaffirmed the natural environment as the source of my spirituality.

My founding of the Colorado Holistic Health Network (CHHN) in 1978, and serving as its General Coordinator for three and a half years, were an additional source of self-discovery. Once again, serving others provided significant growth and healing for me. CHHN became one of the largest and most successful volunteer networks in the nation concerned with connecting traditional medicine with emerging health, wellness, and healing practices from around the world. I received a 9Who Care Honorable Mention Award from the Denver television station for my volunteer organizing efforts.

Those experiences assisted me in my reestablishing core feelings of being valuable, capable, equal, powerful, and lovable, the very roots of my self-esteem. Recovering my soul and becoming a more loving father also resulted from the discovery of self-care books, and participation in self-help groups and seminars. The culmination of this growth process in self-reflection was spending three months in 1976 at the Esalen Institute, a human potential growth center in Big Sur, California, as a small portion of my doctoral program. An important outcome was my participation in encounter group formats, ultimately facilitating them. Those experiences provided me with an important realization: Despite vastly differing stories, people have similar feelings; universal themes exist regarding love, spirit, and the human condition. Sharing my feelings and stories with others brought love, perspective, resolution, and peace into my life.

Involvement with my emerging friends in the human potential movement taught me to be more open-minded, communal, collaborative, and relational. Also, I learned to be more expansive and inclusive, to blend being with doing, seeking the beauty, goodness, and truth in myself and in others.

Reviewing my parental upbringing, my father's life was measured more in terms of good and bad, and right and wrong, while my mother held a more laissez-faire approach to life. Righteousness in attitude or behavior felt oppressive and adversely affected me as a child. As an adult, giving voice to some of these uncomfortable feelings that I kept unconsciously inside of me proved freeing. Furthermore, I began to undo cultural scripts concerning what a man and woman were intended to be individually and together in marriage. I sought to blend masculine and feminine qualities in myself and (as an astrological Libra) championed that balance in others.

At the age of forty-three in 1980, I had the good fortune of meeting my second wife and soul mate. Parental alienation of my children toward me as their father, fostered by their mother, had been festering for several years. With my own growth as a person, I felt fully capable of giving my whole and healthy self to this new relationship. My soul mate came with three children—a boy eight, a girl six, and a boy four years of age. After three and a half years of being together, we married and with love, brought two additional children, a boy and a girl, into the world. Upon her visit to our home, Virginia Satir, an internationally renowned family therapist, proclaimed us "the ultimate new age couple."

My next significant insight centered on recognizing that alienation could be overcome through love, in both intent and deed. Redemption as a parent was possible. Thanks to my new wife and her strong support, the healing began with my older children who were twenty, eighteen, sixteen, and eleven at that time.

In 1987 my wife was diagnosed with cervical cancer. The first of four major surgeries began about six months after the birth of our second child, and three months after we moved into our new home. In 1990, she passed away at age forty-four, two and a half years after her shocking diagnosis. My dreams were shattered and my responsibilities overwhelmed me for the second time in my life.

Another key insight was that who I thought I was becoming, no longer existed as my new life, my new family, and my new vision of the future disappeared. I had reached another turning point in my life, wondering how to move forward from these major losses. I began by letting go of my postdoctoral work and beginning private practice in marriage and family therapy and consulting work with drug and alcohol programs.

During the first two years after my wife's death, I had no time to grieve. Settling my wife's estate and the children's guardianship, involved legal conflicts over three years. The resulting estrangement from my wife's family seriously challenged my ability to raise the five children together as a family. The biological father never accepted financial responsibility or provided emotional support for his children. When the judge asked him if he wanted his children, he remained silent. As the guardian for the three older children, I had no legal standing in court to enforce financial support of those children.

My heartache was how to raise these five motherless and three fatherless children aged two, five, twelve, fourteen, and sixteen. How was I going to recreate a sense of family? How could I honor my commitment to their mother? The answer required both an experimental and experiential process that progressed one day at a time over the next eighteen years. The greatest expression I have ever read of this passage of time was the fine book titled *Grace and Grit: Spirituality and Healing in the Life and Death of Treya Killam Wilber* by Ken Wilber, her husband. It was published a year after my wife's passing, recounting his experiences and journey between the diagnosis and death of his wife, also to cancer.

I was challenged on every front. Having lost their mother and abandoned by their biological father, the three older children were drifting without a discernible rudder. The tragic realization of their mother's deteriorating health and impending death was overwhelming and incomprehensible to them. The oldest had left home at sixteen to live with another family, as the pain of watching his mother die was too great. I had to place the older daughter in a safe house. I was extremely concerned about her physical and emotional well-being. The youngest was the only one present and assisting me with his mother's needs before her passing. He remained very angry for the next several years. Drugs or alcohol deadened these children's feelings for some time, until I gradually earned their respect and appreciation over the next several years. Also, my two-year-old and five-year-old required my full attention. I was in a very deep hole emotionally and financially at this time in my life and I could not see a path into the future, or any relief in sight during those two years. My life was about reacting, not acting, on a daily basis between ages fifty to fifty-two.

Two years after my second wife's death, I came to the vital realization that I had also effectively died. I required two years to accept that I no longer could live the beautiful life I shared with my wife. The next eighteen years, between the ages of fifty-two to seventy, I began to act. One new beginning involved opening my large community home over the next few years for six to twelve others, including single parents, to live with my family, for both financial and emotional support. In one six-year period I was in a warm, supportive, and loving relationship. After six years together I was again devastated as we separated, in part, for lack of support from some of our children.

Furthermore, realizing that I was embarking upon a new life—for which I had no experience—serving as a really present, compassionate, and loving father to each of the nine children became my mission. I decided to become 100 percent committed to their growth and development into loving and productive individuals who cherished life and living, despite the tragic circumstances in their own lives with both sets of parents. Over the course of those eighteen years, anger and conflict shifted to mutual love, respect, and appreciation. The gift of being a loving parent has repeatedly been returned. There is seldom a day that I am not in conversation with one or more of my children. My oldest daughter began calling me the "option king," as I made myself available and offered ways to view and resolve individual and collective concerns and challenges in their lives.

At a gathering for the 80th birthday of the five younger children's grandmother, she took me aside to share her gratitude and appreciation for all I had done for her grandchildren after the loss of their mother. Despite our estrangement over the settlement of the estate and placing her granddaughter in a safe-house, I felt loved and valued by her acknowledgment of me. Similarly, the children's grandfather has been singing my praises at family gatherings in recent years. He has referred to me as "Superdad." All nine children came together, inspired by my non-blood-related daughter, to honor and surprise me on my 69th birthday. Along with the grandparents' testimonials, that surprise gathering felt like my redemption as a father. I was very moved and proud. Even my first wife was in attendance, because she often cared for my two youngest children on weekends after my second wife's passing. That gathering with all the children was truly a peak experience.

As of today, I am appreciating my ninth year in a relationship with my spiritual partner and together we have successfully bridged the generation and gender gaps of our large blended family of eleven children and eight grandchildren with love and peace.

Having landed on my feet through all my tribulations, I am truly blessed. I am reminded of Scott Peck's opening sentence in his great book *The Road Less Traveled* regarding his spiritual journey. He states, "Life is difficult."

Rick Tidrick is a cultural creative. He loves connecting needs with resources through networking. Rick values balanced and sustainable interactions among and between natural environments and human cultures. He founded The Great Gathering Place, a center for cultural change education that supported seminars, workshops, and gatherings for environment builders, social architects, community artisans, and spiritual pathfinders. He was the co-creator of The Circle Sanctuary, a community for transformation: giving permission to consider and gain access to possibility—for connecting with ourselves, with others, and with the Earth as our sanctuary. Rick has a master's degree in experiential education and a combined doctorate in holistic health, psychology, and counseling with experience in coaching individuals and couples, and facilitating groups and circles. Email him at ricktidrick@yahoo.com.

Masterpiece

by Jason Vitello

With every gentle nudge of my shoulder, coherence spiraled to the forefront of my mind, like a wisp of cigarette smoke toward an open window. My throbbing brain felt like a sponge that had been used to soak up alcohol and broken bits of glass from the countertop of a bar at the end of a ramshackle evening of revelry. Ah, yes, the bar. That's where I was last night. But where the hell was I now? And who was shaking me out of my peaceful slumber? I groaned and rolled over. My eyes watered at the invasion of blinding shards of daylight as I blinked them open. After a moment, the offender came into focus: three feet tall, backpack strapped tightly to his narrow shoulders, hair combed, shirt tucked in haphazardly, and holding a lunch pail.

My six-year-old son, Angelo. "Dad," his voice wavered as he asked in earnest, "can I go to school now?" My wits snapped to attention and my heart sank as my eyes scanned the nightstand for the alarm clock. It was on the floor, where I had apparently flung it hours before in unconscious fury. 12:41 p.m. Damn.

Seven Years Earlier

"I'm late," she said. "What do you mean you're late? I drove," I replied dismissively. "No. My period. It's late. I think I'm pregnant." Those words, uttered by my girlfriend, would alter the course of my life forever. I was seventeen years old and in a highly volatile and unhealthy high school romance that I had anticipated abandoning as soon as I graduated. I was an accomplished artist with good grades and scholarships. I had big plans—and a child was not among them. I would study at a fine arts school, travel the world, and become a famous and influential painter. I had a few friends who had faced the same predicament. They shirked the problem by paying for an abortion or by refusing to acknowledge it at all. After weeks of anguished deliberation and a fatalistic series of events, I could not bring myself to do either. My parents had always instructed me to take responsibility for my actions and do the right thing, no matter the cost. My big plans would have to change.

All of my options seemed like mistakes, thus I would thus have to choose the *best* mistake from among them. For the sake of my son, I decided to do two things I always swore to myself that I would never do—marry young and join the military. I did love my girlfriend but I knew we were young and clueless and that the odds against us were likely insurmountable—but I would do my part. And years later when my child would ask me what went wrong, I could look him in the eye and tell him that I had done my best. I had no idea that things would turn out as they have.

Years passed and I had settled into the role of family man quite comfortably. By all accounts, my girlfriend had become a good wife. Our son, Angelo, was bright, charming, and good-natured. I enjoyed my work as a military graphic designer. I was content, even happy. I thought my wife was too. When she informed me on our fourth anniversary that she intended to leave, I was stunned.

While life had not been what I had imagined it would be, the pieces seemed to fit, and suddenly, they did not. I had done the right thing and sacrificed everything for the sake of my family, and now it was being ripped apart. After my incessant pleading, I was astounded further when my wife agreed to leave Angelo behind in my care. Then she was gone.

At twenty-one years old, I found myself in the awkward and unfamiliar role of primary caretaker to a toddler. My wife had always been the nurturer. Having spent the crucial months after his birth in military training, I did not have as strong an emotional attachment to Angelo and alternated between discipliner and giant play-mate. In optimistic naïveté, I assured him that "Mommy is going to come home." Beyond hope, I actually believed that she would. In the meantime, I tried to be stoic and strong, never allowing Angelo to witness my sadness and confusion. This did little to alleviate his own. He began to cry more frequently and wet his bed nearly every night, almost a year after having been fully potty-trained. Many nights I would open his bedroom door to find him sitting on the edge of his bed, peeking out the window at the driveway, waiting for my promise to come true. I would lay his head on my lap until he fell asleep, sometimes biting my own lip until it bled.

Days turned into weeks and then months. The raw and sharp emotional pain had subsided and was replaced by a sporadic dull ache. So it seemed for both of us. We settled into new routines and despite the occasional loneliness, life went on. One night I sat in my living room, numbly gazing at the pictures of my wife on the wall. Perhaps it was time to take them down? I felt a presence and turned my head to find Angelo standing at the edge of the couch in his pajamas, hours after I had put him down. We stared at each other in silence before he came and sat next to me. Moments passed before he looked up from the floor and into my eyes.

"Dad," he began softly, "Mom isn't coming home, huh?" The pain came flooding back. I turned my head away from him, blinking back tears and swallowing hard. I took a deep breath and faced him again. "No, son. She isn't." He stared back down at the floor and nodded his head gently. Then he looked up at me again and said, "Don't worry, Dad, you will find another mommy."

I do not believe he was talking about a mother for him, but a new companion for me, as he curled his little arm around me in an embrace, patted my back, and laid his head on my shoulder. In that moment, I felt a rush of every emotion imaginable. All I could do was laugh softly at the truths, the lies, the rapturous joys, the melancholy sorrows, the cold cruelties, and the beautiful sweetness of life.

In the years that followed, while I kept my eyes open for a "new mommy" I was actively engaged in a much more profound search for meaning. Ousted from my role as family man, what was I to be now? Upon finishing my military stint, I became prominent and successful in the field of graphic design, a responsible and economically viable profession for the artist with familial duties. However, I began to feel unfulfilled, and believed I was using my talents to dazzle consumers into buying stuff they probably did not need. I had become a "square" and a sellout by necessity. I attempted to enhance my identity by taking on numerous other roles such as writer, bartender, bouncer, playboy, missionary, activist, party animal, and student. I was in a perpetual state of flux, never finding my center. Of course I was also a father, but since the age of seventeen, fatherhood had seemed to me like a mere noble obligation. I was frequently told I was, and believed myself to be, a great father, just because *I was there.*

I still held to the notion that I was meant to be an artist, a grand creator whose work would inspire and influence others. But it seemed that my creative mind had given way to my calculating and analytical mind. The imaginative dreamer in me had been supplanted by the realist. I tried to paint again, but it rarely seemed intuitive or natural to do so anymore and my home was filled with blank and unfinished canvases.

I developed a strong affinity for a friend who seemed to be living the romanticized life I had imagined for myself long ago. He had spent years studying at a notable art institution. His work had been admired in fine arts publications and in the halls of prestigious galleries around the country. Never tied down to one place and shunning the nine-to-five grind, he lived on the road, frequenting New York City, Los Angeles, and San Francisco. He slept on couches when he had to, and made a living via talent and passion alone.

My friend was possessed by a ceaseless and contagious need to create. In the middle of our bar conversations, he would often impulsively grab a napkin and begin to draw with intense fervor. He'd then pass it on to me and proclaim, "Now you!" And for a brief moment I would freely tap into the elusive remnants of artistry within me and draw without distraction or fear of tomorrow, as I had as a child. From my perspective, my friend was the embodiment of such freedom—free to live life with a reckless abandon and make mistakes from which only he would suffer. He was free to pursue his ultimate dream of creating a breakthrough work—a masterpiece—the impact and significance of which would outlast his own lifetime.

All of these musings surfaced one night in a bar, where I watched him from across the room. I had been drinking heavily and was feeling sentimental. I decided that I would tell him how I felt. I would let him know how lucky he was, how he had it made. I would tell him how I envied his freedom, his life. It was then that he noticed me and waved. We smiled, stood up, and began walking toward each other through the crowd. After exchanging drunken pleasantries he said, "I have something I need to tell you, man." "Yeah, I have something I want to say too," I replied. He placed his hand on my shoulder and went first.

"Every time I wake up in the morning, I don't know what to do with my day, let alone with my life. I look everywhere for inspiration and meaning and I have only managed to discover it in passing moments and fleeting relationships. I have tried finding it in my own work … but the things I create end up on a stranger's wall somewhere and I will likely never see them again."

His eyes misted and his voice began to shake as he continued, "The other day I saw you drive by—and *your* meaning, *your* purpose, *your* inspiration was sitting right beside you in the passenger seat of your car. He is with you every day. You already know why the hell you're here. I just wanted to tell you how lucky you are."

Despite my inebriated state, I experienced a heartrending moment of salient lucidity. My knees nearly buckled at the weight of his words. He sighed, lifted his hand from my shoulder, and asked, "What were you gonna say?" "Never mind," I answered weakly.

The following day at 12:41 p.m., I sat on the edge of my bed, finally awake. My son stood before me, ready for school—ready for *life*. I looked at his face, so much like my own. I arose and placed my hand on top of his head, like some instinctual ancient act of blessing. I walked into the bathroom, looked into the mirror, ran the faucet, and splashed waves of cold water upon my face—a baptism of sorts. The words of my friend from the night before came to mind. My "meaning," my "purpose." My "inspiration." My son. My "*masterpiece.*"

Present

Today I work as a counselor, mentor, and advocate at an agency called Fatherhood Support Services. Our mission is to empower men to become better fathers and more fully involved in the lives of their children. That is not to say that I have become the model of fatherhood. I have met men here who want nothing more than to have even a portion of what I was given long ago, a fraction of what I once took for granted. Their greatest desire is to be afforded the mere chance to be an involved father, a role that I have come to understand is as important as any in life.

Jason Vitello is a student at the Graduate School of Social Work at the University of Denver. He is husband to Priscilla and father to two sons—Angelo and Luciano Vitello. Not long ago you could find him under the night sky, somewhere between the disco and the revolution. Now, on most nights, chances are you will find him happy at home. You can reach Jason at jasonvitello@gmail.com.

My Brazilian Daughter

by Chuck Roberts

It is December 26th, 2008, and it is nearly 90 degrees on this midsummer afternoon as I walk along Avenue Rosales on my way back to the hotel. We arrived in Buenos Aires a few hours earlier and I decided I wanted to take some pictures of the Casa Rosada, the office of the Argentinean president. It is less than a mile from our hotel and a nice walk. As I continue back toward our hotel through the park with its brightly colored flowers and freshly mowed lawn, I notice a street named after a very famous Argentine leader, Juan Peron. I remember the movie, *Evita*, which I enjoyed so much. The song that touched me so deeply, "Don't Cry For Me Argentina," runs through my head as I remember the many dramatic gatherings depicted in the film that actually happened right here where I'm standing. I loved the passion that Eva Peron—Evita—had for life. As I approach the shops and restaurants that line the water of the Puerto Medero, my thoughts turn to my Brazilian daughter, Camilla. She will be arriving from Sao Paulo this evening. I can hardly wait to see her.

Gathering in the tenth-floor lounge of our hotel, my family laughs as we talk about the fun times we've enjoyed over the past eight days of our Argentinean adventure. It has been great to have Juan, my daughter Andrea's boyfriend from Argentina, traveling with us. We had just come from a wonderful Christmas visit with his family. As I take a sip of wine and eat one more bacon-wrapped date, I savor the rich flavor of the Malbec wine for which Argentina is so famous. The sun is setting on this warm summer afternoon as I look out across the rooftop pool at the Buenos Aires skyline. I think to myself, "What an amazing Christmas holiday this has been and it is about to get even better!"

It will be at least an hour before Camilla arrives. As the afternoon fades to evening, our conversation keeps coming back to Camilla; she touched all of our lives in such a special way. She should be arriving anytime. We take turns walking over to the balcony that overlooks the ten-story open lobby to keep an eye on the front entrance. I can just see it past the forty-foot-tall Christmas tree that adorns the spectacular lobby. The bellman holds the door open and greets the guests as they enter. I wonder if Camilla will look different. It was June 2004, more than four years ago, since we were last together, when we visited her family in Sao Paulo. As we wait and talk, I think about the day Camilla arrived and how she became such an important part of our family.

It is six-and-a-half years earlier in 2002, on another warm summer day, but this time in the northern hemisphere. I'm standing with my wonderful wife, Leann, and our two teenage daughters, Sharla and Andrea, at the Denver International Airport watching every face that emerges from the arrival gate near the fountain. We are about to meet the young Brazilian girl who, as part of the Rotary student exchange program, will be living with us for the next several months.

I'm hoping the picture I have in my mind of our new student is accurate. Another group starts walking from the top of the escalator, turning and searching for a familiar face in the crowd. Suddenly, there she is. I am immediately surprised. As I see Camilla, the recognition is instantaneous. How can I already know her? Camilla has already spotted us. A very confident and beautiful seventeen-year-old girl, who obviously recognizes us, is moving quickly toward us. The first thing I notice is her beautiful smile, then I hear her enthusiastically call out, "my family!" Camilla has tears in her eyes as she hugs each of us and greets us in the traditional Brazilian fashion, with a kiss on the cheek. In that instant, I have another daughter. It is as if she has always been my daughter and for some unknown reason I am just now meeting her.

Leann has just walked back from the hotel balcony; still no sign of Camilla. I continue to sip my wine, as my thoughts return to the memories from the full year that followed that day in the airport in 2002. We became a family of five: my wife and I, along with three teenage daughters, all at Fairview High School in Boulder. We enjoyed so many good times together.

We also encountered fresh challenges. We had to adapt to having a new person in our home, especially someone with a personality as strong and intense as Camilla's. There was a sense of having to let go of our family of four as Camilla integrated into the family. Initially, we also felt a sense of having a stranger in our home. Camilla was accustomed to confrontation and to forceful conversations; our family conversations were usually more indirect. My daughters witnessed Camilla's almost immediate popularity at school and how she attracted attention that they had not imagined possible. They each struggled to accept their new "sister."

If I had any second thoughts about taking a new person into our home, those thoughts faded quickly for me. I loved the heightened sense of energy Camilla brought. I admired her love and passion for life and her ability to find the joy in every moment. I also admired her commitment to making her new situation and our new family work. Deep in my heart, I knew Camilla was to become an essential part of our family, even as I was concerned for each of my daughters as they worked to accept the change. Leann and I had some heartfelt conversations with each of our daughters during this time. We had all made the decision to bring an exchange student into our home many months prior to Camilla's arrival. We had discussed the importance of the commitment required to make this work and the potential risks and gains. Each in our own way, and in our own time, began to accept Camilla's presence then started to love her as a daughter and a sister. It's hard to identify the specific moment, but at some point several weeks, or perhaps months, after her arrival, Camilla had become a part of our family.

Camilla also had to adapt to us. We were "too quiet." I learned later, as Camilla and I grew closer, that in those first weeks she wondered if we really liked her and wanted her here.

During Camilla's stay, we laughed and had great times together. There was a new richness and joy in our lives. Camilla was a vital part of this newfound joy. I'll never forget the first time it snowed that fall. Camilla had only seen snow on TV; she had never experienced it before. It was that special day that happens every fall when there is a quiet chill in the air and without any warning, the first snow silently starts to fall. "Look, it's snowing!" I said. "What?" Camilla gasped and jumped up from her chair. She stood looking out the sliding door as the lawn slowly became covered in white. Before I knew it, she ran outside, nearly falling on the snowy deck. Camilla ran around the backyard, screaming and laughing with joy, the quiet snowflakes melting on her face and arms. As her exuberance waned, she realized just how cold it was and quickly returned to the warmth of our home.

Camilla and I had some wonderful talks in our study. We'd sit in the two green high-back chairs and talk for hours, often on Sunday afternoons. Camilla's parents in Sao Paulo were going through a divorce while she was with us. It was a difficult time for her. Often our conversations followed a long phone call Camilla had with her mom in Sao Paulo. I loved to listen as she spoke in her poetic-sounding Portuguese. Even though I couldn't understand what she was saying, I could tell from the passion in her voice just how hard these times were for her. I heard all about Camilla's mom, dad, and sister Vanessa, as we discussed just what makes a strong family. The day that we talked about love, marriage, and fatherhood was one of those rare days when I knew in my soul that I had really made a deep and meaningful connection with Camilla. I remember there were a few tears on that day, mine and Camilla's.

All this time Camilla was so focused on improving her English skills. She would often say, "Tell me if I make a mistake; it is the only way I can learn." Working with her on improving her language was an important way that she and I built our relationship. She worked hard to win the spot in this exchange program, with the primary goal of mastering English, and she did not want to miss any opportunity to learn. I admired her dedication and focus.

As spring warmed into summer and our family grew closer, I was beginning to feel a twinge of anxiety. It took me some time to figure it out, but it became clearer with the passing days. I didn't want to face it, but I knew that this precious family time would soon come to an end when Camilla returned to Brazil. For me, it was a time of unexpected internal turmoil. I didn't want to miss a minute of the limited time we all had together, but my anxiety increased as August approached.

Late one night after everyone was asleep, I let down all my restraints and went deeper into my soul-searching than ever before. The seemingly endless tears kept coming as I wept alone in the dark of the night. The depth of my sorrow surprised me. I knew I had to dig deeper to discover just what was behind these intense emotions. In the days that followed, I began to realize that my feelings about Camilla leaving were just the tip of the iceberg. Camilla was only the first of my daughters that I would have to let go. My oldest daughter, Sharla, would be leaving for college in less than a year and my baby, Andrea, would be gone the following year. Of course, I always knew my daughters would grow up and leave home someday, which is what I wanted for them, but I had no idea just how hard it would be to let go. Releasing them is one of the most difficult things I have ever faced.

Back on the tenth-floor lounge of our hotel, the tears well up again as I reach for my wine and let those feelings surface. I know that I become very deeply attached and have been intensely passionate about many things in my life since I was a child. My love for my daughters and my wife is the deepest of all. I know that letting go of a child is one of those all-important, but oh-so-difficult responsibilities of being a good father. I knew as I watched the birth of each of my daughters, twenty-six and twenty-four years ago, that I had been entrusted with the responsibility of being a father for these two beautiful human beings. I remember the tears of pure joy on those "birth days," as the doctor handed me my minute-old daughters wrapped in warm delivery blankets. I looked into their eyes and experienced that miraculously instant recognition. Of course, I had no idea that I would be given the opportunity to play a small part of this important role for an amazing young girl who was being born almost six thousand miles away in a hospital in Sao Paulo, Brazil, at nearly the same time. For this, I am eternally grateful.

This time it is my turn to check the hotel lobby. I look past the Christmas tree and I see Camilla walking into the lobby as the bellman holds the door open. I am excited as I return to the lounge to gather Juan and the girls. We rush quickly into the elevator. Fortunately, it is a glass elevator that looks out across the lobby. As we start our descent, I can see Camilla talking to the receptionist at the front desk. The receptionist points up toward the top floor and Camilla turns to look. After a moment, she sees us all waving from the elevator. The smile on her face is incredible. The elevator seems to be taking forever to finish its descent to the lobby, and my heart is racing with anticipation. Finally, as the elevator door opens, I see an amazing and beautiful Brazilian young woman running toward me. She throws herself into my arms, sobbing. All I hear is, "Daddy." As I wipe the tears from my face, I know our family is reunited.

Chuck Roberts lives in Boulder, Colorado, with Leann, his wife of thirty-two years. Their daughters are living in Hollywood, California; Rosario, Argentina; and Sao Palo, Brazil. Chuck and Leann have also been privileged to have another "adopted" daughter in their lives for the past eight years, Jennifer. She is now a medical student in New York City and will be married in the fall. Chuck works as a business development executive for IBM's worldwide health care practice. This role allows him to combine his deep caring for others, and his years of experience in the field of health care, with IBM's resources and integrity to facilitate real change in the lives of many people. Write Chuck at CharlesJRoberts@gmail.com.

Growing Together—A Father's Story

by Jeff Klein

I didn't plan on being a full-time single father, but when circumstances called me to become one, I wholeheartedly accepted the call. As I reflect on the past four years since I received "the call," I recognize that I learn as much from my daughter Meryl Fé as she does from me, and the lessons I have learned through single parenting serve me in every aspect of my life. They have profoundly informed the work I do through my business, Working for Good, and have prepared me for a deeper level of intimacy and connection with others.

Lesson One: Connect First

I vividly remember one day when Meryl Fé was eight. As was often the case, I was in somewhat of a hurry and needed to get her moving out of the house, to the car, and on the road. Meryl Fé did not share my sense of urgency or need for speed. The more anxious I was about leaving, the slower she moved. The more I beseeched her, the more belligerent she became, until she ended up standing still and said something to the effect of, "Dad, if you want me to move, then connect with me first. Don't just try to pull me along." Needless to say, that was like having a bucket of ice-cold water dumped on my head. I immediately stopped, took a breath, got down onto my knee so I could be eye to eye with her, acknowledged what she must be feeling, and apologized. Then I told her how I was feeling and explained where we needed to go and why. I asked if she understood and if she had anything to express. She responded that she didn't, and said, "Let's go!" which we did, with ease, joy, and great flow.

Lesson Two: The Power of Listening

Homework has been great grounds for mutual discovery—especially about the processes of learning and relating. When we began doing homework together, Meryl Fé would almost always end up in tears—and I in utter frustration. While we would invariably find a way to make it through the work and our emotions, it was never easy. She would admonish me: "You don't understand. I just need to get the answer. I don't need you to tell me more than is necessary for that." And I would respond: "I need to know the context. And I want to support you to understand what you are learning, not to just get the right answer." It often felt brutal—to both of us. As time passed, I began to let her emotional outbursts fly past me, without reacting. At the same time I listened more deeply to her words and framed my questions and comments in ways that reflected understanding of and respect for her requests. In time her tears and my frustration became exceptions rather than the rule.

After I recently gave her a dynamic (as in "moving") visual illustration of the run and rise of a slope and successfully imparted the relationship between ratios and percentages, she said to me, "You should be our math teacher, Dad. You make it so much easier for me to understand."

Lesson Three: Hold the Space and Stay with Emotions

Another context for some of my deepest lessons from parenting have been that of boundary setting and being with the expression of intense emotions. Fortunately, over the years of being a parent before single parenting, I learned how to stay present for strong emotions—like tears and tantrums (though Meryl Fé is not prone to those)—rather than to retreat from them. Being alone with a young child who is totally dependent on you for pretty much everything calls forth a certain kind of presence and balance—to cultivate a sense of boundaries and appropriate behavior, while at the same time comforting and building sustainable trust. So what do you do when your child is acting out, behaving like she is itching for an argument, pushing the boundaries beyond acceptable limits? I learned to hold the line in the face of gut-wrenching tears and wailing, not giving in to the verbal accusations and occasional physical assaults, while remaining compassionate and loving; witnessing her internal struggle between exerting her will and complying with the boundaries I set.

Sometimes I felt like running away or caving in, but somehow I was able to listen to the voice inside— "Hang in there. This will pass. You are doing the right thing."— and stay the course.

When the storms passed, the skies were so clear, as we invariably felt closer, with deepened trust and no residual charge.

Lesson Four: Lighten Up

One of greatest lessons I have learned from and with Meryl Fé is that of lightening up—of finding humor and playfulness in the face of tension and intensity. When one or both of us are wound up and getting intense, we often move from a heated moment to a light one in an instant as one or the other of us will break out in laughter or add a twist of humor—poking fun at ourselves or each other—to turn the fire into steam and then into a warm breeze.

Lesson Five: All You Need Is Love

Fortunately for Meryl Fé and me, one thing we have always been able to do is end the day with love. Regardless of the confrontations or stresses we may have had along the way, we end up with a hug (usually at least three), a drink of water (I hand her water bottle to her and take it back when she is done), and "I love you, *duerme con los angelitos.*" In some ways, it feels like this has almost become a ritual. It is our way of saying "I love you"—no question about it. We affirm our connection, respect, and love for each other and set the foundation for tomorrow.

Lesson Six: Slow Down and Be Here Now

As I reflect on all of the previous lessons and on the experiences they represent, I recognize that one theme running through all of them is that of slowing down and showing up for the moment. Not only is Meryl Fé asking me to be there for her, she is giving me the opportunity to be there for myself and for whomever or whatever else might be present. At times, when I have been particularly wound up for one reason or another, she will even say (as I have said to her) "Dad, take a few breaths. Relax. It's okay." What a delightful reflection and invitation. Hard to resist!

What all of the lessons reinforce for me is that not only is Meryl Fé growing up and I am witnessing and participating in her growth, but I am growing up too, and she is witnessing and participating in my growth. And we both witness and participate in the ongoing growth and development of our relationship.

I delight in the experience and lessons from this passage and feel infinitely fortunate to have had this unexpected opportunity. As Meryl Fé enters her teens and we enter new passages in our journey, I have no doubt that we will continue to grow, together.

Jeff Klein *is CEO, Activator, Producer, and Process Facilitator for Working for Good®—A Conscious Marketing and Business Development Company. He also serves as a Director of the Baumann Foundation, whose mission is to explore the experience of being human in the context of cognitive science, evolutionary theory, and philosophy to foster greater clarity about the human condition, and is a founding trustee of Conscious Capitalism, Inc. Jeff authored his award-winning book,* Working for Good: Making a Difference While Making a Living, *to support conscious entrepreneurs, "intrapreneurs," leaders, and change agents at work. For more information visit www.workingforgood.com.*

The Turning Point

by Robert William Case

Two roads diverged in a wood, and I—
I took the one less traveled by,
And that has made all the difference.

—Robert Frost

Well-known lines from "The Road Not Taken." The words come from the perspective of an older man looking back on the course of his life. The poet focuses on a seemingly insignificant historical event and a choice made there. Somehow over time that single decision point and the actions that followed became the destiny of his life.

Now consider this … Here's a different man with equally famous words, again spoken from the perspective of someone past his physical prime, looking back at a decision point in the road of his life that only he can see, and saying, "I coulda been a contenda. I coulda been somebody! Instead I'm a bum."

That's a line from a performance that won Marlon Brando an Oscar for his role in the 1950s black-and-white movie, *On the Waterfront*. But this time when the actor looks back to the choice made and acted upon, he concludes that from that point onward, his life became increasingly smaller.

So I have to wonder, what is it about these forks in the road that causes old men to look back with joy or regret, or perhaps some other deeply held belief? And what is it about these seemingly irrelevant times and places and the corresponding events that unfold and evolve into turning points, that when the elder looks back, he remembers a power that shaped the man that he became?

I wonder if most men have such moments, because I did. There was a day and a night in my own life that stands out like no other. It was not a time of notable achievement or passionate romance. It was just one of those turning points at an insignificant time and place that has made all the difference. That day I unknowingly stood at the tipping point of a fulcrum in time and met my own future. It happened like this ...

In a time before cell phones and laptops, on a warm August evening, a dark-haired man on the edge of forty sits with two small children in a Goodland, Kansas, diner. Through dusty eyeglasses he gazes out the window at dusk, watching the sky transform from blue-gray into primrose, orange, and red. They are all tired, heading home, and the Colorado line is just down the road.

Home. The kids are out of school for the summer. He needed to get away from Denver for a while and to find a place that didn't cost too much: somewhere like Ohio, the home of his parents, still living together in the house he grew up in, some-place like home. It had been a long couple of years for him and his family. He got laid off from his job. Soon after that, his wife explained that it was her time and turn to go for the brass ring. But she fell into a bottle and never came out.

And now the man and the children sit on the inside of a diner window, watching the leading edge of a bright harvest moon rise up out of the asphalt and brown prairie. It's coming up right at the end of the street and just visible out of the corner of the window. The little boy stands up in his chair and points. They all turn their heads and pause, watching the light slowly coalesce into a glowing arc that seems to be resting upon the pavement. Then over hamburgers and milkshakes, they plan the rest of their trip.

"Where would you like to wake up tomorrow morning?" the man asks, pushing back on the fatigue and doing his best to sound lighthearted. "We can get a motel right here, start out fresh in the morning, and be back in Denver by lunchtime."

The children keep right on eating, neither one very interested in a night in Goodland, Kansas.

The father continues, "Or we can keep right on going. I'm feeling pretty good. A couple cups of coffee and we'll finish the drive tonight. You can wake up in your own beds in the morning. So what do you want to do, rest here or go on?"

It is not a close call. The two kids look at each other and grin, homemade French fries showing on their teeth. "Go home!" they say, almost in unison. Less than two years apart, they are very close and sometimes seem to have their own, completely nonverbal form of communication. However it works, they understand exactly what the other one is feeling and quickly announce an accord, without hesitation. They want to be home; to sleep in the warmth of their own beds, in their own room, surrounded by all of their familiar comforts and playthings.

So they continue their dinner with purpose, eager to be underway once again. Soon the father is holding open the door of the diner like a threshold for each of them to pass through. And they do, only to stop in their tracks, turn, and stare up at the ball of the ascending moon, sorrel and huge, hanging in the sky directly over the center of the main street. The storefronts and signs are aglow in a numinous half-light. The moment does not last; it gradually fades as the globe rises and shrinks before their eyes. The colors fade like shadows, bleeding into gray and brown.

Slowly they walk toward that end of the street, watching the moon's changing display and following a course that takes them to a GMC pickup, the beige one with the green license plates and the tail-wagging lab in the back. He has his own turn at dinner and then gets a chance to sniff the parking meters and take a short stroll.

With one last look at the rising sphere, they climb into the truck for the last leg of their journey. The little boy arranges his pillow and blanket on the floor of the cab. He rubs his fingers along the yellow satin fringe, humming to his own song. Higher status due to age, his sister adjusts her backpack, pillow, and books on the seat above. Finally, she snuggles into the warmth of her own blanket. And the truck begins to move, heading west out of town.

Eastern Colorado is a very big expanse at night. They drive on and on under the rising moon, across a rolling sea of prairie and sage. And every time the truck travels over a small rise, the man wants to see mountains in the moonlit distance. And each time all he gets is more sage and another low hill up ahead. In this way the truck rolls on and on as the miles slide by, the moon growing smaller and smaller, silver now and still ascending into the sky.

As the pickup truck rolls along, the only sound is the warm rushing wind coming in through the open window, keeping the man awake. From time to time he looks over at the sleeping children. He knows deep in his heart that everything he cares about in the entire world is traveling down the road that night in the moonlight. Their lives are on wheels. He could take them anywhere. Back to Ohio with its safety and predictability, back to the raw uncertainty of his life in Denver, or anywhere. He has only to choose.

It feels as though there is no fitting in for him in Denver anymore. Everything he does or wants seems out of sync and there is no end in sight. He feels caught up in a harsh ambiguity, as if standing on the edge of a cliff with long beautiful wings where there once were shoulders and arms, now longing to feel the wind on his face, steady and strong and knowing it would be perfect for flight. If only he had the strength to extend and raise the wings out to their full length with just the right rotation, then the same wind would lift him up and away from the earth. But he cannot move. He cannot will the legs to jump.

The miles go by and the moon rises higher, a small white globe now, directly overhead. The summer air is cooler, still keeping him awake. Inside the truck there is another sound, like a very low hum, just barely audible. It might be something mechanical showing some wear. Then it passes and in the stillness that follows he wonders if he just imagined it. But then the sound returns, a little deeper and louder, but still the same tones—only this time the hairs on the back of his neck tingle. He listens hard. It is definitely not a sound made by the moving parts of a truck. It is too deep and sumptuous for that.

Then it stops once more. In the quiet he looks around, his senses fully alert. "Could it be one of the kids?" he wonders. He turns his head and looks over, first at one and then the other. They are deep in sleep and very still. So the man waits in the stillness, calling it back, asking for the enchanting sound to return. And in a few moments it does, like a gift, fuller and richer this time and definitely coming from outside the moving truck. Then it passes once more.

Once again he waits in the silence. All of his senses wide-open and keenly alert, not out of a sense of danger, but out of hope for the mellifluous sound to return just once more. And then it does, this time filling up the night, a beautiful voice carried on the wind, calling out to him now, saying just two words, over and over, "Come back. Come back."

It is a voice that fills all of his senses, as if there are ears in the center of his heart, an irresistible attraction pulling the father, and through him the sleeping children and the truck, down the road, back to Denver, back to all the changes.

Late that night the truck pulls into the driveway of their home. Fatigue and relief wash over him. Their long drive is over. The voice is quiet now. It left them out on the highway, fading away when the harsh lights of the city came into view. But the sensations of that sound still fill up his senses and he does not want to lose the memory of it to sleep.

Happily, he picks up each child and their blanket from the cab of the truck, and carries them into the house. He tucks them into bed with a smile and a kiss, then says the goodnight words, the ones he always says to them just before turning out the light. The words never change. He has said them every night for as long as each of them can remember. And he will continue to say them for a long time to come.

 ***Robert William Case*** *speaks, writes and inspires with stories about real and legendary heroes and the art of being and becoming more. In addition to being a father, husband and son, Robert is a Colorado author, speaker, and lawyer. His award-winning first novel is titled* Daedalus Rising: The True Story of Icarus. *It is available in fine bookstores and online at www. amazon.com. Robert also writes a weblog that can be enjoyed at www.Edgewaterdad.wordpress.com.*

Part Two: Adventure and High Achievement

The Day I Became a Sailor

by Coy Theobalt

For a number of years people would hear me chatting about my time on the water and ask, "So you're a sailor?" I would find myself hemming and hawing, trying to tell them yes, I sailed, and that I loved sailing. But it was very hard for me to actually speak the words and reply with certainty, "Yes, I am a sailor."

My resistance to this declaration comes from having read many books about the adventures of sailors around the world. Real sailors were men and women who had faced death and destruction many times, only to emerge from the cold salt waters, beaten but rescued to live another day. These people were sailors, in my mind. A "person who sails" is someone who takes out his boat on a pleasant and benign day, weather-wise, and tacks back and forth across the lake, while enjoying a favorite beverage along the way. "Sailors" are made of grit and salty air. Their hands are calloused and red from the wind and sun.

The day I can say I became a sailor started out routinely, riding the wind across Santa Barbara Channel for a four-day trip around the Channel Islands just off the coast of Southern California. The channel is only about 35 miles across, and according to my sail plan would have us in a safe harbor in five to six hours. It was a beautiful day, with the weather channel reporting 18-to-20 knots of wind and 5-to-7-foot seas—a perfect day for a sail with two crewmates. One of the crewmates was a novice sailor, like myself; the other was a complete rookie.

We motored out of the Santa Barbara Sailing Center in a relatively new 32-foot-long Hunter sailboat. We had gone over the pre-trip list in the morning over strong coffee and bagels and made our lunches before heading out, so we would not need to be below deck any longer than necessary. Our sail plan called for us to motor northwest from Santa Barbara for about an hour, then turn due west and set our sails so that we could ride a nice leisurely breeze across the channel.

All was well as we unfurled the sails one by one and felt the surge of the boat underneath us pick up speed. The best sound in the world to a sailor is that of turning off the engine and hearing the wind in the sails. We set our course of

285 degrees west northwest, trimmed the sails, tidied up the boat, and sat back to enjoy what was to be a great day on the water.

At this point in my sailing career, I had sailed up to 50 miles in a day across open waters without being able to see the destination. This trip was much shorter and we could make out the high hills of Santa Rosa Island in the distance.

As we sailed along, I began chatting with our newest crewmate about the physics of sailing, a subject that continues to fascinate me the more I am on the water. He asked the typical questions about how we can go into the wind and yet go forward. I began to notice the swells getting deeper as we talked, but I had no thoughts of worry at that point, as the little sloop glided up and down with ease. My thoughts returned to teaching.

Somewhere about two hours into the trip the wind picked up from 20 to 25 knots. This is a perfect wind speed for someone who sails often, but I noticed my friend's knuckles turning a shade of blue-white as he gripped the side of the cockpit. The boat was leaning over more in the wind than he was comfortable with. I gently eased the line that controlled the mainsail so that the boat took a more upright position on the water. Then I gazed up to see the ocean looking more menacing. The swells were getting even deeper than before and the wind had increased once again, to almost 30 knots. I saw my first mate reaching for the deck bucket, not to swab the deck but to use as his own personal "puke" bucket. His face was developing a sickly appearance; he looked greener than the sea.

By now, when the boat reached the bottom of a sea swell, all you could see on either side was a wall of green seawater. The wind had begun to howl and I started thinking about what we needed to do next to keep ourselves on course and safe, but I realized I had no crew able to go up to the front of the boat and accomplish this task. So I decided to drop the mainsail completely and try to get at least one sail tie on the back of the boom to hold it in place.

In my mind, the next few minutes of the trip became the point in time when I realized I was indeed a sailor. I looked back toward the coast of California only to see nothing but a sky filled with sea salt as the wind-generated waves blew the tops off the swells and into the winter sky. Looking forward I saw the same thing. We were 20 miles offshore and 18 miles from our destination. My assessment was that I had one crew member so seasick he could not walk, another scared out of his mind, and me. I gathered my crew and told them we were going to be okay, but we needed to continue toward the islands rather than turn back. I needed them to stay focused, do as I said, and hang on. We found life preservers and jack lines to keep us from being thrown overboard. I shall never forget the moment I stood at the helm of that boat and made the choice to continue on.

The sea raged in winds over 40 knots and 15-to-18-foot swells. I stood at the helm of the boat with my eyes filled with salt and started the engine. Then I turned the boat into the wind as we motored up the side of a huge wall of green water. As we approached the top of the swell I released the line that held the jib sail and had a crew member crank it in with the winch as quickly as possible.

At that point the worst thing that could have happened did happen. The line became caught on a forward part of the boat and the pressure on it was too strong to free it, so the sail became trapped against the mast. This was dangerous in a howling wind. I eventually was able to release the tension on the line, holding the sail just as we reached the top of the next swell. The sail filled with air instantly and sent the boat screaming down the next wave, nose-first into the bottom of the swell. The boat buried into the swell and I screamed for everyone to duck, as a wall of ice cold seawater came racing down the deck and across the cockpit. I looked up afterward to see one crewmate clinging to his tether and the other with his head buried in the deck bucket, releasing the last remnants of his breakfast bagel.

The good news is that the impact of the swell freed the line that was caught and I was able to furl in the jib sail to the point of creating a small patch of sail that we used as a storm sail to keep the boat's nose on track in the rough seas.

I released a breath of air that I must have been holding for what seemed like an eternity. I had the boat under control and we were on our way out of this very difficult, challenging day. The ride became easier as I steered the boat at angles up one swell then down the other side.

After a couple more hours, I spotted what I thought was land in the distance. Sure enough, it was the vague outline of Santa Rosa Island looming above the horizon. My shoulders began to release the tension that had built up over the past few hours. As we got closer to land, the seas began to loosen their grip and we were able to steer into a safe harbor. When we set the anchor and tidied up the boat, I looked at my watch and saw we had been on the water for almost nine hours. This changed my life forever.

To me, a life-defining experience is one in which, afterward, you see yourself and your world somehow differently. At that instant, one has more clarity about himself and his relationships to the world around him. That winter day on the waters of the Pacific Ocean was certainly one of those times in my life. Today, when someone approaches me and asks if I am a sailor, I say, "Yes!" without question, while in the back of my mind I recall that perilous day many years ago.

Sailing, to me, is the most exhilarating experience in the world. It requires relying primarily on the wind to take you to worlds unknown, whether you are crossing the Santa Barbara Channel or the Caribbean Sea. When I am sailing, my entire world becomes focused only on what is at hand, in the moment. I have learned more life lessons from my sailing experiences than from any traditional teacher. Those lessons have occurred on every level, from purely physical experience to the more subtle spiritual awakenings that have transpired over the years. I believe that my time on the water and following the wind have made me a better man.

Captain Coy Theobalt left the world of corporate consulting to live a dream he had held in his heart for forty-three years. He pulled the proverbial plug on his business and ventured into an unknown world as the captain of a sailboat, offering day sail trips to tourists in the Virgin Islands. During his four-year odyssey he sold his first boat and bought a 60-foot pirate ship, which he began restoring to her glory days on the Caribbean Sea. The Gypsy Wind became his teacher and mentor. She taught him many life lessons that he captured and shares in his book, Gypsy Wind Speaks: Life Lessons from a Sailboat. *You can contact Coy at ctheobalt@comcast.net or call him at (303) 618-1265. He is available for keynote speaking, transformational leadership workshops, and of course, sailing adventures.*

Big Goals and Olympic Dreams

by Chuck Darling

Tossing and turning in my Kansas City hotel room in 1956, excitement coursing through my veins, sleep will not come. Tonight we play the College All Stars, led by two all-time great players, Bill Russell and K.C. Jones. Bucky O'Conner, my basketball coach at the University of Iowa, is coaching the College All Stars. The twelve-man team representing the United States in the Melbourne Olympic Games will be selected based on tonight's performance.

The road to reaching this defining moment of my lifelong love of sports has been challenging and has had its ups and downs. At a little over six foot nine, I am very fortunate to be tall for my generation, to have good coordination, and to be motivated at a young age to do what is necessary to be the best I can be. Athletics come naturally and easily, but there is also an element of good luck involved.

As a sophomore at Helena High School in Montana, I started the season as a six foot two, second team forward. I began growing an inch a month, so that by Christmas I was on the first team and at six foot seven made All State in March. We easily advanced through the quarter- and semifinals. However, in the finals we lost to Missoula, who full-court-pressed us the entire game, repeatedly stealing the ball before we advanced beyond midcourt. My team and I were devastated.

In 1946 our family moved to Denver, Colorado, and I enrolled at South High School. My initial goals were to win the state basketball championship, be selected all-state in track and field, and make the scholastic honor role. In my junior year we had an outstanding team and were undefeated state champions. Denver University was a short walk from South High and on a number of days we scrimmaged their varsity, playing half court. Needless to say, competing at that level was a big help in improving our basketball skills. The following year, with the graduation of four of our starting five, we were chagrined to be ranked number three preseason. However, we again went undefeated until the finals of the state tournament, when we lost to a very good team from Manual High School, our only loss that season. I was selected for the all-state team both years.

Researchers have shown that kids who are protected from grappling with difficult tasks don't develop what psychologists call "mastery experiences." Kids who have this well-earned sense of mastery tend to be more optimistic and decisive. They've learned they are capable of overcoming adversity and achieving goals. Basketball presented these challenges, and by doing well in sports I developed the confidence to excel in other areas. I made the honor role at South High, graduating tenth in a class of six hundred and sixty-six graduates. Also, I set a state record in the discus, even though the distance of 156 feet would not have medaled in today's competition. With encouragement from Mr. Holms, the South High principal, toward the end of my junior year I added a new goal. I would run for student body president—and be elected. Campaigning for the election and fulfilling the duties was a new and broadening experience, far different from participation in athletics, but would have been unlikely without first doing well in sports.

The next decision was where to go to college. My final selection came down to Yale or the University of Iowa. I was impressed with Pops Harrison, the Iowa coach, and decided, probably correctly, that I was really not the Ivy League type (although my mother never forgave me for not going to Yale). My family also had other ties to Iowa. An only child, I was born in Denison, Iowa. My dad had graduate degrees from the University of Iowa and we had many relatives living in Iowa. When I was a Boy Scout in Helena and tested for the geology merit badge, I had the good fortune of meeting the chief geologist for the Montana Geological Survey. I was so impressed that I decided early on to be a geologist. Both Yale and Iowa had excellent geology departments. Considering all factors, Iowa won out. I had three new goals: to be All American in Basketball, to win the Big Ten Basketball Championship, and to graduate Phi Beta Kappa.

My freshman year at Iowa was also Bucky O'Conner's first year as the freshman coach. Freshmen were not eligible to play on the varsity then, but we did get a lot of good experience scrimmaging the varsity. The following year on the varsity was the only time I ever played on a losing team. In my sophomore year at Iowa we won 15 and lost 7, winding up fifth place in the Big Ten. I was on the second team until mid-season when Bucky replaced Pops as head varsity coach. We were on a road trip to play Ohio State and he told me to be ready to start. I scored 21 points and from then on was the first-team center. The next year, my junior year, we had a better conference record, ending up third place in the Big Ten. I was selected to the All Big Ten first team.

About this time I began thinking, perhaps a bit wishfully, that just maybe I could have a shot at making the Olympic team in my senior year. My graduation year, 1952, was an Olympic Year and the basketball team would be selected from the National Collegiate Athletic Association (NCAA) and Amateur Athletic Union (AAU) championship teams. But in order for me to be eligible, Iowa would first have to win the Big Ten. In my senior year, we were in a season-long battle with Illinois for the Big Ten title. With identical records, it came down to a rematch in Champaign. Extremely bad weather totally disrupted Iowa's travel plans, delaying our arrival. The game ended after midnight on Sunday morning and is the only Big Ten Basketball game ever played over a two-day period. We were leading at halftime, but ran out of gas the second half, dashing our goal of a Big Ten Championship and squelching my dreams of making the Olympic team, at least for 1952.

Iowa wound up with 19 wins and 3 losses, a good record but a very disappointing second place in the Big Ten. Individually, I had a great year, averaging 25.5 points and 22 rebounds per game. I was selected first team All American and won the Chicago Tribune Big Ten MVP award. Although failing to win the Big Ten Championship, I achieved my other two goals at Iowa: I graduated Phi Beta Kappa in geology and made All American.

Upon graduation from Iowa I went to work for Phillips Petroleum Company. Phillips was the sponsor of the best amateur basketball team in the nation. They played in the NIBL (National Industrial Basketball League). It was a great fit, whereby I could play ball a few years while gaining experience in the oil exploration business and preparing for a career in geology. Overall, we had a fantastic win-loss record over the five years I ended up playing for Phillips. Gerald Tucker was coach of the Phillips team my final three years and did a superb job. Gerald was All American at Oklahoma, had a fine basketball career with Phillips, and was very basketball-savvy. He really improved our team's scoring and rebounding by moving six foot nine Burdy Halderson, an outstanding center at Colorado University, to power forward. This gave us better scoring by adding height and strong rebounding with the two of us being able to be on the court at the same time.

The next hurdle was the March AAU National Basketball Championships in Denver. We had no problem reaching the finals but then ran into the Buchan Bakers and lost 59 to 57 on a last-second shot at the buzzer. However, we still qualified for the Kansas City Tournament, which was held in April to select the 1956 Olympic team. In addition to our Phillips 66 team and the Buchan Bakers, the other two teams were the College All Stars and Armed Service All Stars.

So, this is it. Here we are in Kansas City and twelve hours from now I will know if my Olympic goal is just a dream or a reality. Although I don't feel like I even closed my eyes, I must have drifted off after a long sleepless night because the phone is ringing and it is time to get going. Tonight's game against a powerful College All Star team, anchored by Bill Russell and K.C. Jones, of later Boston Celtic fame, is a must-win for us. A team meeting is scheduled after breakfast to fine-tune our game plan. The only thing we are changing is that my main assignment is to block Russell out, keep him off the boards, and let the rest of the team take care of the rebounding. We are to relax, take a nap, and be ready in the lobby at 5:00 p.m.

The strategy worked for the game. I was able to outrebound Bill Russell 12 to 7. Against the College All Stars, I played the best 20 minutes of my basketball career, scoring 19 points in the first half against Russell, perhaps the best defensive center who ever played the game. The scoring opportunities were just there. We beat the College All Stars 79 to 75. By winning the Kansas City tournament, the first five of our Phillips 66 team were automatically selected for the Olympic team and our coach received the honor of being appointed as the Olympic coach. Unlike the so-called "Dream Team," which was comprised of NBA professional players and represented the USA in the 1992 Barcelona Games, our 1956 team was composed entirely of amateur players selected from the NIBL, the Armed Services, and graduating college seniors.

To prepare for the games, the Olympic Squad gathered at Bunker Hill Air Force Base in Indiana for two weeks of practice, plus four intersquad exhibition games. Going one-on-one against Russell, I was playing the best basketball of my life. The team then played ten games in different cities against the best amateur teams in the country, winning all quite easily. We developed a great sense of team unity and spirit.

Then it was off to Melbourne, Australia. With the reversal of seasons in the Southern Hemisphere, the summer games were held in November and December. We were housed in the Olympic Village, which was a really exciting place. We had a chance to mingle with other athletes from all over the world. A popular activity was exchanging pins with athletes from other countries.

Participation in the opening ceremonies was a highlight of my life. We gathered for two hours outside the Melbourne Stadium. The time flew by as we exchanged hats and posed in small groups for photos. All too soon, it was time for us to march into the stadium and gather in the midfield. To this day, I vividly remember the wonderful feeling of hearing the announcement as we entered the stadium, realizing I was really there in Melbourne to represent the United States of America. Awesome! We couldn't help ourselves, but broke ranks to cheer on the final torchbearer as he circled the track and lit the Olympic torch.

Bill Russell not only anchored our defense, but also led all scorers. We won all of our games by more than 30 points. Our closest games were against the Soviet Union, defeating them by 30 points in round robin pool play and by a score of 98 to 55 in the finals. In the 1956 games our team played in Converse shoes, which were state of the art at that time. The Soviet team played in really poor-quality shoes. After the competition we visited their quarters and gave them our game shoes, which were accepted with sincere thanks.

Fourteen years of competitive basketball, many hours of training and practice, first-rate coaching along the way, and being very fortunate to be teammates with some of the hardest working and best amateur players in the world paid off. The experience has had a very positive impact on almost every aspect of my life, including maturity, confidence, and goals in other areas of my professional career and family. It was a long road with many setbacks and challenges, but my goal to play in the Olympics was transformed from a wonderful dream to an incredible reality. What a thrill to mount the podium to accept the gold medal while our National Anthem played! In 1986 we received yet another honor and recognition when the team was inducted into the USA Olympic Hall of Fame. It was a long time ago, but what a life-changing experience that has given me a slew of great memories!

Chuck Darling *is a retired petroleum geologist. In 1952 he was an All American basketball player at the University of Iowa and graduated Phi Beta Kappa. He played on the Phillips 66 team for five years and in 1956 was a member of the USA Basketball team, which won the gold medal in the Melbourne Olympic Games. He capped a twenty-nine-year career with Phillips Petroleum as Chief Geologist for Europe and Africa in London, followed by four years as Phillips manager in Alexandria, Egypt, and six years as Vice President for Celeron Oil and Gas Company in Denver.*

Twin Voices

by Bill Green

"Three Feet from Gold." Anyone who has read Napoleon Hill's book *Think and Grow Rich* immediately will recognize that title from one of the early chapters in the book. For those who have not read it, here is the "Cliffs Notes" summary:

> A man from the East Coast goes to California during the gold rush to seek his fortune. He buys a claim and proceeds to dig. He digs ... and digs ... and digs. What seemed initially promising, quickly evaporates into nothing. He gives up and returns home broke and broken. The person who bought his claim picks up where the first miner left off and strikes gold in only three more feet. That's right, the first miner gave up, packed it in, and called it quits, just three feet from gold.

"Three Feet from Gold" has become a mantra that I have repeated over and over in my head. It means keep going, don't give up, almost there. While I'm sure it was meant as an inspirational, if somewhat cautionary tale, for me it has become almost an undoing. Sort of a call to ignore intuition and keep going no matter what. I'm a smart guy when compared to your average American hamster, but I have never been a fast learner. However, I did rapidly learn to adopt "Three Feet from Gold" as my personal doctrine.

"Three Feet from Gold." I have usually preferred to repeat that mantra and chalk up my intuition (which is usually whispering, *"Run!"*) to simple fear, aka False Expectations Appearing Real. Typically, I dismiss that intuition as fear, rather than yield to it. The mantra has kept me in personal and professional relationships much longer than were healthy or reasonable, and has put me in some scary situations in the backcountry that I was ironically able to work my way out of, using the same dogged determination that got me in.

"Three Feet from Gold," however, has rarely applied to following my intuition, but rather going against it. Fighting the flow, being determined, not giving up, digging deep into my suitcase of courage (insert your favorite cliché or sports metaphor here). As a result, I usually have felt like I spend my life spinning my wheels, going nowhere fast, while my intuition whispers that I should be doing something else.

As a bit of background, I work with my partner Nathan on a web-based magazine, *Pangaea Expeditions*, which educates and inspires people to explore the world through adventure travel. To further that, we offer a few guided trips a year. Before each trip, we pre-run the route to scope out current road conditions, fuel availability, photo opportunities, and the like. We take detailed notes and GPS waypoints to make sure that anyone who comes on one of *Pangaea Expeditions'* trips has a wonderful experience with some clear-cut adventure, but not excessive risk.

During a recent scouting trip through the Utah desert, common sense took "Three Feet from Gold" out behind the shed and beat the crap out of him. But "Three Feet from Gold" didn't give up without a fight. The word "desert" is generally used to describe a dry, desolate environment. However, four days of constant rain and snow had replaced southern Utah's normally dry environment with washouts, mud, deep snow, and overall difficult conditions. For such conditions, the loaned Jeep I was driving was not well equipped.

Shortly after leaving camp on the first day, we discovered that the all-night rain had transformed the trail from its usual desert dirt and rock into epic mud—vehicle-swallowing mud that with every step tried to suck the shoe right off of my foot. The further we went, the more difficult the conditions became. Finally, one mud-covered hill halted my progress. I slid into the ditch and got stuck, not once, but three times. I radioed ahead to Nathan to alert him of my predicament and that I was going to give it another try. The voice that came back over the radio said something I had never heard before: "Hang tight, I'm coming back down." I protested, "I think I can make it up with another go," but there was no response.

In that moment my companion was something I had never had before: a voice of reason further up the road—with a map. He could see things that I couldn't. He was able to see that if we followed that road it was only going to get worse and we would soon be committed in a potentially life-threatening situation. "Three Feet from Gold" was feeling pretty beat up. Score one for common sense, even if it came from someone else.

The situation played out a second time just a day later, only this time, replace mud with snow and ice. We were on a shelf road, at night, and every time we rounded a corner the 700 watts of artificial daylight blazing from Nathan's Land Rover would shine off into the abyss with no reflection to return it. We were climbing a cliff wall. As we rounded one switchback, the trail turned from diffi-cult, but doable, into something altogether different. Thoughts began swirling around my head like post-flush toilet water as I got a hint of what lay before us on the next couple miles of trail. In no particular order, my thoughts were: "This is not my truck to destroy … Living is good … There is very little room for error … It is a long way down … This doesn't look particularly safe." And finally, "Three Feet from Gold."

Before returning to my predicament on the snow-covered trail carved in the side of a cliff, let me ask you a question. Do you know any identical twins? Twins that dress alike and speak alike? I went to school with several sets of twins and one set of triplets. Some I could tell apart after several years of getting to know them. Others, I can't tell apart to this very day.

Fear and Intuition are identical twins that I still struggle to tell apart. Is the voice telling me that this is wrong or that I should quit and turn back, coming from Fear or from her twin sister Intuition? When I take a stand against Fear, am I really fighting my own Intuition, all the while plugging my ears to their voices and yelling the "Three Feet from Gold" mantra? To be honest, I rarely know. Their voices are too similar. Perhaps it is because I have shunned Intuition for so long that her voice is unrecognizable to me.

A few years back, a quick run up Colorado's Mt. Elbert turned into a daylong, 15-mile, 10,000 foot vertical "adventure" when I followed bad directions and took a wrong turn. I can't really blame the person who gave me the directions because every 50 feet I would turn around, thinking, "This can't be right; I should head back to the main trail." But every time Intuition whispered, "Turn around, you are going the wrong way" in my ear, I would shout back "Three Feet from Gold!" (not just in my head, I said this out loud) and press ahead. I really thought she was Fear. Just a few hours later I knew I had made a mistake, but it was too late to turn back. I was well past the point of no return. I was committed.

Back on the icy switchback in Utah, along with the thoughts swirling in my mind was the voice, "Just turn back; this isn't safe and there is a better way." After carefully walking the route to the next switchback, we decided it was doable. Nathan went ahead in the Land Rover and I followed along in the Jeep. That lasted about 50 feet before I got stuck, then got unstuck and began sliding into the massive sandstone canyon wall. Traction was regained just before metal met sandstone and I made it to the top of the climb. Clearly it was the voice of Fear telling me to turn back, but I showed her!

We approached the next climb exactly the same way, but without the same success. Just a few feet shy of the top, the Jeep lost traction and began careening back down the mountain. It was all I could do to keep the truck on the narrow shelf road, knowing that the slightest miscalculation would, to borrow a phrase from *Hitchhiker's Guide to the Galaxy*, "end in tears." I got lucky, but Intuition was waiting for me at the bottom of the hill with her arms crossed. "I told you so" was all she said. Three more times we tried to get the Jeep up the hill under its own power and three more times we failed. We scouted ahead on foot, barely able to stand up on the slick surface, realizing that if we tried to press on, we would be committed. Now was the only time to turn back. And so we did.

That was one of the first times I was able to discern the different voices of Fear and Intuition, and it got me to start looking at other areas of my life where I was advised by both Fear and Intuition, and occasionally bitch-slapped them both with the "Three Feet from Gold" mantra.

We make thousands of decisions every day. Should I get up or one more snooze? Shave or scruffy? Shaken or stirred? Every decision has consequences, some big and life-changing defining moments, some small and forgotten. The cost of each decision we make is the opportunity we forego. All we have to guide us are the voices of twins.

Just because we make a decision out of Fear doesn't always mean it is the wrong decision, but it usually means that we will make multiple trips back to the past to sit with Fear by her fire and wonder if we made the right choice. Then, we cling to what might have been and openly invite the haunting from the ghosts of possibilities past, preventing us from being fully present in our lives. Just like a martini cannot at the same time be shaken *and* stirred, and just as we cannot choose both door number one *and* two, we cannot fully live our lives while wishing for what might have been. Our lives, while shaped by the past, cannot be lived there. Intuition, like my friend's voice on the radio, lives in the future. When we follow her guidance, we know it is right and we can live without regrets. We go through life surrounded by voices. Some are our own. Some come from friends or family. Some come from Fear and some from Intuition, but there is only one voice we need to heed.

Many people would suggest that the reason I heard my friend's voice on the mud-covered hill in Utah is because my radio was tuned to receive the same frequency that his was transmitting. Perhaps the reason I so often hear Fear is because I am more tuned to her frequency, to her voice, rather than to that of Intuition.

My good friend and coach, Carole Billingham, once told me that Fear shouts, but Intuition whispers, which is why it takes patience and practice to recognize her voice. She is always there, but I know I have rarely listened.

Bill Green *is a writer and active lifestyle and travel photographer who is passionate about telling stories of people, places, and things (or of people going places and doing things). He currently is working on two books with* Pangaea Expeditions *about adventure travel destinations. You can find him on Twitter, @bill_green.*

A Shipwrecked Mariner

by Ilan Shamir

I hadn't planned walking forty days across remote Iceland solo; then again I hadn't planned not to. A journey across a land of ice and fire and into the heart of what lay in my soul. One step at a time.

As a photographer and coleader for twenty-five-day Swiss Alps treks in spring and summer, I was on my way back to St. Louis. Our plane flew into Keflavik. Soon, my traveling companion Rob and I would land and begin our exploration together. That is until he surprisingly said, "I am going back to Chicago." "Rob, buddy, friend, we're doing this together!" I pointed out, but I could tell he was clear and headed home.

I thought to myself, "I could go back to sweaty, hot, end of summer in the Mississippi river valley or put on my fierce Norse explorer mode and see what this place is all about." Life was continually presenting me with situations, asking me to choose: Either bring me farther away from my dreams or closer to them. I had been on the best adventure of my life since April. Why compromise my adventure spirit? "I'm in!" I shouted to myself.

Walking across Iceland wasn't part of my plan even a day ago, but now suddenly it was. Roaring rivers, waterfalls, coastal cliffs and puffins, rain, fog and more rain, geothermal hot springs, green grass in this short summer season, wild Icelandic ponies thundering across the openness; the wildness of this land that I was soon to befriend.

The more I walked, the more I could feel the geology of the land, rather than merely view it as a casual observer. I snapped photos to capture the journey with my precious remaining three rolls of Kodachrome. The daily routine—wake, eat, write, walk, rest, eat, sleep—and the days obediently lined up one after another.

Toward the end of the thirteenth day when it was time to set up my tent, I panicked. "Where is my backpack?" I couldn't help but laugh when I realized it was still on my back. It had become a part of who I was, and no longer a heavy burden. Days later I would look at my tent all set up and wonder, "How did *that* get set up? I don't remember even taking it out of the pack." It had all become so second nature.

Step by step the journey continued, as I spotted mountain ranges or rivers far in the distance and felt exhilarated to arrive stronger to meet my next goal. Thoreau's quote, "Go confidently in the direction of your dreams. Live the life you have imagined," took on new meaning.

Now thirty-three remote days on foot, I was more part of the land than I was of the cities. No electricity or roads, the patterns of the Earth were my guide. I had worked out many of the traveling details and felt solid in each step—comfortable with my well-worn boots on the volcanic rocks, grasses, and beaches; comfortable with my blue, tubular-frame backpack and its secure fit.

I was alone, yet so un-alone in this vast terrain. The rock and sun and sea and rivers were my true companions. The sun did not appear to set each day, rather it was the Earth turning that I felt—this enormous globe spinning through time and space causing the sun to disappear. I felt deeply connected; steps became prayers, and breath the rhythmical waves. I walked farther and farther away from the constant bombardment of stimuli from my city life. The noise in my head had come to a halt, a simple gift and a welcomed relief.

In this island of fire and ice and rock, the Vatnajokull glacier in its prominence and powerful forces dominated the landscape. The idea of a road encircling the perimeter of Iceland was only a dream of the Norse and Viking inhabitants of this mass of land floating on the shifting plates of the north Arctic sea—that is until 1976, just one year before I arrived. "Good timing, what *good* timing!"

I had hiked up to one of the icy fingers of this massive glacier that covered 10 percent of all of Iceland. The white and blue creaking ice was peppered with gravel of black lava rock, its prize for moving slowly and powerfully. Car-size icebergs crashed off the glacier and were bobbing up and down in the cold blue lake making their way to the north Arctic sea a hundred yards away. The forces of the Earth were right before my eyes. The pitch-black lava beach was being pounded by the churning ocean. And only a narrow passage of tundra lay between the two—no trees, no bushes, a flat terrain scraped clean. A black bird caught my eye. Its flight was a pattern I had not seen; it was out of the ordinary and erratic— more sideways and upside down. The wind picked up slightly.

In the distance, a dark line appeared hugging the Earth. The air cooled. The blue and wispy white sky turned gray. Suddenly, a gust of frigid wind and a drop of rain appeared. I yanked my tent from my pack for shelter and scanned the horizon. The dark line had doubled in size. The adrenalin poured into me instantly. Raindrops drummed on my pack and parka and on my face. There had been no visible sign of civilization for miles, for days. My thin, blue ripstop nylon tent would be all that was between me and nature, now only the illusion of protection.

The black horizon grew. The wind blew through my body. "Is it the ocean or my pounding heart?" Desperately scanning the horizon, I saw a rectangular shape. Miles away? I started running toward it. Sky growing darker. Thicker. Fighting the wind. Fighting my fear. Into the wind. A tsunami of air. Running with seventy pounds on my back. Crawling across the ground for the last fifty meters to this solid corrugated metal building. I pull on the door. "No, it's locked!"

I fall against the heavy wooden door, exhausted, push on the door again and it swivels, propelling me inward. The sign on the wall reads: "This shelter is for the exclusive use of shipwrecked mariners."

"Oh crap, no ship, no shelter!"

I continued reading: " … and others who have to seek refuge in bad weather and distress."

Good! I'm not going back out there," I thought to myself.

I read further: "These surroundings are remote and difficult to pass for strangers and very misleading. The National Lifesaving Association of Iceland welcomes all those who stand in need of help and care and authorizes them to make use of the provisions stored in this shelter. Slysavornafelig Islands, Breidamerkur Sandour, 64 degrees N. Latitude, 16 degrees W. Longitude. Nearest farmhouse 123 Km." A map on the wall: "1952. Published by the USAF Aeronautical Chart and Information Center, Saint Louis, 18 Missouri." "St. Louis?" I thought. "You've got to be kidding!"

Gray wool blankets were piled on a gray painted bench by a long, well-worn wooden table and an old wooden chair, near a wooden platform for a bed. There were two glass jugs of drinking water, bowls, wooden spoons, an empty box of tea, heavy wool jackets, sea clothes and overalls, five pieces of firewood, and a rusty old woodstove in the corner of this 7-foot by 9-foot room. Four walls, a wooden floor, and a roof—"a castle," I would later write in my journal. The wind howled and roared and shook the corrugated metal hut while I made soup, unrolled my sleeping bag, and gave thanks for this exquisite shelter.

Day 34. Oatmeal and dried fish for breakfast. Soup, crackers, and a cream filled cookie for lunch. Journaling, napping. Hovering above the landscape like a surveying eagle and imagining myself a tiny speck in a remote outpost. Outward movement had come to a stop. I was anchored. I was here to stay and listen and let life catch up with me.

I wrote in my journal, "I have seen the beauty of the Alps. I have been free and carried everything with me on my back. I have touched the fire of my inner soul … I am so much larger than my limited surroundings of the city life I had created for myself. It is *time* to move out of St. Louis to connect more deeply with nature and live more of what my life has to offer."

I began shaking, not from the wind, but from knowing that I would be making one of the most difficult changes in my life—going beyond the fear, beyond the unknown, and totally in the direction of my dreams.

"If I write it down it will be real," was my soulful commitment. I'd leave loved ones, contacts, familiarity, a failed marriage, career success, and eight years of establishing my life. Surely I could take the best of it with me, but uprooting takes courage.

Day 35. The wind continued with force, then stopped as abruptly as it had started. When the wind abated to just blowing hard and cold, I packed up and walked the blustery path toward my final destination. I continued on foot for five more days to the small town of Husavik on the coast of Iceland. I definitely became a different person than I had started out: strong, thankful, clear, with a deep and unexpected exploration of the truth of myself. The closer I got to nature, the closer I got to my own true nature.

The green grass overlooking the town where I camped was a soft welcome mat of enormous proportions. I was home, home with myself. Sure, there are risks associated with the outdoors: disease-bearing insects, aggressive or protective predatory reptiles and animals, avalanches, hypothermia, storms with flooding, unstable terrain leading to falls, glacial crevasses, disorientation and isolation in remote terrain, misidentification and ingestion of poisonous plants, severe and unexpected cold weather, large hail, erratic geothermal eruptions, human attack or theft, choking on food, lacerations with one's own knife, explosion of fuel or cooking source, impure water, exhaustion of food sources, medical issues requiring major and immediate care, being struck by a meteor or just plain stumbling, leading to broken limbs. But my choice is simple; the greater risk is of being tamed, losing my wildness, not using my unique talents and never truly living.

"I can do this!"

The bus whisked me and my backpack around the newly completed road and back to the airport. I pitched my tent in the tall, waving grass right next to the jet runway. The aurora borealis put on quite a show for my last night in Iceland. A true celebration!

In the early morning that crispy cold September, the arriving plane from Europe touched down on the runway to wake me. "Pretty cool alarm clock," I thought.

The end of an amazing journey.

But truthfully, it was just another beginning.

Ilan Shamir started his career in promotion and advertising for 7UP the Uncola and product design for Willy Wonka Confections before escaping the world of sugar and candy to do his true life's work. He changed his name to Ilan Shamir, which means "protector of trees, life, and celebration," and used his talents to create the Advice from Nature series of products found all over the country. Ilan is a gifted drummer and storyteller and has planted more than sixty thousand trees to repay the Earth for all the paper used in his company. Learn more about his inspiring work at www.yourtruenature.com. See pictures and hear an interview of his Iceland journey at www.yourtruenature.com/iceland-travel.

Part Three: Sexuality

The Fallen Soldier Rises

by George Ira Carroll

An eight-year-old boy was in a deep sleep one early morning, only to wake up to something he had never seen before. As he lay still, his eyes slowly began to creep open. What he saw on the television was something so foreign and new, he couldn't help but stare in awe and bewilderment.

His eyes were glued to the television, unaware of what he was watching. Little did he know that what he was seeing would powerfully shape much of his future in profound and potent ways. He didn't realize that what he was observing was going to create his deepest pain, and was going to give him the greatest gift of his life.

A few of the neighborhood children had discovered hidden stashes of their parents' erotic magazines and adult movies and showed them to other kids in the neighborhood, including the youngest one. As he was observing and absorbing the content on the television, his young, malleable mind began to create a belief system that would forever change his future. Only eight years old and still undeveloped physically, the young boy was watching his first pornography film, and behind his conscious awareness he was comparing his eight-year-old body to the pornography actor on the television. In that comparison, he unconsciously formed the idea that he was sexually inadequate.

As the young boy grew into his teens, he developed a voracious appetite for sports. He imitated NFL wide receiver Jerry Rice and aspired to be just like him. He soon excelled and seemed to be a star in the making. As he began to go through the first stages of puberty, he started to notice his interest in the opposite sex. He was quietly flirtatious and, like most teens, curious to explore his sexuality.

Transitioning from middle school to high school he started to experiment with girls, and the more he explored, the more an anxiety would overtake him as he approached sexual intercourse. The seemingly harmless erotic films and magazines absorbed by the young child catalyzed what the medical community calls erectile dysfunction.

That young boy was me.

I grew up in a seemingly normal environment. My parents worked hard to pay the bills; we had everything we needed to survive and get through life. I was the youngest of three, and my brother and sister had their own challenges growing up.

I never told anyone about what I was experiencing because I was so ashamed of what was happening. I felt so helpless. I didn't want anyone to know my weakness, and I used football as a way to feel masculine and powerful. But when it came to romancing and pleasing women, I was the first to tell myself how worthless I was and how I could never be good enough. I continually sabotaged relationships because of these deep-seated feelings of inadequacy. I made it through high school and fortunately, my football prowess got me into college.

At the University of Northern Colorado in Greeley, I excelled academically and became the starting wide receiver in my sophomore year. I was all-conference that year and felt great on the football field, but plummeted in the romance department. I deeply yearned for close connection and sexual pleasure with women, but my intense self-judgment and deeply rooted insecurities prevented me from meeting my needs.

Enter: Viagra

One of the players on my football team, who had access to a seeming pharmacy of drugs, introduced me to Viagra. He didn't know about my dysfunction, but he told me he could last for many hours on this stuff. Knowing that I couldn't last for minutes, I was intrigued, to say the least. I bought some pills to try out at the next opportunity.

When the moment arrived, I was like a kid in a candy store. After my first dose of Viagra, I felt like I could puncture walls and flip tables. I was a marathon man, as my little soldier held strong all night long. I felt so proud of myself. I called my pharmacy friend the next day to order another shipment.

I became addicted to Viagra and started using similar products like Cialis and Levitra. After a month or so of successful sexual interactions, I contracted major headaches anytime I took one of these pills. Over time, they became effective only about 70 percent of the time. I kept asking myself what I was missing.

I continued to excel at football, and at the start of my senior year I was closing in on the school record for career receiving yards. Toward the end of the season, I entered the final home game just 157 yards shy of that goal.

As the game began, I was "in the zone," catching three passes for 63 yards by the second quarter. Well on my way to breaking the record, if not in that game, definitely the next ... then ... disaster struck.

The next play was a run in my direction. As the ball was snapped, I began ferociously blocking my opponent. I planted my right foot in the ground to gain leverage. All of a sudden, crash! The runner was tackled from behind and both the defender and our running back landed on my lower leg and ankle, applying four hundred pounds of body weight plus momentum, shattering my leg and shattering my dream to play professional football. That ride suddenly came to an end.

After graduation I decided to move to Denver, Colorado, to explore other opportunities. I found myself in a corporate selling environment, excelling fairly quickly. I moved up the ranks and became a manager in just over a year with the company. I noticed that as I blossomed in my career and was making lots of money, my penis slowly began to work. So I thought, "Make more money and my penis will follow suit." Magic formula!

Enter: Falling in Love

During my sales manager success, I met a woman with whom I eventually fell head over heals in love. The problem was she was one of my sales reps—and I had a semi-functioning penis. Over the course of three months, we avoided anything sexual and just had fun exploring our connection. The relationship eventually became so strong that we could no longer avoid exploring the physical dimension. I had this little voice in the back of my mind the whole time asking, "What if it doesn't work?"

You may have already guessed ... the first time we attempted to have sex, it lasted no longer than a minute before things went "downhill." I was devastated and began blasting myself with self-judgment. A week later she cheated with one of my friends right in front of me. My buddy didn't know we were dating at the time because we had kept it a secret.

Needless to say, my heart was shattered. I fell into a deep state of depression. I had to quit my job because I was emotionally unfit to lead a team of salespeople. I began drinking heavily and using drugs as a way to escape my pain. I took a one-week trip to Australia to visit a good friend and get clear about who I was and what I wanted to do next. During that trip I was so broken inside I could barely think straight. Somewhere along the line I made the decision that I was unwilling to settle for a mediocre life.

Upon returning home, I went to the Denver Public Library and began reading Anthony Robbins' *Unlimited Power*. Little did I realize that what I was reading was going to change my life forever. In this powerful book, Tony Robbins talks about how we have complete and utter influence on our life experience. The primary message I took from that book was that if I could manage my emotional state, I could create whatever life I want for myself. That book opened the door to the world of personal development. I was hooked.

Robbins introduced me to human change technology called Neuro-Linguistic Programming (NLP). *Unlimited Power* is an experiential book. While experimenting with the various tools and processes described by Robbins, I noticed some fairly rapid shifts in my internal experience. I became even more hooked. Any book Anthony Robbins recommended, I read. And I also read many of the books that those books recommended.

In the movie *The Silence of the Lambs*, Hannibal Lecter asks Clarice why she wants to stop the women from getting murdered by the rapist serial killer. She replies that she grew up on a farm where she could hear lambs being slaughtered. Those lambs would squeal and scream and this created a deep sense of pain within her mind. Hannibal then responds, "Oh, I see ... you think that if you can stop these women from being killed, you can silence the lambs in your mind." After personal development and NLP deepened within me, I began to recognize wounds that I wanted to heal and transform. I believe NLP came into my life because at a profound level, I was asking for healing—to be fixed. Now, I don't believe that any human being is broken, but I sure felt broken after years and years of my penis not operating properly.

After studying NLP for about two years, I decided to get formal training. Fortunately, there was an NLP school right in my backyard, in Boulder, Colorado—NLP Comprehensive. I was so impressed with the immersion course, I decided to pursue hypnosis certification. After these two trainings I felt a sense of freedom I had never experienced, and I now had a structure to uncover the deep belief systems that were creating my sexual anxiety.

One day, I was reading quietly in my room, and something very powerful came over me. I became aware of the three beliefs that were at the root of my erectile dysfunction:

1. I am not worth loving.
2. I am sexually inadequate.
3. All women want men with big penises.

When this powerful awareness came over me, I realized a huge shift had taken place, but I didn't know the full magnitude as yet. I had a relaxing massage after that awareness occurred and didn't think about those beliefs again until I got home later that night. A huge surge of emotion came over me and I began releasing emotion like crazy. Floods of tears ran down my face. It was like a volcanic explosion of emotion rushing through me and I kept thinking, "Oh my God, is this it?" Not yet knowing what "it" was, I knew that whatever "it" was, involved my sexual anxiety.

As soon as I was aware of the programming that was creating the sexual anxiety, I went to work on it using the NLP and hypnosis tools I had learned in my training. Every night, I would apply certain tools and would use hypnotic suggestions as I slept.

Within thirty to forty-five days of applying the tools, I started noticing my little soldier being more stimulated by things that wouldn't normally stimulate me, and not long after that, I attracted a relationship … and guess what? That's right, the sexual anxiety that had been running my life was discharged (pun intended) and no longer adversely affected me.

Once I was able to break through this limitation, the biggest limitation I've faced so far, I knew what my path was. Not long afterward, I decided to become a personal development coach specializing in breakthrough NLP coaching, and I began to pursue my vision of becoming an inspirational speaker.

I now run a growing professional coaching and speaking practice, where I have the great privilege of helping people to overcome limiting beliefs, so they can live their optimal lives. I'm currently building the life of my dreams and, after overcoming my tenacious obstacle, I now believe that I can overcome anything.

George Ira Carroll, *a professional speaker and Certified Master NLP Breakthrough Coach, intertwines humor, insight, and passion in his style. He majored in communication at the University of Northern Colorado, where he played collegiate football and learned the power of goal setting and of motivating himself and others. His energetic spark and deep insight create uplifting inspiration and deepened understanding for his audiences. He has a natural ability to teach. His presence provides powerful calmness and his unique style keeps audiences riveted*

and reaching for more. In coaching individuals, his compassionate nature and in-depth awareness and understanding of human behavior and belief systems has allowed him to help hundreds of people break through limitations to reveal deeper levels of potential within themselves.

Two Seasons

by Aaron J. Luttrell

In each individual the spirit has become flesh, in each man the
creation suffers, within each one a redeemer is nailed to the cross.
—Hermann Hesse

"This is your cross to bear," she said, referring to my homosexuality. She was a close friend and a religious leader in my community. Her eyes softened, her jaw squared, her lips closed acutely, sternly. I sat there exposed, my secret laid bare before her, before the café that is just outside the doors that lead into the auditorium of the church, before God. Ashamed. Sullied. I did not know how to respond at that time to her, to myself, to God. My innermost secret, now confessed, chilled me the same way one feels upon stepping out from a warm house into the chill of winter. My "hour of lead," as Emily Dickinson says.

This would be the beginning of an emotional and spiritual winter in my life: the spring and summer of my childhood and early youth now passing and with them the feeling of certainty, replaced by a fundamental crisis of my identity as a person, as a man. How could a homosexual be a spiritual man and be loved in the eyes of God?

I wandered and searched for answers, as anyone does having left a home where everything is given out of love, with little question for intention, and now I had to journey alone. I studied philosophies, read scriptures and interpretations of scripture. I scoured the thoughts and opinions of friends, mentors, the Church, family, professors. Sometimes the answers were similar, but mostly they were inconsistent and borne by conflicting points of view. What became apparent to me was the observation that, when one spends enough moments listening to one's fellow human in conversation, one sees that each of us bears a kind of cross and that its burden infuses our respective points of view. I now realize these varying points of view are beautiful and fulfilling in their own ways. One can see the challenging aspects of one's life as a cross of death or as a certain kind of redemption and life.

Several months after my revelatory conversation in the café outside the doors to the church auditorium, the theme resurfaced. I received a phone call from a friend who worked at the church. He was clearly upset, even frantic. A local radio station had interviewed a man claiming to have participated in homosexual acts with the pastor of the church, he said, and it proved to be true. Our pastor's secret exposed his cross, which was on display for all to see.

I grieved for our pastor, his wife and children, his global ministry. The very man who had championed antihomosexual rhetoric was himself struggling with the issue quite publicly, and his religious community was witnessing it. I felt empathy for him. I had taken up my cross and confessed; the pastor tried to bear his alone. It appeared neither of us could overcome it, at least in the eyes of the Church. How could I overcome or accept my homosexuality if this pastor, who had led thousands of Christian men and women, who was a counselor to presidents of countries, an elevated man of God, could not overcome or accept his? I wondered if perhaps these desires came naturally, are natural, are a part of nature. Nature is immensely diverse and each unique part contributes to form the entire whole. And, does not the Old Testament proclaim that God knows us before we are born and that we are wonderfully made?

I sensed that God still had a place in His heart for me or, perhaps better said, that God had a place in my heart. I wondered if that is what's meant by having faith. Life is full of challenges, crosses to bear, so many of which have no clear explanation. Why me? Why am I homosexual? I just *am*, just as oceans *are* and the wind and trees *are*. There is an infinitesimal diversity in nature, yet it and we are all made of the same elements: one from the many. The idea of this allowed me to accept myself and begin to love myself.

How lovely the winter of my soul was becoming then—lovely in that I embraced my cross like a man embraces the cart to which he is tethered. Rather than dig my heels in and fight, I chose to bear its burden upon my life; to slowly glean the image of my true self; to move naturally with the course of my life. Out of the dark and cool night of the soul, I opened the shutters of my inner self increasingly to others, those like me with similar crosses to bear. I found that many men and women raised in the Church sought reconciliation with what, as homosexuals, felt natural to them versus what the Bible says. Many of them found their reconciliation through faith—faith that God makes no mistakes, that He knows us before we are born and has a plan marked out for us.

I saw the first signs of the spring of my life budding as I embraced my cross and carried it with me. The shame left me like snow melting from the trees on a bright sunny day. I no longer viewed my cross as a victim does, but rather as a man carrying a part of his natural self: his wonderfully made self.

I finished my college studies in the spring of 2007 and moved to Denver, Colorado. It was at this time that my severed ties with my family began to mend. The dialogue was more open, cautiously on their part, but open nonetheless. This was something I longed for and it came like the first spring warmth carried on the breeze.

The cool afternoon wind wisped around my face like a cat chasing his tail: soft, gentle, and playful. The carefree wind, the warm spring sun, the fresh leaves peeking out of their brown and wintry stems, each a harbinger of the fullness and endless procession of living. The world is fine and unsurpassed in beauty during the spring. How suddenly the visceral affection changes from winter; days ago there was chill in the air; snow clung to boots and invaded bare and swaddled feet. The wintry cross the world bore now dropped away, its snowy mantle barely clinging to the trees. The dead of winter, little more than an empty tomb, gave way to the signs of new life rising out of the ground, radiant in redemption. The great and ancient Ouroboros became revealed all around, as the mouth of spring devoured the tail of winter. How sweet and precious, endearing and redeeming is spring.

On my walk that day, I wandered by a cathedral, sat for a moment, and recollected my experience with the Church. There stood a statue depicting Christ dying on the cross. The marble looked cold, like winter; the eyes reached toward heaven, striving toward the bright and warming light. This is what a man looks like when he is drawn from the dark winter of his cross and into the bright, life-giving spring of his redemption, I thought. I cannot help believe that in that very moment Christ accepted his cross not as a shameful thing to bear, or as the instrument of his death, but rather as the means upon which he would find his life and redemption. The cross was the winter of his life. The eyes gazing upward, striving toward the promise of new life, were the glimmering hope of the spring of his life to come. He accepted it and lived with it. It was the mouth of the Ouroboros consuming the tail of winter and heralding spring. Could it be that the story of Christ, his cross and crucifixion, was his way of demonstrating: This is what it means to *be like Man*?

An ordinary statue in an ordinary garden reveals the extraordinary and sacred truth: The story of Christ is the story of us all, each of us crossbearers, each of us redeemers. Truly, I thought, this is a lovely and grand image of being human and reflecting that which is all around us. In this way, I have learned to welcome with open arms the seasons of my life and the seasons of my inner life.

After finishing my walk that early spring afternoon, I came home and continued to recollect the last few years and seasons of my life. A sense of joy and redemption filled me. I embrace my cross. I no longer see it as a burden or as my crucifixion. Rather, my cross stands upon a certain hill in my heart, a vanguard and reminder of the icy countenance of winter and the warm redemption of spring. I had finally found my reconciliation and redemption: I am a homosexual man and I have faith that God made me intentionally, lovingly, knowingly. I am one particular part of all that is wonderfully made. My life and my willingness to live it depend upon how I choose to accept its challenges, its crosses—as an avenue of death or a journey to greater freedom and redemption.

I made dinner for us that evening. We watched a movie, laughed together, as he and I often do, and enjoyed each other's love. Then we fell asleep embraced under the warm comforter and caressing sheets, surrounded by love and in love.

Aaron J. Luttrell was born and raised in Western Colorado. His college studies were in phenomenological philosophy from the University of Colorado. Growing up in an evangelical Christian family, traveling abroad, and studying philosophy and science have helped shaped his worldview: one in which objective science reestablishes itself as secondary to the realm of the subjective, qualitative experience of what it means to be human.

Part Four: Health and Healing

Healing Like There's No Tomorrow

Through Cancer into Conscious Manhood

by Michael Vladeck

The sight of that sun-bleached payphone standing alone against the faded-pink side of the rundown gas station fills me with nervousness and intimidation. I step out of my jeep and into the piercing silence of this sacred, open land in the middle of the remote, southern Utah desert where the gray sage of a summer's past is standing pure and still in the breezeless morning. The warmth of the low-angled sun on my skin brings some relief to the burdensome question that I've been carrying with me for the last six days, while adventuring amidst the sandstone walls and canyons: Will the hospital's latest test results give a clear answer as to whether or not I have cancer?

"Hey, Ma. It's me."

There is a pause, and then, with forced enthusiasm, she says, "Hi." I feel the touch of anxiety in my body.

"So?" I ask, because at the moment I'm too anxious to utter anything else. "So?" I repeat, creating a vacuum that hovers in the air, awaiting an answer to fill it.

There was a brief pause that seemed large enough to swallow both the whole history of my life as well as the entire desert clear to the far line of the sandstone horizon. Then, with a deeper tone of gravity in her voice, she replied, "So ... yes, it *is*. It is cancer."

And just like that, I was suspended in a place inside myself, disconnected from the timelessness, spaciousness, and indifference of the desert, overtaken by waves of sadness, numbness, and humor that came crashing down on me all at once.

Two years earlier, at the age of nineteen, I'd had a series of powerful insights that brought an end to a decade-and-a-half-long spell of intense, eventually suicidal depression. I was able to connect to and then release deep-seated beliefs and feelings of unworthiness and unlovability that I'd been carrying. I saw for the first time that I *was* unconditionally enough and lovable. With this shift, the consistent throbbing ache that was depression came to an end, though I still had to work out other hidden levels of insecurity and unhealthy core beliefs about myself, my relationship to life, and my place in the world.

I began to see that in my childhood I had created behavior patterns in an unconscious attempt to give myself a temporary sense of security, safety, and control. It seemed true to me then that having needs was a sign of weakness, so I convinced myself that I didn't need or want anybody's help. I'd figure things out and work through challenges on my own. On a deeper level, I believed that I needed to be right in order to prove that I had value and deserved love.

I had developed what a great therapist I saw called an "enlightened ego." I could even make judgment sound like compassion. I could impress myself and others with my deep spiritual insights, but it was all coming from my head rather than my actual experience. Meditation and spiritual books were being filtered through unseen layers of ego and fear. To be fair, it was as good a start as any. And though I was limited by my illusions, I was clear about my commitment to healing myself emotionally and connecting with the truth of who I really was underneath all these made-up beliefs and patterns.

I decided not to drive straight back home to Boulder, but instead to be alone for a few days in a place were I could be with myself without any distractions. That first evening, once I'd set up camp, was pressurized with the incredible intensity of this unknown thing that stood before me.

What would the cancer do to me? Would I die within a year? Within a month? Would it be painful? Would I lose limbs? Would I be taken to a place to do treatment and never return? Would I live long enough to ever be in love? Long enough to be thirty, or even twenty-five? Would I need surgery, chemotherapy, and radiation? Would I climb the mountains I'd dreamed of climbing as a child? Of course, I didn't yet have answers to these questions, which proved to be an enormous blessing, as I was able to let them go and focus fully on processing my thoughts and feelings during those three days.

The cold and calm desert morning brought the realization that the *only* way to deal in a fully present way with this situation, with this mystery that I was facing, was not to ask, "What am I going to do about this disease?" but rather, "How am I going to relate to it and all its challenges and outcomes?"

This new mindset about how to approach my experience was a true blessing. It opened the door to the deeper levels of healing—the emotional and spiritual. This healing, I figured, might improve the odds of ridding myself of the physical disease.

Or, perhaps I'd still die, but then at least I'd die with more acceptance, love, and gratitude for this life, even if it were shorter than I would have liked. This was my attitude and my way of engaging what would turn out to be a seven-year journey with cancer, a journey through what turned out to be a widespread and late-stage form of cancer, which four top oncologists in the United Stated told me was "incurable" and ultimately, "terminal"—that, inevitably, it would kill me.

I tried just about every kind of treatment, both in the U.S. and abroad, that seemed to hold some promise—from Western to Eastern, from clinical trials to shamanism. None of these methods was effective enough at shrinking the tumors. But on I went and kept searching for something that would reverse the tide of cancer advancing throughout my body.

My first brush with deeper healing occurred with the realization that I had a hidden agenda—I wanted to prove that conventional Western medicine was not as effective as natural medicine. This was really a rebellion against my father, who was a medical doctor, as I was carrying pain around not feeling smart or intellectually acknowledged by him in certain ways.

When I realized how attached I was to being right about this view, I faced this essential question, "Would I rather be right, or be healed?" I needed to let go of these lingering beliefs that I wasn't enough, so I could release the patterns of trying to convince the world that I was right and therefore worthy. My heart was telling me to let go, but I was afraid to do so. It said, "Stop fighting, Michael. Surrender these patterns so you can heal."

Over time, I also began to see how I used judgments to try to feel better and more secure and how I'd throw that dark net over just about everyone in some way. I saw that *all* needs are important and that, by respecting them, I was able to more deeply understand and love myself. I began to really comprehend that my inherent worth was unconditional, that I didn't need to prove it or manufacture it by acting or looking a certain way, such as by saying wise, insightful things, being successful, or even by healing from cancer.

"Does it bother you that people keep looking at your neck?" I'd be asked—a reference to the baseball-sized tumor that was pushing my earlobe out at a strange angle. I looked deformed and freakish. To live like this without suffering, I had to accept the fact that I did look a bit weird, that I had serious amounts of cancer, and that I was, in a word, vulnerable. This was big medicine and a huge gift to be in the prime of my twenties and be able to cut through attachments to my physical identity and vanity.

For months, the scans had been showing that the arteries feeding blood to my kidneys, liver, intestines, and legs were being compressed by the mass of tumors.

My doctor warned me, "While you may have only a month or two to live, you are certainly in the *red zone* now for a serious medical problem, like losing your legs in the event of developing a blood clot."

By that point, I'd been told for years that I had only a few months to live. These somber declarations were getting old to me. Yet, it was impossible to ignore the severity of the situation. I had so many tumors in my abdomen, some the size of softballs, that I couldn't take a deep breath for years. The blessing of this discomfort was in keeping my mortality so central in my awareness, which led me to make peace not only with the life I was living, but with the likely possibility of an early death. Through the support of a few healers, an amazing therapist, and regular meditation, I continued to see through the fabricated reality I had built around my identity.

I began to feel the freedom that existed in actually feeling my fear. I started taking responsibility for being shut down or dishonest. I felt the peace and wisdom in accepting that I did not have everything under control and figured out.

I began to dissolve my righteousness and arrogance, and the perpetuation of "The Michael Show"—the act designed to get me love and acceptance.

As I let go of effort and struggle and simply relaxed into myself, I became softer, more loving, powerful, and beautiful. I began to live my life more authentically, allowing myself to show up as vulnerable and raw. Instead of seeking strength from external approval and successes, I started feeling the strength that comes from simply being connected with myself.

In this way, I was able to open a channel of communication with the wounded little boy inside me. "Michael, hi! I'm here. You can let go of trying to be special. You are enough as you are. I know it was confusing growing up. It really seemed that you needed to be smarter, cooler, and more popular. But you didn't. And you never do. I love you exactly as you are; you don't need to prove anything to me or to anyone else. Let them have their own opinions about you. Let them be who they are. You're safe, really! You can relax. My love is here for you. You can just be you. I'm here and I'm not going away."

While all this deep healing was wonderful, I still preferred to survive, but appeared to be running out of time. I was about to undergo a type of chemotherapy that might dangerously weaken me. As a final shot, I once again researched the world over to find what cutting-edge or experimental approaches were out there for me. After much research and education, I found a brilliant team of doctors in Germany and hopped on a plane to see them.

About five months into this amazing treatment, I received an unexpected phone call from one of the nurses. "Michael," she said, her voice calm yet infused with joy, "I have great news. Your scan is completely clean. There is no evidence of cancer in your body." As I took that in, time completely evaporated. What remained was a feeling of expansiveness and the greatest sense of relief that I have ever experienced in my life. Every cell in my body rang with gratitude for my life and for the powerful, enriching experiences of the previous seven years. Hallelujah!

I have now been cancer-free for almost a decade. My health and longevity are still not guaranteed, of course, but no one's are. And it's this uncertainty about life that invites us to connect to our own humanity, humility, and fragility and, by doing so, to connect more authentically and sincerely to each other.

Of course, it's not necessary to experience a terminal illness to discover that. Any challenge can become an opportunity for healing, but it won't be unless we choose to see it in that way. I'm aware that my growth as a man depends on how I engage with the difficult experiences of my life, whether they be relationship challenges, health conditions, financial issues, or challenges that seem trivial and small. The strongest and wisest men I know understand this power of working with their own perceptions and attitudes.

In this awesome life journey, we are all in the same boat. The winds of change and transformation are always blowing, and our work is to set our sails of humility, openness, and resilience to the fullest that we can, so that we may arrive home to the experience of who we fully are as men.

Michael Vladeck is in love with life, plays outside as much as he can, and feels blessed to be within a community of conscious men and women who are passionate about living authentically. His purpose is channeled into working as a personal coach and counselor for families with teenagers, couples, and individuals, helping them deeply connect with themselves and to each other. He lives in Boulder, Colorado. For more information on him and his work, visit www.MichaelVladeck.com.

Crying for Columbine

by Craig Knippenberg

What unfolded that evening, and over the days to come, completely tore apart every notion I'd ever had for about fifteen years about predictable emotions coming from socially prescribed actions. I had been guiding children and teens toward greater emotional and social well-being.

We circled up and I asked the kids to simply share what they experienced. Chaos, terror, fear of missing friends, a dead classmate lying outside in a pool of blood comprised the starting themes.

While I remember the impact April 20, 1999, had on me at the time, it wasn't until two years later that I felt how deeply it had wounded me. I was in Las Vegas for a mental health conference and some much-needed R & R. I would engage in that all-too-male routine of blocking my emotions with golf, good food, gambling, and a few martinis. Having just heard my favorite therapist guru, I was totally excited and decided to attend the closing talk on secondary trauma before heading out for a five-star dinner.

The speaker was interesting as she discussed some clinical information, then everything changed when she asked us to do a guided exercise. I made myself comfortable on the floor, closed my eyes, and joined in. As she led us through an image of "hope" meeting "despair," my plans for an emotional break were turned into a complete immersion into the pain inside me that had been building over the last two years. In tears, I approached the speaker to seek additional guidance. She knew immediately where my pain came from when she saw the name of the town on my nametag—Littleton, Colorado.

The day of April 20, 1999, started out like any other. I was on my way to my office inside a Lutheran church where I had a private practice as a child and family therapist. I stopped by Foley's to pick up a new suit and heard the cashier talking about a school shooting somewhere in the southwest metro area. My first thought as I headed out on the highway was, "I hope the shooter is not one of my patients."

The closer I got to my office at the church, the louder the buzz from the half-dozen choppers flying overhead. It took me five years to disassociate that sound from that day. Pulling into the parking lot, I realized something was going on at the high school nearby. Still not aware of the magnitude of the tragedy, I walked up the center walk only to find the doors to the church locked. Surprised, I then heard the side door open and a woman call out, "Get inside quick! There are gunmen running around the neighborhood!"

The church was filled with youth group members, along with Columbine students who had run to the church for safety. It was a chaotic and confusing time. Still not fully aware of what had happened and needing to provide financially for my young son and wife, I was torn between going down to the school or seeing my patients. I decided to honor my appointments. Thirty minutes later a mother came into the church and announced, "There are a dozen dead at the school!" After my last patient left, tens of students streamed into the church, a church where one of the shooters had attended confirmation class.

Later that evening, the pastor announced to everyone that he would be meeting with parents and that my graduate student and I would be leading the triage group process with the teens. My graduate student turned to me and said, "What do I do? They haven't taught us this in graduate school." I replied, "Just follow what I do. I haven't been trained in this either."

A group of black-clad teens, many of them church members, were sitting in a circle in a corner of the room. One of the young men talked about how he had lost his friend. Then a young man across the room screamed, "Yeah, but your friend killed my friend!" Struggling to stay composed and worried about a fight erupting, I reminded them that everyone had suffered a loss and we needed to listen to each other.

A young girl said in a soft voice, "My teacher said she was going out of the room to see what was going on and that she would be right back for us." After a pause, with an abandoned look in her eyes that I will never forget, she continued, "She never came back." Her eyes told the story of every kid in the room. Everything her parents and counselors like me had taught them had collapsed like a house of cards in a matter of fifteen minutes.

What transpired over the next several weeks is a blur, albeit with numerous memories etched in my brain. As part of my daily counseling duties I ran groups for younger kids. They told stories of being locked down in their elementary schools, and heard about the fear and terror of their older brothers and sisters imprisoned within the high school—siblings who, no doubt, had been arguing just the day before.

A sweet young lady whom I knew for several years shared how she was being blamed for turning down one of the shooters for a prom date the week before. On her way to the library that day, she thankfully accepted a lunch invitation off campus. A former student of mine was later awarded the Boy Scout Honor Medal for lying on top of a classmate in a science room closet as they listened to footsteps just outside the door. He had whispered to her, "Stay quiet; if they come in they will shoot me and never know you are here."

I reached my tolerance for despair when on the third night a young man shared his experience with our small group. He told a story about the girl hiding next to him in the library who was asked if she believed in Jesus. When she said yes, one shooter put a gun to her head, asked, "Why?" and pulled the trigger. "It wouldn't have mattered what she said," he cried. "They were going to kill her anyway." At that point, I felt myself slip out of my body. I was floating above the room, completely disconnected from what was going on around me. Only the voice of my therapist friend saying, "Craig, are you OK?" brought me back to the room.

In the weeks that followed, my pain and sadness turned to outright rage as I watched the media circus surrounding the school. So much attention was being paid to two young men whose rage had destroyed so many lives. I couldn't read the papers or watch TV for weeks and found myself hemorrhaging emotionally and disconnected from my wife. Long walks and sitting in the dark on Rebel Hill, the mound overlooking the school where the memorial now sits, were my only consolation. Even my preschool son could tell something was wrong when he begged me one day to take off the purple and gray ribbon I wore on my suit coat.

While the despair was overwhelming, I continued to move on, providing care while questioning my own long-held beliefs and values. Did hope still exist? Or was despair the winner? How must it feel to be the parents of Eric and Dillon? Would this community, which had turned on itself in grief, ever recover? If I had been in that school, would I have stayed with my students or left in the chaos?

Two years later I sat in one of Vegas' finest restaurants, eating a fabulous dinner and crying my eyes out as I wrote down my experiences and planned for an anniversary memorial service at the church. I was facing a divorce and the prospect of raising a child as a single dad. While our marriage had been struggling for years, the shooting impacted both of us deeply. My wife was a newspaper editor and was reading all the stories every day. The Columbine tragedy revealed that our styles of grieving and healing were completely different. Neither one of us could soothe or support the other in the way we needed.

I also knew something inside me had changed forever. I had always been fairly even emotionally. However, this sadness and pain wouldn't subside. My neurochemistry was shaken to its core and remains disrupted to this day. A bout of depression came quickly and resurfaced at the loss of my father five years later. Neurochemically, I will be forever vulnerable to the pain of loss, abandonment, and the lessening of my emotional resiliency.

I still shudder when I see our state flower, the columbine, or hear about another school shooting. Yet, I hold onto the image from that secondary trauma workshop exercise, of hope meeting despair: the picture of a baby representing hope encountering the pain, loneliness, and disconnection of youthful death.

I still feel rage when I see front-page photos in the news that glorify despair and seduce countless others to express their pain in violent ways. Yet I believe that each day I go to work is ripe with moments of beauty where hope does overcome despair, as I watch people change their lives.

I've learned that while I continue to struggle with the debilitating power of despair, it is those moments of beauty, many of which were carried out by the students and families at Columbine, that truly make me cry. I still believe that when hope meets despair, it is despair that pauses and steps aside.

Craig A. Knippenberg, LCSW, MDiv, is a child and family therapist and president of Knippenberg, Patterson & Associates in metro Denver, Colorado. Following the shooting at Virginia Tech, he started the Enough! campaign to fight against the glorification of violence in the media. He is also the founder of AdventureDad.org, a blog and website dedicated to helping dads connect with their kids through shared adventures.

The Worst-Case Scenario

by Jared Ediger

I moved out to Colorado in 2001. After wrapping up a summer job with some coworkers the following July, I decide to join them for dinner and drinks at a local bar. It is a typical, nice summer evening and we are all sitting out on the patio enjoying a few cold beers and margaritas. As the hours pass, more and more drinks are consumed, and the conversation is getting increasingly louder as people begin to lose their inhibitions. The beer starts getting mixed with hard liquor, more by the minute, and my consciousness is fading into a deep fog. The conversations of those around me become mixed with the lively music and chatter of people sitting throughout the building. I am slowly losing my grasp of what is going on around me, but there is nothing I can do to reverse the process. It is as if people's actions and voices are in slow motion. My behaviors and words are no longer under conscious control. Despite this, the euphoria continues to fuel my drinking and there is no reason to stop. Combine this with the antianxiety medications I'm on and you have a pretty lethal cocktail for inducing bad judgment. Next thing I know, I am driving aimlessly and entering a convenience store for food. Other than these few tidbits of recollection, the night is a blur.

Most people could read the above story and chalk it up to the mistakes of growing up, but in this case I'm not the average person. It is different for me because I have obsessive-compulsive disorder (OCD). With OCD, unless I can prove the worst has not happened, in my mind the event has already occurred. I consistently imagine that I have run over and killed someone, or at least caused a harmful accident. Two of the worst-case scenarios, right? Therein lies my problem: I cannot realistically process dangerous circumstances and properly evaluate risk. What for most people would seem like a moderately reckless life decision, I interpret as a tragedy for which I am solely responsible.

When I woke up the day after this event, I could not believe the decisions I had made. My mind locked onto the scenarios of death and car crashes. After all, stories of people killed by drunk drivers pervade the news. That very disturbing thought not only settled into my head that morning, but seemingly has remained to this day. While there was no reason to believe that I had run over or killed someone, my mind went to the worst outcome possible, and it continues to fixate as I recount the events of that night. This thought will not go away; it repeats itself most days and continually haunts me.

Usually, the quickest way out of this kind of intense concern would be to produce evidence that I had not committed the horrid act. Ordinarily, that would be easy, but because I was intoxicated I could not prove the worst had not happened. The information I desperately sought to reassure me was lost along with the night of drinking. I dug through newspapers and checked out my car multiple times for blood and other signs of an accident. My behavior may sound extreme, but I could not stop the compulsion to do this. In my mind, those actions were the only way to come up with evidence to calm my worst fears. Seeking to clear my conscience and reduce my anxiety, I needed an answer. To no avail, I repeatedly tried to relive the events of the night before trying to come up with a way to prove my innocence. I was hoping that by meticulously reviewing the situation, I could somehow get sufficient information to disprove my doubts. That is where the compulsion comes into play in obsessive-compulsive disorder.

I cannot remember exactly when I first became aware of OCD. I remember the summer after my freshman year of college, when I was struggling with depression. Looking back on it, I can recall some distressing thoughts that I could not get out of my mind. After receiving some counseling, I was able to get through this event and my life straightened out. I did not know this was just the start of things to come. During my daily fixation with responsibility for some hit-and-run accident, I even questioned whether I should turn myself in to the police.

Once again, I turned to counseling in hopes of relieving my symptoms. The counseling helped for a little while, but my doubts quickly returned. What my mind desperately needed was reassurance and sometimes counseling was the best way to get it. The thought of having possibly killed someone was at the forefront and I could not contemplate any other possibility. The harder I tried to suppress these thoughts, the stronger and more persistent they became. At the time, I had no idea how much power this disease held.

A good analogy for those unfamiliar with the condition might be that of a faulty alarm system that goes off even if nobody has broken into your home. In the case of OCD the alarm repeatedly goes off when there is no obvious threat. The only way for someone with this condition to beat it is to learn how to shut off the alarm. If you cannot figure out how to do this, OCD can be quite persistent. You can imagine how hard it is to focus when an alarm is continuously going off in your mind.

It has taken me quite some time to figure out how to shut down the false alarms of OCD. Only in the past two years have I felt I have gained a decent amount of control over these symptoms by anticipating intense feelings and being able to dispute my obtrusive, repetitive thoughts. Learning to tolerate or come to terms with these feelings and thoughts has been the key. When I expose myself repeatedly to the issues that trouble me, facing them head-on instead of running from them, the issues have a tendency to lose their power over me.

Today, I am much quicker to recognize when my thoughts are heading out of control. I have realized that I have spent much of my life seeking reassurance and approval from family, friends, and acquaintances that I am a good, likable person who has not done anything wrong. I failed to realize that by seeking reassurance, I was reinforcing the problem.

For me, one of the biggest fears I have and continue to have is the fear of being infected with HIV or other bloodborne viruses. This wouldn't be such an issue if I weren't a nurse and didn't work with needles all the time. The fear of accidentally being stuck by an infectious needle is downright debilitating for me. The chances of my being stuck by a needle are relatively high; whether it is virus-contaminated or not is out of my control. As someone with OCD, I neutralize this anxiety by rigid control and double-checking everything that I do when I am in these situations. It can be quite tiresome to always have to be on guard against possibilities that may never occur.

Uncertainty is not something I deal with well. I would rather live in a boring, scripted manner than lead a life of frequent ups and downs. Of course, I know that life carries no certainty or guarantees, but my life is less anxiety producing when carefully scripted and thought out. The trouble is that this is not how life works, since there is an element of human error in everything we do. Of course, eliminating every risk is not going to happen, regardless of what my mind might try to tell me. The only way to decrease some of the anxiety associated with the fear of being infected with a needle is to repeatedly imagine the event happening to me and how it might feel. By repeatedly exposing myself to the thought of having stuck myself with a dirty needle over and over, I might over the course of time become accustomed to the idea and lessen the anxiety it produces.

This is also how I have approached the drinking and driving scenario. The worst outcome for me was possibly having killed someone. I used to avoid all local news shows and newspapers, fearing they might have some story about someone being killed by a drunk driver. I could not tolerate possibly having to relive the situation that I so desperately wanted to avoid. I have realized that the best therapy for me involves sitting with those uncomfortable emotions of drinking and driving. By doing so over time, my mind adapts and the event produces less anxiety. I have only been able to adopt this practice over the past few years, and it has been quite a challenge.

I imagine that I will always remember this drunken event in my life. After all, it is pretty hard to forget an event like this that carries so much emotion with it. The solution for me, and probably for most OCD people, is to try to avoid any situation or event that could possibly trigger such uncomfortable emotions again. People who have anxiety disorders like OCD tend to have a very low threshold for anxiety-producing events like these. That was why it was so difficult for me to write about it. Every time I tried, I was reopening an old wound that has never fully healed. That became apparent after multiple attempts to actually sit down and express my thoughts. However, I'm amazed to realize how much it has helped to get this story on paper and to openly disclose the details of my chronic struggle. I know I have improved considerably in my ability to deal with OCD, but I also know that I have much more to learn about healthy coping mechanisms.

Jared Ediger was born and raised in Newton, Kansas. He currently resides in Highlands Ranch, Colorado, with his wife Suanne and their children Miles and Kelsey. As an oncology nurse at Porter Hospital in Denver, he helps people who are chronically affected by cancer. He also helps facilitate the cancer support group at the hospital. Jared has found the opportunity of working with people and families affected by cancer to be his passion. Feel free to contact him through email at edigerd@yahoo.com.

A Leap of Faith

by Rob Ivker

Let the beauty we love be what we do.
There are hundreds of ways to kneel and kiss the ground.

—Rumi

As I write this story in March 2011, describing the pivotal events of my life-changing journey, I'm currently four decades into my evolution as a physician/healer and closer to the realization of my childhood dream … to become the best family doctor I can be. At the age of sixty-four, while many of my colleagues are contemplating retirement, I'm thrilled to be launching my second family practice: Fully Alive Medicine (FAM), in Boulder, CO. How I got here has been quite an exciting adventure.

Following a twenty-four-year hiatus from full-time practice (teaching and writing about holistic medicine and a part-time respiratory healing practice comprised the bulk of my professional life), FAM represents the manifestation of the vision I saw for myself at the age of twelve, shortly after letting go of my dream of stardom as an NFL quarterback. Medicine, my father's passion, looked like a good back-up vocation/avocation, but I wasn't sure it would be nearly as much fun. That uncertainty was dispelled during my first seven years of practice—the happiest period of my professional and family life.

After starting a solo family practice in 1975 in suburban Denver, my journey along the medical road less traveled began in 1980. I was led down this path by my sick sinuses. After three years of a worsening case of chronic sinusitis (recurrent sinus infections), I was told by my ENT consultant that he could offer me sinus surgery, but couldn't guarantee that it would cure the problem. His dismal prognosis: "Rob, you're going to have to live with it." Although it's not a terminal disease, I felt like I'd just been given a death sentence. I was thirty-three with a wife and two young daughters, and sinusitis was making it challenging to enjoy life. I was often irritable and felt depleted of energy. The thought of living this way for the rest of my life was depressing and unacceptable. Although I had no clue how I'd do it, I believed it was possible and made the commitment to cure it.

"Incurable" sinusitis, my father's Parkinson's disease, and my daughter's nephritis, all contributed toward diverting me from conventional medicine, which offered no hope for any of these ailments. But what put me over the top was an article I read titled "Death Does Not Exist." It was a lecture by Elizabeth Kubler-Ross, M.D., who at the time (December 1984) was medicine's leading authority on the subjects of death and dying. Her conclusions resulting from her many years of research were:

- Death doesn't exist … all that dies is a physical shell housing an immortal soul.
- Our existence in these bodies is a very brief part of our total existence.
- Our primary purpose while we're here is to *learn to love*.

Wow! I was stunned by these conclusions and even more shocked to hear them spoken by a physician. What made it even more noteworthy was that Kubler-Ross was investigating a subject that was neither discussed nor taught in medical school, perhaps because it represented failure to the medical profession. Even the words *love* and *soul* were rarely, if ever, mentioned in a medical setting. But this was a medical researcher relating her scientific conclusions about death and the meaning of human life. Essentially, she was saying that *we are spiritual beings sharing a human experience, with the collective intention of learning to love ourselves and one another.*

As much as I wanted to, I was unable to dismiss her findings as irrational or conclude that Kubler-Ross "had lost it (her mind)," as many members of the medical profession had assumed. Although it totally shattered my worldview, her beliefs deeply resonated with me and subsequently had a profound impact on curing my sinusitis, transforming my medical practice, healing my life and my relationships, and experiencing a dimension of health I never knew existed.

Simultaneous with my first reading of the Kubler-Ross paper, my thirteen-year-old daughter, Julie, was preparing for her Bat Mitzvah. Her Torah portion, Leviticus:19, was considered the essence of the Torah: *You shall love your neighbor as yourself*. It sounded remarkably similar to what Kubler-Ross was saying about our life's purpose. But her informed opinion was derived from her experience as a twentieth century psychiatrist, and this passage had come from a three-thousand-year-old text.

At about this same time, my practice had increased fivefold in just over two years, and was considered the highest-volume family practice in the Denver metro area. In 1983, based on a vision of providing greater continuity of care, I borrowed what for me was a huge amount from a local bank and expanded to become a family practice/minor emergency center. Columbine Medical Center (CMC) was open seven days a week, from 8:00 a.m. to 9:00 p.m. I was wearing multiple hats—family doctor; business manager; budget, marketing, and personnel director—while administrating a staff of twenty, including five family doctors. Maintaining quality of care in a facility seeing more than a hundred patients per day, while still trying to fulfill my family responsibilities as a husband and father, proved to be too much for me, my sinuses, and nearly my marriage.

Although I had initially made some progress in improving my sinusitis with dietary changes and saline nasal sprays, the stress of working more than sixty hours a week at a job I no longer enjoyed was triggering more frequent and severe sinus infections. On paper CMC was a success, but for me it was a tragic loss of the job of my dreams. In fact, after only three months of operation, I felt as if I'd made a huge mistake and began trying to sell the practice to a Denver hospital. After more than two years of frustration with no sale, I was depressed and angry (with myself). I desperately needed a break.

My brother mentioned an ad he'd seen for a 35-acre uninhabited island for sale in Fiji. I called the owner, who lived in Aspen, Colorado, and told him I was interested in seeing the island and would like to spend a week camping there. He readily agreed and sent me a map with the location of the only freshwater spring, and provided me with a couple of options for reaching the island. It was about two miles off the coast of a remote, road-less part of one of the largest of the three-hundred-plus Fijian islands. He hadn't been there in eight years and recommended that I "find a Fijian in a village near the end of the road, with a motorboat to take you there."

In late May of 1985, I left Denver for the South Pacific with a backpack loaded with camping gear and freeze-dried food. It took four days, along with the help of several Fijians, to reach the island. Shortly after arriving I was greeted by a startled fisherman from a nearby village, who came ashore in his small fishing boat. He wasn't used to seeing anyone on the island, let alone a Caucasian. He spoke excellent English and was quite excited to meet me and to introduce me to his family and the approximately one hundred people in his fishing and farming village. Nearly all of the villagers are Methodists and related. Upon entering the village several young children ran away crying ... they'd never seen a white person before.

What struck me most about these people and their culture was that the entire native Fijian population seemed to be living by the *Law of Love*—treating others the way they wished to be treated. They followed Jesus' lead and lived according to his (and the Torah's) core teaching, *Love thy neighbor as thyself*. Since I'd never met Jesus, and they'd never met a Jew, to me they were the most Torah-like people I'd ever known, and to them I was called "a man of God." As a total stranger in a place that felt otherworldly, I was welcomed into their homes and villages as if I were part of their family.

By our standards they would be considered a third-world country—poor, underdeveloped, and with few material possessions. However, the truth is that this population, guided by the belief that *God is Love*, was clearly happier, healthier (physically, emotionally, spiritually), and much more strongly connected to the Earth than our wealthy, urban, technologically advanced culture, where self-worth is often measured by net worth.

On that first trip I also experienced traditional Fijian medicine—hands-on healing, prayer, and herbs. I had a bout of severe abdominal pain and was treated by the "stomach specialist." Every family in Fiji has a particular part of the body that they heal, and at least one member of the family has the "gift," i.e., a healing touch. After kneeling beside me and reciting a prayer, the stomach healer lightly touched my abdomen, and within about ten minutes the pain was completely gone. I was blown away! They explained to me that the healer is simply a channel for Divine Love, and that it's God doing the healing. Whatever it was, it sure worked well ... far more effective than any prescription drug and with no adverse side effects. I was away for only twelve days, but that trip, at a time when I most needed a shift in perspective, changed my life forever.

Rapid and radical change became the norm after returning from Fiji. I spent all of 1986 working with Myron McClellan, a spiritual psychotherapist, who was instrumental in teaching me to love my nose, sinuses, and myself while helping me manifest my heart's greatest desires. Surprisingly, I also heard from him that I was a visionary, a talented writer, and had a "remarkably powerful healing touch." Within three months of meeting him, I had agreed to a deal selling CMC to Porter Hospital. Within sixteen months I had cured my chronic sinusitis, and in less than three years self-published *Sinus Survival*, describing my holistic approach for treating, preventing, and curing sinusitis. It became a best seller and has sold over 400,000 copies.

Although it initially felt awkward and uncomfortable, I also started doing healing touch on nearly every patient. Beginning in early 1987, until August 1988 (I stopped when I was threatened with the loss of my medical license), I was in a continual state of disbelief. I worked with a series of patients who experienced miraculous healings. Among them was a woman with metastatic breast cancer given three months to live (she's still alive and quite well), and a totally blind seventy-three-year old Fijian man with glaucoma. After one brief session with him he was able to see all of his fingers when he held his hands up to his eyes. As he related this incredible news, we embraced in a flood of tears. In that instant, I was overcome with awe, humility, joy, and gratitude, wanting only to serve God with this amazing gift. As I left his house and headed back to Colorado, I knew I'd never practice medicine as I had before.

In selling my practice to the hospital, I signed an employment contract to work as Medical Director of CMC. In August 1987 (just three months after working with the blind man), during a meeting with Porter's CEO, when I expressed a strong desire to practice holistic medicine at CMC, he responded, "You can't do it here."

That rejection and my subsequent resignation marked my official departure from conventional medicine, and fueled my commitment to transform medicine and heal our ailing health care system. Much to the disappointment of most of my family (especially my father, who considered it a completely irrational decision), I decided to walk away from a lifetime of financial security and pursue a mission that I strongly sensed was central to my life's purpose. In taking this life-changing step, I felt supported by tremendous faith and the belief that if this was what I was meant to do, my family's financial needs would somehow be met. And they were, mostly with book advances (but just barely). Taking major risks, following my heart and visions, creating a new medical model, while living on the financial edge has at times been quite stressful, but it has truly been a labor of love and an exhilarating spiritual journey.

During the past two decades I've dedicated myself to co-creating and teaching the new specialty of Integrative Holistic Medicine to both the public and the medical community. It's an evidence-based curriculum built on the fundamental belief: *Unconditional love is life's most powerful healer*; and its corollary, *the perceived loss of love is our greatest health risk.*

There are currently about fifteen hundred physicians (M.D.s and D.O.s) certified by the American Board of Integrative Holistic Medicine. This part of my mission has now been completed. I've also become a certified Healing Touch practitioner, while practicing what I teach on myself ... walking the talk. I'm feeling more vibrantly healthy than I ever have.

I'm now in the process of synthesizing all that I've learned from taking risks, experiencing pain, manifesting visions, and living my dreams during this magical evolution as a healer and teacher. With great passion, it's all being integrated into a new model for family practice and a new foundation for twenty-first century health care. *Love heals* and the *loss of love makes us sick.* These truths, *the heart of holistic medicine,* were repeatedly presented to me during the height of my transformational journey in the mid-1980s, and now they're being installed as the cornerstone of my new practice ... *Fully Alive Medicine!*

Dr. Rob Ivker *is a physician/healer, health educator, and bestselling author. He is the co-founder and Past President of the American Board of Integrative Holistic Medicine (ABIHM), a Past President of the American Holistic Medical Association (AHMA), a Fellow of the American Academy of Family Physicians, a Healing Touch Certified Practitioner, and a former Assistant Clinical Professor in the Department of Family Medicine and Clinical Instructor in the Department of Otolaryngology at the University of Colorado's School of Medicine. Married for forty-two years to Harriet, a psychiatric social worker, they have two daughters and sons-in-law and four grandchildren. His website is www.fullyalivemedicine.com.*

S.O.S.

by Steven Schwartz

As I sat in my parked car, drifting in and out of passive thought, the radio was broadcasting a 9/11 memorial. At that moment a wave of memories flooded my mind, as I thought back to the early days of my chiropractic career. It was the day after that fateful day in 2001 that I began a new practice in Denver, Colorado. Ironically, eight years to the day later, I found myself in a very similar situation. Suddenly, my phone rang. It was my lawyer approving my resignation letter and clearing me to send it to my soon-to-be-former partners. My own personal twin towers were falling down around me and I had no place to run. All I could do was look back at the situation and try to learn from my past.

This is a story about listening to my heart and following my inner guidance. As a young doctor, I thought I knew it all and, at the same time, was completely clueless. The story I am about to share is a journey of finding myself. The experiences and lessons I learned during this time have helped to solidify my life and bring peace to my soul.

The day after the biggest hostile attack that ever took place on U.S. soil, I had just left a chiropractic practice at which I spent two years. During that time I had found the niche that would be the foundation for my career. I was having great success using various vibrational healing methods to treat allergies and autoimmune diseases. As our nation was glued to its TVs watching the Twin Towers aftermath, I was busy building a successful practice. I was young and very motivated to establish myself; even a plummeting economy was not going to deter me. In fact, the first week at my new office the receptionist commented that people were already calling to schedule appointments, before I had officially started. Within a year, my success led to the opportunity to create the clinic and life of my dreams.

Business was good and we were growing quickly. I felt a burning desire to keep pushing, to grow bigger and bigger. The creative side of me continued to evolve as well. The more I became familiar with the underlying pathology of allergies and autoimmune conditions, the more I started thinking of innovative ways to remedy them. I was an avid student with an unquenchable thirst for learning everything I could about quantum physics, human bioenergy fields, and ways to work vibrationally with disease. Over the next three years, I honed my craft and became clear about how I could bring my gifts to the world. I traveled abroad, seeking out different kinds of healing modalities. I studied healing principles from indigenous cultures and even explored lost technologies used by Atlantis and Lemuria.

Even as my business was growing, something inside of me still yearned to be expressed. I knew it was much bigger than me and I knew I needed more help to manifest it. I was envisioning a holistic center that would use vibrational healing modalities to help people resolve chronic illness and allergies. Seven years into my practice I traveled to Peru, at a crossroads in my life.

While in Peru, I traveled with a shaman friend to the highest altitude lake in the world, Lake Titicaca. A boat took us across the vast lake to a remote island called Amantini. We stayed among the locals and were escorted to the top of a mountain peak, where we participated in a ceremony that revealed the next step in our lives. It was clear that it was time to launch my dream center. I was eager to return to Denver and move forward.

Immediately upon returning, we made the decision to begin looking for the ideal office space. My model was far from perfect. I had a lot of ideas, but my systems were not solid; my practitioners were not ideal ones; and I knew I needed to hire an office manager. The clinic was still generating a healthy income, but it demanded all my energy. Patience was never one of my strong suits. My East Coast mentality always had me pushing and driving forward. Unfortunately, I was so stuck in my head that I was ignoring a major part of me that made me successful in the first place: listening to my heart and following my inner guidance. My head said, "Go forward," but my heart and gut knew something was not right.

Things did not go well in the months to follow. Whether I didn't see it coming, or chose to ignore it, the wheels started to loosen on my business. I hired an office manager, who I knew was not right for the job, but she was persistent and I needed a manager. I learned a big lesson: we attract things into our lives that are familiar to us, not necessarily right for us. But because it is familiar, it feels right. I foolishly turned over my entire business to her, so I could focus on other things. She replaced my existing staff with new staff, and passed off responsibilities that should have been her own. As payroll skyrocketed, revenues began to fall, ultimately leading to IRS issues. We did not see eye to eye on the new location and we had major problems with designers and contractors. As bad as this was, the worst was yet to come. Little did I know that a major storm was brewing and I was heading directly into it.

During 2007, I finally took occupancy of my dream clinic. Instead of starting out with money in the bank and a staff of committed individuals all on the same page, the opposite occurred. My office-manager issues were coming to a head, my savings were depleted, and the IRS was knocking on my door. My staff was split between people loyal to my office manager or to me, and I hated going to the office each day. If that weren't enough, I was about to embark on a three-week trip to Peru. All this, and the country was embroiled in the worst economic recession in eighty years. I was more stressed than ever.

I never even considered the possibility of failure. I was consistently successful at anything into which I had put my mind and energy. This was no different. I hit my lowest point that September, with the clinic barely getting by. The staff morale was very low and the tension was palpable. I had to drain all my savings to get the IRS off of my back, and my girlfriend of two years had just left me.

This was supposed to be a divine project. What did it all mean? How could all of this be happening? This clinic and experience *was* divine. I was so hardheaded and overly focused on the things that didn't matter in my life. The universe put me through the hardest time and lowest points of my life, all so I could connect with who I really was. My mask covering my true self was really stuck, and the process of removing it was extremely uncomfortable. A smashed ego made me realize what was really important to me.

A glimmer of hope shone right around the corner. In April 2008, I was invited to speak at a health symposium. My presentation was a huge success. I made a lot of contacts and once again got excited about the clinic. These contacts pumped new life into my dying business and brought much needed support. My original vision of having a flagship alternative health care center once again became a real possibility.

The floodgates opened. My struggling clinic all of a sudden expanded from a single-owner business to a four-member corporation. Private investors were giving us money to grow, and people were actually approaching us about locations around the world. There was only one problem. I was extremely stressed and even more unhappy than ever before. My partners, all of whom knew little about health care, had a different plan from mine. I was outvoted on every idea and was basically forced to follow their agenda. The energy that rejuvenated me through the early summer had turned sour again by August.

On September first, my original company was replaced with our new business entity, which had plans for global expansion. The very next day, I was presented with legal papers naming me in a potential lawsuit involving my former massage therapist, whom I had fired months earlier for allegedly inappropriately touching a patient. I was named solely because the alleged incident occurred in my clinic.

This brings us back to where this story began, sitting in my car, readying to resign from my own clinic and walk away from my life's work.

I felt defeated, but I knew that my vision was bigger than me. I was willing to take myself out of the picture in order to breath life into it. As CEO, I could not afford to be linked to any potential legal improprieties while investment money was being raised. Sadly, over the next month, my former partners ran the clinic into the ground and totally withdrew from our business arrangement, leaving me with a shell of a clinic and with my dream shattered.

That September was one of the most emotional months of my life. Everything I'd worked for over the previous ten years was gone, with nothing to show for it but a huge financial hole. However, I received something that was way more valuable, my freedom. The day I left my practice, as emotional as I felt, I also felt as if I just got released from prison.

I delivered my resignation, and flew back home from Denver for a chance to completely remove myself from the whole ordeal and reconnect with who I am. Who was I as a child? What was my purpose for going to chiropractic school? Being around my friends and family helped shed light on the answers.

Returning to Denver was a huge undertaking. I had to clean up the mess that I had left behind. I had to make sense of my previous life and start over.

During this period in 2009, I got to see who my true friends were. My mom, stepfather, and sisters were so supportive. My old roommates from chiropractic school helped remind me who I really was. They gave me strength and confidence to come back and face the biggest fight of my life. A colleague of mine offered me a place to work until I got back on my feet. Another colleague offered me an opportunity to be the clinic director of a new company that uses advanced laser biofeedback technology for relieving allergies and autoimmune conditions. In a time when my ego and confidence were completely shattered, these fine individuals were there for me. Through this experience I was able to move forward, remembering the lessons and reinventing myself. A year later, I am much wiser, grounded, and closer to realizing my dreams than I ever have been.

Looking back on this experience, I would do it all over again, but in a different way. I was given an opportunity, and I went for it. I look back to when my practice was the most successful. I was working with patients and helping them get better. I was following my inner guidance in my life and helping my patients follow theirs. When the ship was sinking, I was pushing my way through life instead of flowing with it. Even during tough times now, I have great appreciation for where I am in my life. I feel so blessed to be out from under my other situation. I find that by believing in myself, and surrounding myself with people who believe in me, manifesting the life of my dreams is much easier.

When I relax, enjoy life, and exercise patience, I am more apt to realize powerful insights. Daily meditation and breathing practices help me stay centered and grounded. I am now more open to seeing the signs the universe provides. I will be forty in two years and anticipate that my next decade will be the most important and meaningful years of my life. My beautiful ship sank, but I survived and was rescued. Given a second a chance is an amazing gift and one of which I choose to take full advantage. I am truly a blessed man!

Dr. Steven Schwartz *is the co-founder of The Allergy Stop, in Denver, Colorado, which uses advanced biofeedback technology for treating allergies and chronic inflammation, and clearing cellular memory patterns. He is also the CEO and President of Bioharmonic Technologies, a "sound healing" CD company that uses frequency, geometry, mathematics, and music to create change in human physiology. Dr. Schwartz is an avid snowboarder and adventurer, who loves traveling. He has a strong passion for helping people to achieve their highest potential and to create optimal health. For more information about Dr. Schwartz, visit www.bioharmonictechnologies.com and www.theallergystop.com.*

Eating Desserts First

by Keil Oberlander

A crispy chicken-tender melt, breakfast potatoes with melted cheese on top, and a raspberry iced tea. My cousin Christine shared the secret of that little plate of heaven when she took me to Perkins roughly a year before. Now my friends and I stand in line before the cashier to pay for our meals. I am third in line. While we chat and giggle aimlessly, I glance at the marquee board behind and just slightly above the short cashier's head. A simple message displays crookedly across the midsection, "Life is uncertain; eat desserts first." I smirk at the words. My first thought is, "You people have no idea." My second reaction, which occurs simultaneously, is that of being thunderstruck by the marquee board's revelation. It speaks to me a truth I have been breathing ever since March 17, 2009, a truth of which I was unaware and unable to put into words until this exact moment.

When I eat a meal, like tonight, I cram myself full of food to the bursting point. Dessert is often out of the question, but more often out of my budget. Despite watching the latest Harry Potter just before the glorious meal, the meal is almost as exciting and enthralling as the movie—and that is saying something coming from a guy who has read the entire series eight times. Food simply enamors me. If necessity did not force me to consume food in order to maintain energy and life force, I would declare food as my most prized hobby. When I was going through nine months of cancer treatments, the highlight of the week occurred whenever Aunt Caroline and my two cousins, Eiel and Anika, would bring over Chinese food, or according to Anika and me, Chinese "mind-nourishing enhancement." My thoughts are put on hold when the cashier calls, "Next," and it is my turn. Once I pay, we exit and hit the road.

Cruising down the city streets, I sit quietly in the passenger seat. My mind wanders back to the saying on the board directly behind the baked goods and pies, "Life is uncertain." I know this firsthand. When trying to remember which movies I have seen with my friends, I always ask myself, "Did I have hair when we went to that one? Was I balding, or was I shiny bald at that point?" The amount of hair on my body at any given time period allows me to remember what time of year something happened and in what order. Streetlights zoom by and I try to move my eyes across the window fast enough to catch more than their blur. A thought hits me: I have been lugging cancer around far longer than since diagnosed; the diagnosis was only the initial and official knowing. Boy, did the ugly beast ever rear its ugly head! The devastation of the diagnosis shook my world and cured my teenage disease of knowing it all. A new disease replaced it and it was not an illusion this time. Fortunately I am a fast learner. I adapted quickly.

Uncertain. The word does not hit the spot. I want to use something more eloquent ... *Foggy? Vague? Ambiguous?*—that is the word I like. Some people cannot cope with the ambiguity of life. They are too caught up in Hollywood dramas, mediocre-paying jobs, inconsequential relationships, and the like. The reality they create for themselves is a false and unfortunate reality. Those who cannot cope with the unknown are in for a long and difficult haul. For those who cannot eat dessert first, many memories fade before they have a chance of being made. Cancer is no little thing. As I have written from the get-go in my journal, it is unbelievable. Cancer is something you might catch in a daytime soap opera. It does not happen to anyone in real life—let alone a sixteen-year-old life.

So many things are left undone because of cancer. So many things that I chose not to do when I was healthy are now off limits. Attending open gym to work on basketball during the summer was too much of a hassle. It was summer! It was my time to be lazy. I could actually get away with playing video games, watching television, and gluing my eyes to the screen all day. Well, congratulations, Keil. That is all you can do now. You cannot play basketball now. You cannot play baseball with your brothers. You cannot help out on the farm. You can't do diddly. I did not eat dessert first when I had the chance, and I cannot change that.

I catch the opaque reflection of remorseful eyes in the window as I stare at nothing. I, along with others, should have eaten dessert first. Indulging in dessert is natural, but we are taught from a young age that there is a logical, chronological, and strict order to eating a meal. This order is as follows: hors d'oeuvres to entrée to main course to salad to dessert. Perhaps the habit of playing it safe and conservatively following the meal etiquette, instilled within us by our parents who likewise were instilled with the same ideology by their parents, and so on, is wrong. What is life when confined to a strict structure that safeguards against all mystery, all chance of adventure? People who do not eat dessert first may never do so unless they realize what they are missing in their unfortunate habit.

Allow me to introduce my mother. I look at the driver and the two "macking" in the backseat. I wonder how my friends are able to dine. My mother is one of the strongest people in the world, a true warrior and a fellow cancer survivor. If you are unfortunate enough to find yourself in a disagreement with my mother—which you inevitably would one way or another—you need not wait long to discover that she is as brave as a lion, stubborn as a mule, and tough as nails. Now that you are acquainted with my mother, I present Exhibit A: her home office. I once thoroughly cleaned her office, throwing away what I thought was trivial garbage. One of these articles of "garbage" was an email from one of us kid's baseball seasons in 2004, which I carefully scrutinized. Mom came home one day and discovered that email in the garbage. One might have thought I had broken the picture window in our living room from her reaction. I was promptly grounded. I cleaned and Mom grounded me—irony, anyone? As things pile up, they become hidden and lost. One cannot enjoy the dessert if it cannot be found. It will get slightly stale and a little less appetizing. The dessert is not likely to be eaten. Things lost lose their value—out of sight, out of mind.

My mother has a set of china for special occasions. Their use has never in my lifetime been witnessed. There is also a special set of silverware that we use only for Thanksgiving and Christmas dinner. None of this eatery will wear out in a million years. Oh, the woeful injustice! We should be using that to devour the dessert! What purpose lies within continually saving when at any time life's ambiguity could take us for a roller coaster ride? What happens after the chance to use what we have been saving for that special occasion, is lost in the rush? Every breath and every day is a celebratory occasion. This cannot be forgotten. If celebrating is so difficult, why not make the effort to rejoice at least once a week with a family dinner followed by a card game or movie? Better yet, why not play a refreshing game of volleyball?

Before heading into the operating room to remove the chemo-blasted tumor, all I wanted to do was play volleyball with my friends. I knew a long recovery process would follow the surgery and that my friends would all be in school by the time I was able to play again. But I never got around to it. In the pre-operational meeting with the surgeon, I was forced a dose of toxic reality: My arm's function was likely to be lost. Paralysis would prevent me from lifting it. All of my life I have participated in sports. All of my life my friends and family have teased me about being a monkey. Would it all have to just end? To save my life, yes, it would.

We slowly creep within sight of New Underwood, my hometown with a population of something around seven hundred. My driver taps the steering wheel with his finger to the beat of the radio, the two in the backseat are still ambitiously aiming for first place in their make-out marathon, and I am still enraptured by the mystical marquee board. We pull off the interstate and onto the exit. We are almost home.

I was lucky. I pulled through the surgery better than anyone had expected; even my surgeon was flabbergasted by my recovery. I smile as I remember the physical therapists who came in several hours after the surgery. I blew them away when they told me to very carefully touch my left shoulder with my right arm. They told me in advance that it would be okay if I could not do it, because it was something that would most likely come a week later. I confidently took a deep breath and touched my left shoulder—just like that. I rendered them speechless. Their eyes widened. I beamed.

We drive down the highway until passing A Avenue, then B Avenue, and finally C Avenue. Turning right onto C Avenue, I can see the basement and living room windows ablaze with light. I crane my neck to observe the starlit sky. Life is uncertain; ambiguous. We all need to take advantage of it. Wait a minute. My thoughts stop cold. Why say "we?" This is something about which I may only speak for myself. *I* should do things I would not ordinarily do. *I* need to do those things I would shrug off for the only reason of "just because." *I* must live loud, wild, and proud. But most of all, I want *you* to hear my message. I want you to change with me, to resist that meal structure we were both taught at a young age. Eat dessert as much as you can, and eat it first. The bellyache sure to come is so much more satisfying than an empty stomach full of regret.

We have pulled into my driveway and it is time for me to enter my domain. My brothers will be playing video games, Dad and Sierra probably watching a movie, and Mom sound asleep. A well-known person once unkindly advised, "Let them eat cake!" I agree anyway. Go on, have a bittersweet bellyache on me! I step out of the car into the chilly November night. I bid my friends and you, my reader, with the same respect as a brash woman outside of Perkins screamed to her boyfriend, "Peace out, I love you face!" I leave you now, but not without beseeching thee to remember: *Life is uncertain; eat desserts first!*

Kyle "Keil" Oberlander *grew up in Elm Springs, South Dakota—a town that consisted of his household of four siblings and his parents, and the neighbors across the gravel road. He moved to New Underwood, South Dakota—a huge upgrade to about seven hundred people. Keil participated in basketball and baseball before he began kindergarten. He took up football for a few years in junior high, track during middle school and high school, and cross-country his freshman year. Excelling in athletics and involved in a plethora of extracurricular and volunteer activities, he was always determined to do what would be best for him in the future. Keil will be attending Brown University in Providence, Rhode Island, in the fall of 2011. He only knows thus far that he will major in Spanish and either premed or some form of social work on a global scale. He pretty much just "goes with the flow."*

Part Five: Spirituality

Light in the Cell

by Roberto Wahid Lewis

Each person who has ever lived has a story about some event that forever changed his life. Mine is no different, except for time, place, and circumstance.

I will never forget the night my mother walked into my bedroom and told me my father was dead. I was nine years old. At first, I wasn't quite sure what she meant, but as the day unfolded the story of his death was revealed to me, my four brothers, and two sisters. At the time, my mother was pregnant with my youngest sister. My father was stabbed during an argument in a bar. I remember my mother telling me, "We will be alright; we will make it."

As we prepared for the wake I remember feeling very sad. At nine, I realized I would never see my father again. The night of the wake, I went up to the casket and saw my father lying there, lifeless. I touched his face and hands for the last time and as the tears streamed down my face, I vowed never to cry about anything ever again in life. Filled with rage, I pledged to my father that I would kill the man who took him from me. As a nine-year-old child, I didn't really understand anger or how detrimental it can be if not addressed. As they lowered my father into the ground, I would not allow myself to cry nor would I allow myself to grieve. All I wanted was to kill the man who had taken my father from me. It wasn't until fifty years later, while talking with a dear friend named Fatima, that I finally grieved my father's death.

As far back as I can remember, everyone always told me I was just like my father. My uncles would tell me stories, that nobody would f--- with my father because he would jump off his feet and knock them out. Growing up, I took no s--- from anyone, either. I would fight at the drop of a hat. I felt no pain, so being hit didn't affect me. If I was in a fight, I would be as brutal as I possibly could be to the person I was fighting. I remember one time, after beating a guy senseless, I dragged him to the curb, took his foot, laid it on the curb, and jumped down on his leg. I left him there screaming in pain. I believed what everyone had always told me—that I was just like my father. I had also internalized that, like my father, I would not live long (he was thirty when he died). My only prayer to God was that I live to be fifteen; that was the age I had set to kill the man who had taken my father's life.

Between ages nine through fifteen my anger and disrespect for the law grew even stronger. The man who stabbed my father was never prosecuted, so I lost all respect for society's laws. By now I was stealing cars, burglarizing homes and businesses, dealing marijuana. I had also joined one of the most powerful street gangs in Chicago. Being in a gang made me even more reckless, and I had the reputation of shooting first and asking questions later. Among the gang members, I was known as someone you did not want to cross. I was able to convince a couple of my gang brothers to help me carry out my plan to kill the man who took my father's life. We had access to just about any kind of available street weapon.

By the time I reached fifteen, God had already brought more suffering on my father's killer than I could ever have inflicted. I guess the thought of taking a life was more than he could bear. By now he was homeless and could often be seen in the streets, smelling like urine and feces. The day I approached him to kill him, he was drunk and smelly. My gang brother told me that I would be putting him out of his misery if I killed him, that I should merely let him suffer the way he was. So we just turned and walked away from him. I never thought about taking his life again after that. I asked my father to forgive me for not following through on my pledge to him.

The next few years I found myself immersed in the life of the underworld. I was shaking down tavern owners, selling protection to business owners, and controlling a prostitution ring. All the while, the idea that I wouldn't be here for much longer pervaded my thoughts, so I was going to do whatever I wanted, whenever I wanted, and no one was going to stop me. The more I got away with, the more emboldened I became. The anger never left, nor did my contempt for the laws of society. I missed my father and I often wondered what my life would have been like had he lived, but I constantly thought, "This is my life now and I'm in it for the long haul, however long that may be."

There is a saying, "Man plans and God plans, but God is the best of planners." I know now that God had a plan for me that was beyond my comprehension. At the age of nineteen, I was charged in a twenty-count indictment, subsequently convicted on two of those charges, and sentenced to one hundred to three hundred years in prison. At the time, the special prosecutor told the judge and jury that I had no respect for the law. In prison there is a "law" that prisoners live by, and I would not respect even the prison code. The prosecutor added that the only way I should ever leave prison was in a pine box. The next day I was in a maximum security prison, immediately wondering, "How can I escape from here?"

I settled into prison life fairly easily. At that time, the gangs literally ran the prisons. I had the status of a gang chief in charge of one of the most powerful gangs, so I was able to get just about anything I wanted. I needed movement in order to plan my escape, so I got a job working in the maintenance department. I started as a plumber and later learned how to weld. My job took me all over the prison, even into high security areas. All the while, I was looking for an escape route.

In 1978 the government decided it was going to take back control of the prisons. In the middle of the night, they went from cell house to cell house, gathering who they considered top gang leaders. They loaded us onto a bus and transferred us to various other prisons. Some were transported out of state. I was sent to another maximum security prison. As I stated earlier, "Man plans and God plans, but God is the best of planners." I did not realize it at the time, but God had already planned my destiny; I would soon meet my spiritual teacher.

My future teacher came to the prison offering a "lifestyle program" to anyone who wanted to participate. I remember walking into the room where the orientation was to take place. The moment our eyes met, I felt something shift inside me. The program consisted of yoga, meditation, health, hygiene, and organizational skills. I took to the yoga and meditation like a duck to water. I found myself being more calm and relaxed, and thinking more rationally. The teacher and I would often have one-on-one conversations. We would talk about a wide range of subjects. When I told him that I was never supposed to get out of prison, his response was, "This does not have to be your prison. It can be your retreat, your sabbatical, your church, your masjid—it's up to you." That made so much sense to me. From that moment on, I never considered myself being in prison.

I cherished his friendship, and to this day cherish it even more deeply. I felt supported in a way that I had never felt supported before, even in the gang. No matter where he traveled, he always stayed in touch with me, always letting me know what was going on in his life and always concerned about me. There was never a doubt in my mind regarding his level of sincerity, and I actually began to feel love from a real human being. As my mind questioned my heart as to what was going on inside me, things began to shift externally as well. My meditation became part of my daily routine. I began to read and study anything I could find regarding spiritual life and spiritual practices.

As I settled into my new lifestyle, with the various practices that kept me at peace with myself, I still had to deal with the reality of my situation. One reality was that I had to appear before the parole board. For many years, the board denied me parole, but I found consolation in their denial. Somehow I knew I was not going to be in prison for the rest of my life. I knew that God was not done "cooking" me yet. I found peace and relief in knowing that. There comes a point in all of our lives, no matter where we are, that we must look at our life and then decide if we want to continue in the same lifestyle, or change. No matter what one's status is or the amount of time and energy one has dedicated to a particular ideology or concept, if that no longer feeds the hunger inside, one has to have courage enough to let it go. That's what I did. I resigned from the gang, relinquishing my title and authority. I knew and accepted the inevitable consequences of my actions—retribution from the gang. I survived the attack on my life. I was stabbed in the neck, back, and head and almost lost a finger.

I am remorseful for all of the bad and wrong things I did in life, but I cannot undo any of them. God has given me another chance to become a fully-realized human being. With the support and guidance of my Sufi Sheikh and my community, I hope to reach my destiny. I have been out of prison since 2002 and have been married since 2004. I own my home and business. The same dedication and devotion I applied to being a bad guy, I am applying toward being a loving, serving human being. I love life and appreciate each and every day that God gives me.

Nobody could ever convince me that miracles don't happen—I am living proof, nor could anyone ever convince me that there is not a Divine Plan at work in all of our lives. I lived on the dark side and I know what it's like to be in the mud and slime of the underworld. Now I have the opportunity to experience living life as it was designed to be lived, free of fear. My journey hasn't ended; it has only begun. Through God's Mercy and Grace, I have risen from the depths of hell. I will continue to hold my Sheikh's hand and follow his instructions, because his guidance and God's Grace have molded me into the person I am today.

Roberto Wahid Lewis, having long ago left the underworld, has dedicated the remainder of his life to loving service and continual spiritual pursuit through his participation in an Illinois-based intentional community.

Free Fall

by Jim Sharon

Mount Shasta, California on a warm, late August morning, 1983. Me, alone in the woods, lying in a sleeping bag, looking up at the sky through the forest of trees. Complete stillness, outside and within.

I had done it! Burned all my bridges "for real."

At 36 years old, with a wife, a young child and a doctorate in psychology, I was now homeless, jobless and disgruntled with the spiritual community I'd been part of for over a year and a half. Maybe my marriage was over, too. I didn't know yet.

My family and friends thought I had gone "off the deep end," and maybe I had.

My backpack contained at most a week's worth of casual clothing; I had $16 and one credit card in my pocket. How would I get out of these woods—and where would I go, anyway?

Four notable things remained: faith; the quiet thought, "I am free;" stillness; and a deep, silent "belly laugh."

The seeds of this pivotal moment were sewn more than 10 years earlier. It's September of 1972 and a disheveled, barefoot guy in tattered jeans and a sleeveless t-shirt is approaching our Virginia Beach apartment with two other movers. As we chatted with "Sam the Move-man" throughout the day, my wife Ruth and I learned that he'd recently relinquished a lucrative accounting job in California, given away all his possessions, and sold his book collection for a pittance. Hitchhiking on faith, Sam had followed wherever destiny took him. Now he was 2700 miles from the home he left behind and making a little money assisting our movers. Floating free.

Fascinated by Sam's story, Ruth and I invited him to stay overnight in our new apartment. Listening to him talk, I kept wondering, "Could I ever be that unencumbered? Would I ever have the guts to give everything up? Did I have it in me to take that kind of risk?"

I was content in my role as a mental health center counselor and happy in my marriage and in our cozy little apartment. Life was good. Nevertheless, Sam lingered on the "back burner" of my consciousness for the next decade.

Small Town Life

Fast forward ten years and life continues to be good. Ruth and I had moved to Greeley, Colorado, where I received my doctorate in counseling psychology and co-directed a progressive wellness and human development center that we had founded. We were a vital part of a close community of friends. Having spent my life in and around major cities, I was enjoying the benefits of small-town life. We bought a simple, lovely house, where we were happily raising our daughter, who was attending kindergarten.

Enter onto this peaceful scene, a group of flamboyant characters that I met through a friend. Over the course of their visit, I found their free-spirited demeanor refreshing and contagious. My friend and these seemingly carefree people were giddy about their recent involvement with a California-based group and its charismatic and "outrageous" leader. One night, on impulse, I brazenly decided to call him. I opened the conversation by saying, "I've heard a lot about you; it's high time we met. Who are you?" Without skipping a beat, he replied, "I've been to the bottom of hell and back." Intrigued by that response and our brief conversation, I accepted an invitation to meet the leader and others in his group during their forthcoming visit to Colorado.

Swept Away

As was not uncommon during the heyday of groups and cults in the '70s and early '80s, both my wife and I got "swept away" by the leader's charisma and promises and by the group's energy. We also appreciated their lightheartedness and non-dogmatic spiritual views, so we accepted an invitation to participate in a month-long summer intensive. The crux of this very intense and challenging "training" and the core message of the teachings was that in order to attain genuine freedom and inner peace one must learn to "stand on nothing," as the leader termed it, continually striving to be present and innocent. We were experientially taught to relinquish patterns of defining ourselves, including life roles, and to release attachments. For example, during the training, we were forbidden to engage in "props"—routinized practices and distractions, such as meditation, television, exercise, reading and sex.

We all experienced our mindsets and nervous systems being reprogrammed. In the process, the anxiety and confusion I often felt were trumped by an electrifying sense of rising to fresh challenges—and I was having a blast re-inventing myself and my sense of reality anew.

Following this rigorous and ultra-dynamic month, my soul longed for a greater form of self-expression and I came to regard my small-town Greeley life as mundane and dull.

I convinced my wife that for my continued personal development I needed to head off to Santa Barbara, California to do more with the group and the leader. I was quickly humbled in this posh enclave by having to join other doctoral-level townspeople in accepting a series of minimum-wage jobs. I began to have mixed feelings about the leader and the group, and although I was still learning a lot, I didn't like the frequent drama or effusive energy in the mix. Missing my wife and my daughter, I invited them to rent out our house and come join me at my former Greeley friend's condo. They arrived in Santa Barbara just before Christmas 1982. Ruth and I slept in sleeping bags on the darkroom floor; Alaina's "bedroom" amounted to a corner in the living room. Ruth and I accepted a series of menial, minimum-wage jobs, while participating in various activities with our group. Mimicking "Sam the Move-man" (and many other cult followers of that era) we sold all our furniture and most possessions --for a pittance. We were "in" ... 100%.

In August we engaged in a three-day group program at Mount Shasta, CA. By now, I was growing weary and wary of paying for "freedom" events and personal guidance, in the process, depleting the little I had left in savings. I had also grown tired of the leader's challenges, games and arbitrary rules. After obstinately refusing to "play along" at this retreat, I was asked to leave the event, which landed me alone in the forest where I began this story, my wife having chosen to stay.

Leaving the Cult

I made my way from Mt. Shasta to San Francisco, where I lived in numerous homes over a six-week period, often panhandling, or doing a few one-week jobs. Many days I awoke with the thought, "Where will I live tomorrow?" A few times I almost was going to stay in a homeless shelter, but I was fortunate and resourceful enough to never have to do so. Actively involved with the community, Ruth became increasingly distant from me, as I had minimal contact with the group.

This proved the most intense period of my life; I felt agitated, lost, conflicted and confused. Part of me felt that the group constituted the most loving people

I'd ever known, with a worldview I held and admired, but I was torn. My skepticism about the leader's tactics, concern over changes in Ruth's personality, my increasing unease with the whole ordeal—and my own internal state—mounted by the week. Finally, I sought out some cult experts in San Francisco. They confirmed that a lot was indeed amiss, and felt I had been markedly destabilized and disempowered in an essentially unsavory cult.

In November 1983 I accepted a kind invitation from my sister to come live with her family in Denver and work with a local cult expert until I landed "on my feet." Three weeks later, I met with Ruth at her sister's home. After lengthy, often heated discussions, she agreed to reunite with me. With financial assistance from my parents for a few months, we reconstructed our lives, settling in the Denver area, where we have lived ever since.

Despite the turmoil and upheaval that I had encountered during the last quarter of my cult involvement, I did not regret what I deemed a vital—and "wild and crazy" life experience. I had learned a lot about cult dynamics and celebrated my courage, adventurousness and convictions.

Longing Persists

Though I had learned my lessons and was quite wary of any future involvement with cults or spiritual groups, a hunger remained inside of me for deep connection, both to the sacred (God/spirit/higher self) and to community. When I met my next spiritual teacher in 1991, I was vigilant and skeptically inquisitive for a long time before I accepted him as a trusted guide. Once the teacher had earned my trust, I became very involved in his intentional Sufi and yogic community. I loved the combination of caring for one another, rigorous and beautiful mystical practices, service work, playfulness, environmental consciousness, and support of the householder path, which included jobs and children. By that time, Ruth and I had two more children and they also cherished community involvement.

But then the pattern repeated itself. Despite valuing my friendships and experiencing ineffable beauty, meaning and great gratitude for my ongoing spiritual development, I often had misgivings. I felt consumed by the intensive participation that was required, controlled by the teacher's influence in many of my personal choices, and disapproving of the teacher's periodic sharp and public rebukes of his students. I craved more autonomy and more of a life outside of the community. After 11 years, I painfully exited this group, after an even greater internal struggle than I encountered in leaving my first "cult."

Introspective by nature, I've often reflected on the experiences and lessons I gleaned from my involvement in two spiritual communities. Since my youth, I have held a spiritual longing, a love of sacredness and an appreciation for authentic vulnerability, which I retain to this day. While both communities fed these yearnings in different ways, I continually had to weigh the value of surrendering my will against the questions of whether it served me to relinquish my autonomy and power. Despite the incredible mystical learning and genuine love I garnered in both communities—especially in the Sufi/yogic group—my need for autonomy and for following my own convictions proved paramount.

And yet, I soon realized that living without a spiritual path and practice, without community and without guidance leaves me unfulfilled.

This, I think, is an issue for all who journey on a spiritual path. Why and how does one exchange self-will and autonomy for guidance and community—and what are the healthy and appropriate boundaries for doing so?

Through years of making such discernments, I have come to realize the critical importance of continually refining and following my own inner guidance. I cannot trade my own inner truth and knowing, my inner compass, nor compromise my dignity for so-called "spirituality." And I no longer think I have to do so. I can honor my needs and core values, and still be actively engaged on a sacred path. It is an old precept—and for me, neither a useful nor healthy one—that one must relinquish autonomy and discernment for spiritual connection.

Homecoming

Now approaching my mid 60s, with a psychotherapy practice spanning nearly four decades, a 40+ year marriage, three adult children and a grandchild, I am once again part of a spiritual community. I believe that I have found a comfortable "home" in an international Sufi order that provides an ideal balance of community and guidance without any interference in members' autonomy, and does not seek to compromise members' dignity in exchange for spiritual guidance. This global community embraces values I cherish, and provides the "sacred" and community connection that lights and delights my heart. Ahh, balance at last!

Jim Sharon, Ed.D. *is a licensed psychologist and certified life coach in private practice in Centennial, CO. He has been involved as a leader and participant in men's groups since the inception of the men's movement over 30 years ago. Dr. Sharon serves as the coordinator and editor of this anthology and founder/coordinator of Whole Man Expo. Contact him through his counseling practice website at www.energyforlife.us.*

Angels Along the Road

by Stephen Booth-Nadav

> Israel said to Joseph, "Your brothers are pasturing at Shechem. Come, I will send you to them." He answered, "I am ready." ... When he reached Shechem, a man (angel) came upon him wandering in the fields. He asked him, "What are you looking for?" He replied, "My brothers, I seek. Could you tell me where they are pasturing?" The man (angel) said, "They have gone from here ... to Dothan." So Joseph followed and found his brothers at Dothan.
>
> –Genesis 37:13–17

Throughout our lives there are moments ... an "angel" appears ... if only we are ready to listen. This is a story of some of the angels who have appeared along my path, and the incredible impact they have had.

B'reishit—In a Beginning

This story begins when I was twenty-seven, searching for my soul, listening for the still voice that would help guide my next steps. At a gathering at the Hillel (Jewish) Student Center in Minneapolis, I listened and heard the deep wisdom emerging from Eddie Benton-Banai, Ojibwe elder, touching and sharing the spirit that connects us all. In this circle, Jewish and Ojibwe, his chants were our chants, his spirit our spirit. In this circle of sharing, Jewish and Ojibwe, all paths were enlightened.

Eddie invited me to join a spring gathering of tribes called Three Fires up in the north woods. In this sacred circle, I noticed I was welcome, but not really welcomed. Eddie said, "You are my guest; however, we are used to white folks coming and basically just ripping off our culture and leaving. So we are leery. But you come from a rich tradition. Go back and learn from your tradition. Then come back and we can have a true exchange."

Just as Joseph was propelled by the man-angel into his future, I was propelled by Eddie. Sometimes, even with boundaries, souls join and God's hand is discerned. Thus I began my path to becoming a rabbi.

Twelve years later I met my man-angel again, running into Eddie at a powwow in Lansing, Michigan, where I held my first position as a congregational rabbi. My wife Jan introduced me to him as "Rabbi Booth." Soul to soul again. Eddie said he was not surprised. I thanked him and have never forgotten his gift to me.

Rabbi on the Reservation

In my second year out of seminary, an angel delivered an invitation to join a group of rabbis and native spiritual leaders at Canyon de Chelly on the Navajo Reservation for five days. Once again, we were hosted by a native elder, Chauncey Neboyia (www.acanyondechellytour.com/Chauncey.html).

Chauncy was the last elder still living in the canyon. He and his grandson Daniel welcomed us to his land, where we camped over Shabbat Bereshit, the weekend during which we enter the cycle of Torah, reading again at the beginning, after the fall Holy Days. Over these days we shared creation stories, Native American and Jewish. We prayed, danced, cried, listened, walked, and opened our hearts to this sacred land, to the circle of life, and to each other. Our souls showed up in this sacred circle of trust.

One morning I awoke to the sound of a colleague *daavening* (morning prayers) up on the side of the canyon where the sun was reaching. Crawling out of my tent on this beautiful fall morning, surrounded by the incredible, awesome beauty of the Southwest desert—the rich colors, textures, endless blue sky, and the air that fills not only one's lungs but one's soul—taking all this in, and hearing the joyful chanting of Hebrew prayers, my heart leapt, and I said, "Ma Nora HaMakom HaZeh!" "How awesome is this place!" (Genesis 28:17) *Here I am. I am being physical, "being outdoors," and "doing Jewish"—my favorite things, and I get to do them at the same time! What could be better?*

As I left Canyon de Chelly and went on to serve two congregations over fourteen years, I kept those loves alive, often wishing I could share my love of "doing Jewish" and "being outdoors" together. But for a busy congregational rabbi with more responsibilities than I could ever count, it rarely happened. I moved to Colorado. I prayed and celebrated joyous Jewish life in community, and I hiked and biked and soaked up the outdoors, but found few opportunities to share both at the same time.

Later I created a B'nai Mitzvah retreat program with Rabbi Jamie Korngold (aka The Adventure Rabbi). We took my class up to the mountains one weekend a year for seven years, teaching and sharing experiences of God, community, prayer, and Jewish wilderness spirituality. It was great; it kept my dim dream alive.

A few years later, freed up from congregational responsibilities, working on staff at Adventure Rabbi, my experience at Canyon de Chelly suddenly came back to me. I remembered how much I loved "being outdoors" and "doing Jewish." And that path continues, as I participate in the Advanced Leadership Training Program of TorahTrek: The Center for Jewish Wilderness Spirituality, and lead contemplative hikes. So, add Rabbis Jamie Korngold and Mike Comins to my list of angel-guides.

Wisdom House Denver

Upon reflection, another angel-guide on the journey has been Ariella, my daughter, now age eight. Suddenly, at forty-eight, I became a father. Such blessing, joy, love, and deep ongoing teaching cannot be compared. She continues to point out the way.

I turned fifty, with a two-year-old daughter, and went on sabbatical to Jerusalem (not far from Dothan). Buoyed by the incredible gift of my daughter and the call to fatherhood, and with the support of my life partner Jan, it was a good time for reflection.

Looking at my life I noticed that somehow I had become isolated in a Jewish "ghetto." *Where are my brothers?* Virtually all my daily contacts and relationships were in the Jewish community. I love Jewish community, but this felt wrong, not me, not my path in life. I am a bridge builder. My life is about relationships. I decided it was time to open myself and build relationships with non-Jews.

I wasn't expecting to work on this goal right away in Jerusalem. But again, an angel appeared. This time it was in the guise of Rabbi Yehezkel Landau, whom I recognized at services in Jerusalem one Friday night. I had not seen or heard of him for more than a decade. Over coffee in a Jerusalem café, he invited me to participate a couple months later in a program he runs at Hartford Seminary called Building Abrahamic Partnerships. (BAP brings together Jews, Muslims, and Christians for a week of living and learning together.) Thanks to Jan's (my ongoing angel-guide-partner) suggestion, I created a team of three—Jew, Muslim, and Christian—from Denver, to experience this together. It changed and connected us for the rest of our lives.

Returning to Denver I became increasingly involved in interfaith work. I got involved in several local interfaith committees and continued to nurture those relationships, meeting more angel-guides along the way.

I also took time—two retreats a year, weekly study, yoga, and meditation—as part of the rabbinic program at the Institute for Jewish Spirituality, to renew and listen to my spirit.

It was there that I had a dream ... a dream of building a multifaith center in Denver. I switched to the term "multifaith" partly due to the influence of one my seminary teachers, Rabbi Nancy Fuchs-Kramer (www.multifaithworld.com). It implies dialogue and relationships starting from a deeper place of connection with one's own tradition than is usually thought of in the term "interfaith."

I had spent years building relationships with clergy and lay leaders in many faith communities. It was also clear to me that "wilderness spirituality" and "multifaith work" were/are my spiritual leading edges. And then to my surprise, Canyon de Chelly returned!

I finally realized I had found my dual love for "being outdoors" and "doing Jewish" on the Navajo Reservation, in the context of a deeply Earth-based culture. Although I was not quite aware of this at the time, Canyon de Chelly had shown me years ago the powerful mirror one can access when being hosted by another culture.

Uniting the past with the present and future, I realized the outdoors (wilderness spirituality), Jewish practice, and multifaith work were in fact all a part of the puzzle that was me. And key to my journey, my story, my life, my self, were angels, guides, teachers, and friends, sharing their souls and their wisdom, from Jewish, Native American, Christian, Muslim, Buddhist, and other traditions (in addition to my constant traveling companions-teachers in my life partner Jan and daughter Ariella).

Putting all this together, today I am creating Wisdom House Denver, a network and community of teachers, leaders, and learners committed to multifaith dialogue, learning, and spiritual inquiry.

Shema, listen. I have been blessed by many on the journey. I have been blessed with an open ear and heart to what they have come to share with me, and to reflect back to me. I have been blessed to walk my path. May you be blessed with the same.

I want to acknowledge the many precious guides I have had along the journey: Eddie, Chauncy and Daniel, Yeheskel, Ariella, Jan, Jamie, and Mike. Also

Rabbis Arthur Waskow, Zalman Schachter-Shalomi, Rami Shapiro, Jack Gabriel, Shefa Gold, Sheila Weinberg, and Sylvia Boorstein and all IJS staff and teachers, Rev. Paul Kottke and more.

Rabbi Stephen Booth-Nadav, a native of Chicago, is a former bicycle cooperative co-owner/mechanic. A graduate of the Reconstructionist Rabbinical College in 1992, he served as a congregational rabbi for fourteen years. Currently, he is living in Denver with his life partner Jan Cooper-Nadav and raising his daughter-teacher Ariella. Rabbi Booth-Nadav is the founder of Wisdom House Denver: A Center for Multifaith Dialogue and Spiritual Inquiry. He is also the rabbi of Har Mishpacha Congregation in Steamboat Springs, Colorado. Previously he served as program director at TorahTrek: The Center for Jewish Wilderness Spirituality. Reach him at boothnadav@gmail.com.

Part Six: Miracles

Tell the World

by Sam Fireman (with Jim Sharon)

"You must live to tell the world! Promise me you'll survive," my brother Aaron demanded through the other side of the electrified fence. That sharp command penetrated my chest as fast as it struck my ears. Instantly the resolve that had become my inner companion intensified into sheer determination. A new Auschwitz camp arrival, I was one of the fortunate ones sent to the left after stepping down from one of the packed boxcars on the train. My beloved brother informed me that at most I'd have a six-month reprieve; his time was up and he was slated for cremation the following day. The German *capo* (barracks overseer), who despised Hitler, did my brother the favor of escorting me to the fence to exchange our farewells. Aaron informed me of a conspiracy (with Polish townspeople hiding dynamite in large, wooden food bowls) to blow up the crematorium and gas chamber prior to his execution. The conspirators succeeded, but my brother was captured and shot, along with other escapees.

In November 1939 the Polish government surrendered to the Germans. I was captured as a member of the Polish army and taken prisoner. The Germans had us march for two days to a sugar factory, where we were detained overnight. Along the way Jews were identified by the German soldiers, pulled out of line, and shot on the spot. I probably avoided being shot by pulling my cap over my eyes and keeping my head down. In the morning the Gestapo (German secret police) ordered all soldiers from Oberslazen to step out of line. I quickly decided to join the group because I knew Oberslazen was populated mostly by Germans. Fortunately, nobody knew I was the only Jew in that group of captured soldiers.

We were loaded into a boxcar headed for Krakow, a town where I had been deployed during my army service. The evening of the second day of travel, as we neared Krakow, I calculated my odds and concluded that if I remained on the train I would probably have a 5 percent chance of surviving; whereas I sensed that I had about fifty-fifty odds of living if I jumped from the train moving at about 40 mph. Positioned close to the open door, I gathered my courage and leaped into the black night. Amazingly, I landed safely, but remained motionless on the ground for about ten minutes to be sure I was not seen moving.

Upon rising, I immediately ran to the nearby forest, where I walked about two hours before spotting a tiny light on the horizon. Following the light, I arrived around midnight at a small house. Upon entering the house, I risked informing the man who greeted me that I was a Jewish soldier. Although at first he did not respond, he soon befriended me. I mentioned that I was famished, so he woke his wife, who proceeded to prepare a meal of potatoes and sour cream for me. After devouring that delicious food, this kind man told me that the Gestapo posted at the guard station in Krakow were seeking Jews and soldiers to murder. He told me he worked for the railroad and insisted that I exchange my army uniform for his own tattered, filthy uniform, along with a lunch pail with a slice of bread inside. He sternly warned me not to betray myself by speaking German, for Yiddish is very similar to German, and many Jews who spoke German were betrayed by their Yiddish accent. He then handed me an identification card written in Polish, adding that the Germans would not be able to read it. He also exhorted me to have confidence and refrain from shaking while speaking to the Gestapo at the guard station.

The guard station routine proceeded as my "savior" described. The guard asked for my card and questioned me in German. Pretending not to comprehend, I answered in Polish that I did not understand his question. I heard that guard ask another, "What should we do with him?" I acted confident and did not shake. The other guard replied, "Let him go." About fifteen minutes later I observed countless bodies piled high at the guard station on the other side of town. Again, the guards requested my papers and I continued pretending not to understand German. They looked me over, uttered, "Get lost!" and motioned me away. After I walked about twenty-five feet, a guard called me back. I immediately thought, "I'm a dead man!" and began shaking all over. As I walked back, the guard headed to his truck. Upon returning, he handed me three packs of fine cigarettes. I took one, began smoking it, and walked away, shuddering inside. Although feeling immense relief, I was perplexed as to how my life had been spared once again.

Two days after returning home I received a letter stating that the Germans needed two hundred strong young men to report for duty the following week. Suspecting that I would be executed if I reported, I fled to my fiancée Hinda's home in Pionki, thirty miles south of Warsaw. One frigid day, while I shoveled snow from the sidewalk at Hinda's house, a Gestapo officer approached and ordered me to report to the local office at 10:00 the next morning. Jews were only permitted to walk in the street gutters. Despite my fiancé and her mother's urging, I decided to comply with the order. Removing my hat and bowing, I bid the Gestapo officer, "Good morning." He barked, "Remove your shirt!" I did as the officer ordered and he drew a whip with an attached wire. I was terrified that he intended to cripple or kill me. But, just as he raised his whip, I heard a sharp command: "Do not hurt this Jew!" I turned around and stared in astonishment at the officer of higher rank who had rescued me.

My protector was Johann Kramer, whom I had known from before the war. Having lost his job, Mr. Kramer had struggled to make the monthly payments on a downspout installation I had done for him. Although Johann repeatedly assured me that he would pay me once he obtained a job, I replied, "You have a beautiful wife and children; you needn't worry about the money." Following his continued assurances, I offered Mr. Kramer two dollars and told him, "Buy some candy, sit with your family, and sing together." Johann grabbed me, kissed me, and thanked me profusely.

Now that he was a German officer, Johann continued arranging favors. First, he got me a good job grooming horses, which I had done in the Polish cavalry. Amazingly, when I wanted to invite people to my wedding, he cancelled an edict that prohibited Jews from gathering together in groups larger than four (to prevent conspiracy against the Germans). Johann and his fellow Gestapo officers actually attended my wedding in my home. Shortly after our marriage, Hinda and I were interred in a Pionki concentration camp, where we were forced to work in a munitions factory for nearly two years. Stationed at the camp, Johann made sure that I had enough work to receive meager rations. Knowing that I was a bugler in the Polish army, Johann gave me a bugle to awaken inmates in the morning. My bugling kept Jews from being shot for reporting late to early morning work assignments. Similarly, Johann instructed me to warn adolescents to avoid sex, since pregnant girls were also being shot. Thus, Mr. Kramer proved a godsend not only for me, but in sparing the lives of numerous inmates.

In 1941 we were shipped in a boxcar to Auschwitz after the Germans liquidated the Pionki camp. Upon stepping off the train in Auschwitz, I was separated from Hinda, who was sent to Bergen-Belsen. Obviously, that abrupt separation proved one of the most painful moments of my life. Before long, my workmate "Doc" Raphael warned me that surely I would be killed in retribution once the Germans learned that I was the brother of a man who had helped organize the destruction of the gas chamber and crematorium. Always focused on survival and remaining a step ahead of the Germans, Doc and I concocted an escape plan. While cleaning buses to transport inmates to another camp (far better than my first job of carting off dead bodies in wheelbarrows), we hid our supplies and joined the busload. We were delivered to a camp in Landsberg, near Munich, where I survived a few more years.

In 1945, as the Americans stormed into Germany (freeing concentration camps in the process), the Germans liquidated Landsberg and made the inmates march through snow to Dachau. At one point, we stopped by a lake and were told to lie in a ditch. I looked up and quivered at the sight of machine guns trained on us from a nearby mountain. Once again, I thought, "This is the end!" Turning numb from a combination of terror, cold, and exhaustion, I soon fell asleep. After a while, I was awakened by a *capo* saying, "It's good!" Once I mustered the courage to climb out of the ditch, he explained that the Germans had fled because the American troops were quickly advancing. So we continued walking, now unescorted and half-dazed, in the direction of Munich. Along the way, we ate leaves off trees, gorged ourselves on raw potatoes and carrots from a farm, and even devoured raw meat from a dead horse (somebody had found a few knives to carve the horse). We were ravenous with hunger. Ultimately, we were rescued by American soldiers and the Red Cross. Despite my elation, I was too sick from what I had eaten to even stand up. I was treated for three weeks in a Munich hospital and then released in relatively good shape.

A close friend of mine, a fellow survivor of the Landsberg camp, returned to Poland. He posted my picture (along with others) in my hometown, under the heading, "He's alive!" Within a few hours, my wife Hinda contacted him and learned of my whereabouts. Accompanied by a group of people, she joyfully and tearfully embraced me at the end of my hospital stay. We then rented an apartment in Stuttgart, a lovely city in Southern Germany. Despite continued police harassment of Jews, we lived in Stuttgart for more than three years.

Hinda and I immigrated to America in 1949. We were blissfully married for sixty-one years before she succumbed to Alzheimer's disease and died in 2001. Early in our marriage I told Hinda, "If we ever have children, I will teach them to be the best (they can be)." My two children have made me very proud. Formerly the vice president of a bank, my son now works as a commercial general contractor. In May 2010 my daughter was appointed chancellor of the University of

Colorado Health Sciences Center. One of my grandchildren is now serving as a criminal attorney; the other is employed as a journalist.

I feel so blessed and privileged by God to have survived the Holocaust and to have had such a long and beautiful life. I have gained a measure of peace by relating my wartime experiences to many, and I hope writing down my story will go even further toward fulfilling my promise to my brother to "Tell the world!"

Coauthor's Note: I feel deeply honored that Sam has granted me permission to relate his chilling Holocaust experiences. Although he appeared to be a Holocaust "Houdini," I subscribe to Sam's conviction that he was repeatedly graced by divine intervention. I marvel that Sam shared his story with such passion and emotion, having told it countless times over the years. While detailing events to me, he choked up a few times over missing good friends or regarding a particularly heart-wrenching and gory incident. I am so amazed at how this remarkable man stands upright at age ninety-six.

From a personal standpoint, most of my paternal grandparents' families were eradicated by the Nazis. Furthermore, strange as it may sound, I have compelling reasons and strong feelings to believe that I also was a Jew who was executed in Germany several years before being born into my current life. Hence, Sam's story evoked a lot for me and I am indebted to him for his immense courage and perseverance in the face of repeated horrors. I also honor Sam for his tireless recounting of the Holocaust atrocities he endured and witnessed, most of which have been omitted in this short memoir.

Samuel Fireman was born during 1914 in the small town of Zarki, Poland. He remained a Polish citizen until settling with his wife in Southern Germany after World War II. In 1949 Sam, his wife, and young son immigrated to Denver, Colorado, where they and an American-born daughter have since lived. Initially, Sam was a construction worker in the Denver area, but later he owned three liquor stores and was active in real estate. He is well known for giving speeches about his Holocaust tribulations at high schools, universities, churches, and synagogues throughout Colorado.

A Thin Thread

by Jeff Applebaum

Narrow escapes or situations that turn out for the best, especially against astronomical odds, are inspiring and motivating. However, when these come from personal experiences, our very own existence appears to be supported by a thin thread. In studying the history of my family, I came across an amazing story of survival where literally millions perished. In addition, as we began our quest to build a family, my wife and I confronted many obstacles that we never imagined on our wedding day. In both scenarios, the value and frailty of each and every life is apparent. As I share these stories with you, I encourage you to think about your own life and the incredible number of "random" events that brought you here today. The first story took place more than seventy-five years ago in Eastern Europe. It begins with a mother talking to her age twenty-something son.

"Jump!" his mother told him. "You are young and strong. If they force you onto the train, jump and you will make it."

Little did Shmuel (Samuel) Epplebaum know that the words of his mother would save his life, as his town and the people of Drohitchin, Belarus, were destroyed by the Nazis under the demented and evil rule of Adolf Hitler.

Watching your own family killed is a pain that pierces the depths of your soul and never goes away. Many have asked, "How could a loving God allow this to happen?"

In the *Book of Remembrance* compiled for Drohitchin after the surrender of the Germans in World War II, Shmuel wrote about watching his own mother and sister being shot.

> *On Saturday night July 25, 1942, I experienced the worst misfortune of my life when I lost my mother, sister, many friends and students during that aktsia (a Nazi military operation organized to find, deport, and murder Jews). I escaped from the market under a hail of bullets and automatic weapons fire, and hid out in the Rovno*

Forest for a few days until I was captured and sent to the Radostov camp. In subsequent years I went through many more awful experiences. I was shot a few times, left for dead once in Eastern Prussia, and from 1942 to 1945, I wasn't alive or dead. The gruesome events of the recent past are unbelievable today, and even those who lived through them can no longer conceive of how such things could have happened, and how they could have survived.

Shmuel was born in 1910 and was the youngest of six children. Shmuel was a teacher in several different towns in Poland as well as Drohitchin. As a child, his father died right after World War I, and his mother ran a candy store to support and educate her children. Shmuel's oldest brother Joseph went to America and settled in Brooklyn, New York, to work as a tailor and send money back to his family in Belarus. Other than Joseph, Shmuel, and a sister who went to Palestine (now Israel) before Hitler took power, the whole family perished. Joseph is my grandfather. If he had not come to America to work for his family, you would not be reading this story.

From the Radostov camp, the Nazis put Shmuel on one of the overcrowded, unventilated cattle cars to be killed near the Brona Gora station. This is where pits were dug in the ground and Jews, Poles, Russians, and Belorussians were told to strip off all of their clothing and fall facedown into them. Hundreds at a time were shot and killed. Another layer of people would then follow the previous one. As his train departed, Shmuel recalled the words of his mother, my great-grandmother, and jumped off the train. Despite shots fired at him, he disappeared into the forest, hid for a long time, and eventually joined with the partisans, or civilians-turned-fighting members of the Russian Resistance. He learned to speak seven languages, joined the Red Army, fought the Germans, and was one of the soldiers who entered Berlin.

Shmuel fought for his life and for the memories of his murdered family, but never felt fulfillment from the revenge he took in the army. He loved and cherished the value of each and every life here on Earth.

After the war he made his way to Israel where he married and, at age fifty, had his only child, Gili. Gili lives with her husband and three beautiful children in Israel today. She is one of the world's top pediatric thoracic doctors, presenting her research and work all over the globe. She has helped save the lives of countless children. I learned of her existence shortly before meeting her, during a visit for a talk she gave in San Francisco in December 2008. We made an instant connection, and I have had the opportunity to visit her and her family in Israel twice thus far.

How thin is the thread upon which this woman was given life? And how many lives has she been able to sustain? How many researchers, doctors, inventors, musicians, fathers, mothers, husbands, wives, friends, and children perished from that little town of Drohitchin and throughout the war? How many great aunts and uncles, second and third cousins could I have known?

One person can lead to a nation, and each of us has a seed of greatness within that we must protect, preserve, and nurture. We have been given the gift of life. What will we do with that gift? Why are there times when I feel so unimportant, even though so many thin threads have been woven into a rich and fulfilling tapestry of life that I experience right here, right now?

Perhaps it is the blessing of children in our homes and around us that helps us to truly appreciate life. Perhaps it was the gift of a daughter that helped Shmuel to see all of the goodness in the world, in spite of all he had been through.

The topic of children leads into my second story. My wife and I have a dear son, Josh, who at fifteen years of age continues to bring joy and challenge to our lives as parents. When he was two, we began our quest to have a second child and discovered that we needed the help of fertility doctors. For the next seven years, we (mostly my poor wife) went through multiple procedures that involved varying doses of medications, regular shots, acupuncture, special diet, Chinese medicine, and in vitro fertilization (IVF).

When we were on our sixth IVF cycle, the emotional, personal, and financial stress had taken its toll. However, we remained thankful for the child we had and still maintained tremendous faith in our journey. Some people questioned our sanity and told us to give up and be happy with the one child, or suggested that we adopt. We certainly had adoption as the next option, if our doctor were to tell us that conception was no longer possible. I also realized that unless you are talking to a clinical psychologist, when people tell you that you are crazy, it's often a confirmation that you are on the right track.

We had high hopes for this particular IVF attempt, since initial embryos had looked healthy and we were further along than through the previous five cycles. Plus, each cycle provided guidance on how to approach the next one for greater success.

I remember sitting with my wife as we were visiting with friends at a Starbucks, when her cell phone rang with a call from the doctor's office about some test results. I watched her face as the look of hope turned to an empty and lifeless stare and tears began to flow down her cheeks. I asked our friends to excuse us as we walked outside and held each other for a very painful moment in time. We had lost embryo number six.

Why not stop now? Why push on? We had a wonderful son already. Then we thought about the potential of one life. What if our baby could be the next Einstein? Or Mozart? Or an actor, or engineer, or a doctor who finds a cure for cancer?

Six months later, with great courage, my wife agreed to a final IVF cycle. Three months into it, she called me in a state of panic as I was traveling in the UK, hysterically reporting that she had experienced terrible bleeding and believed we had once again lost a baby. I felt helpless on the other end of the phone, thousands of miles away.

Once I returned home, we went to the doctor and discovered that a strong heart was still beating within her womb. We had lost a twin, but still had a baby.

On Jan 7, 2006, our son Jacob took his first breath. My wife, then in her mid-forties, had delivered our (second) miracle. As we held the baby in our arms, the long, painful journey to arrive at that day instantly vanished.

We initiated an eighth IVF cycle and had our third baby two years later. We remain in a state of thankful disbelief amidst the current sleep deprivation that comes with raising two small children and a teenager.

Today we see each child as someone who can change the world for the better. What if we had given up after two IVF attempts, or four, or even six? What if we had listened to everyone who said we were crazy? What if Shmuel Eppelbaum hadn't jumped off that train? A very thin thread indeed!

My second son, Jacob, now five years old, loves showing pictures of our family to visitors in our home. He even likes the ones from years ago that only have my wife and me with our son Josh. When asked where he is in *that* picture, he points to my chest in the photo and says, "Right there ... in daddy's heart."

And he was always there.

Jeff Applebaum began his career as an engineer with two degrees from Massachusetts Institute of Technology. As an entrepreneur, he developed a marketing business that spans the globe, and is in high demand as a sales and team-building coach. After twenty years in California, this New York City native is finally learning to speak English. Jeff has been pursuing his dream of being a stand-up comedian, making his national U.S. TV debut on CBS's The Late Late Show with Craig Ferguson. He has performed with comic legends Robert Klein, Richard Lewis, and Robin Williams, and was cast in the principal role of Joey Bishop in the musical tribute to The Rat Pack. Jeff is also credited and appears in the blockbuster film The Pursuit of Happyness. He is currently developing the Comedy Channel for Aha Radio, and lives with his wife and three children in Silicon Valley, California. Contact Jeff via his website, www.jeffapplebaum.com.

My Little Miracle

by Eliot Lowey

On a typically hot and humid afternoon on August 31, 1956, the doctor came out to tell my dad, Ernie, that his wife was doing well and he was the proud father of a robust and healthy baby girl. It had been a rough go for my mom, who had been bedridden the week before her labor started. Her doctor was concerned because she was seven weeks from her anticipated due date.

While the doctor and my dad were speaking, a nurse hurriedly came out of the delivery room and anxiously waved for the doctor to come back in. Another infant was arriving. A few minutes later the doctor returned and said, "You have a second child—a son."

"Twins?" Ernie uttered, in a shocked voice.

"Yes, twins," said the doctor.

"But you did not tell us!" Dad exclaimed.

"We didn't know," replied the doctor.

"Is he okay?" Dad asked nervously.

"He is feeble and weak, and we don't know if he is going to make it," the doctor candidly warned.

My sister Eileen weighed three pounds, eleven ounces, and I was three pounds, nine ounces. We were two months premature and, as was typical in the 1950s, we were immediately separated and placed into individual incubators. The doctor informed my mother and father they were not allowed to visit us. He thought our immune systems were compromised and that, if exposed to unsterile things, we would become ill and most likely not survive. My mother said she cried every day for the six weeks we were in the hospital because she had absolutely no contact with her two newborns. After several weeks, she was allowed to come see us on one occasion. The nurses lifted us up so that she could take a look at us. She said numerous tubes had been placed in us. When my parents came to take me home, the doctor said my sister seemed to be doing well, but they intimated that my prognosis was uncertain.

My unstable condition sent a shock wave through our family. My precarious beginnings reminded them of my mom's niece and nephew, both of whom had difficulties resulting from their births. My cousin Terry's case was the more severe. She was institutionalized at age two due to Rh blood transfusion complications. She required round-the-clock care until she died in her fifties. Predictably, my family's emotional response to my condition was high anxiety.

When we finally came home from the hospital, my mother soon noticed that something was amiss with my feet and legs; both turned downward and inward and had a marked lack of motion. When I was two months old, the pediatrician referred my parents to a prominent orthopedic surgeon for a consultation. He suggested that I had suffered from a sciatic palsy, involving trauma to my lower back that led to paralysis and weakness in my legs and feet. I was immediately placed in casts to assist my legs to grow properly. However, I was so active that these did not remain intact for long. I was often back at the doctor's office to have them reapplied.

Over time, my left leg and foot noticeably improved, with the end result of a normal-looking foot that was quite weak in lateral and upward movement, but nevertheless largely functional. However, my right leg and foot were quite compromised with only downward motion of my foot, and no ankle or toe movement. At fourteen months of age, my orthopedic surgeon referred me for a neurological assessment. The sciatic palsy was confirmed, the only physical difficulties being those with my lower extremities. However, the neurologist went on to say in regard to my prognosis, "I do not think anyone can categorically say that this patient will not be a functioning individual; nor is it possible to say that he will not be left with a considerable deficit." As a result, my right leg was placed in a brace as the next step in the corrective process. I was required to wear my right brace day and night. It kept my foot in the prone position, so my Achilles tendon would not tighten up, due to my "drop foot." Given my condition, it was a great relief to my parents when both my sister and I started walking at fifteen months old.

I had other challenges, too. I cannot help but wonder how my parents reacted upon seeing brown teeth coming up through my gums at nine months of age. My sister was developing normally, but my milestones were delayed and compromised. Many years later, my sister shared that she felt resentment with the attention I received due to my abnormalities. Of course, I would have given anything to be normal. One day, my mom noticed that enamel had grown over one of my brown teeth. I remember her telling me when I was older that it looked like a pearl in my mouth.

As I grew, I came to regard my right foot and lower leg as ugly. My right leg was thin below the knee and my calf looked underdeveloped, especially as compared to my left leg. My foot had an inverted arch, meaning I had a big bump from a bone that protruded where my arch was supposed to be. I would pick at the huge callus that formed to protect the area. My toes curled under and my big toe was crooked at the joint at a forty-five-degree angle. My anklebone jutted out like a doorknob.

I remember going to the community pool when I was nine. A film of warm water covered the hot cement. As I walked along, my foot flopped down with a slapping sound. I felt so embarrassed that other people were watching and thinking how grotesque that appendage looked. I really hated that sound.

I thought the brace and shoes I wore were ugly, too. My shoes were coal black. The brace was made of steel with two claws that fit precisely into two slits on either side of my shoe's heel. Two large hinges with springs on opposite sides of my ankle lifted my foot when I walked. A leather strap buckled around my calf to hold the brace in place. It always itched due to sweat and I was constantly pulling up my pant leg to scratch it. Again, I felt so self-conscious.

On a Tuesday afternoon in February 1966, I was at the doctor's office with my mom, who always took me there and attended to my special needs. She had encouraged me from day one that I could do anything I wanted, despite not being able to move my foot, ankle, or toes. As usual, the doctor had me walk down the hall to inspect my gait. I remember the floors so vividly, just as at the swimming pool. This floor was made of cold linoleum. I always felt elated and even proud that my left leg and foot, although weak, looked normal and were strong enough that I could have my heel hit the floor before my toes did.

After the doctor checked me over, he asked me to wait in the waiting room so he could speak with my mom in private. This was unusual, so as I closed the door behind me I listened to what they were discussing. I knew they were talking about surgery for my leg because I had been going to physiotherapy for several weeks, where my muscles and nerves were tested with electric currents. Still, there was no movement in my right foot. Standing outside that door, I was seeing myself sitting in my room on the top of my bunk bed. That is where I would go after each physiotherapy appointment. I would stare down at my foot, willing and commanding it to move. I thought if I wanted it bad enough it would happen. But it didn't and I just could not understand why. I felt despair. I really did not want to have surgery. I knocked on the door, walked back into the office, and said, "I want to hear what you are talking about."

The doctor asked me, "Do you want to have surgery on your foot and leg that will help you not to have to wear your brace?"

"What would the surgery do?" I inquired.

The doctor said I had two options. The first one involved stiffening my ankle. I would be able to walk without my brace, but it would severely restrict my physical activity. The second option, which was less predictable, involved a tendon transplant, so that when I thought to move my foot down, that foot would move up. This had a much lower chance of being successful, but it would allow me to be physically active.

I remember asking, "Will I be able to run and play with the other kids with the first surgery?"

The doctor replied, "No."

"Will I need to still wear my brace if I do the tendon transplant?"

"Only at night when you sleep," said the doctor. "And, you can get your first pair of sneakers."

It was unimaginable to think that I might be able to go to school with sneakers like all the other kids. I felt so scared, and excited.

It became clear to me that the tendon transplant was the only acceptable option for me. I had it done in August 1966. It was marginally successful, as was documented two years later in a letter from my doctor to my dad stating, "The tendon transplant is indeed working well but it does not have sufficient strength nor does it have enough coordination to incorporate into active use of the foot … He will require another surgery in a few years to stiffen the ankle and foot." Well, I never did have that second surgery.

Years later, my brother Eric called out to me, "Let's do this one." We were standing at the top of a black diamond run on an overcast day, no wind, and all we could see before us were the massive moguls and the steep descent. I'd skied throughout my teens and early twenties, so I'd gotten pretty good at it. But this was one run that I had never skied because I felt it was beyond my capability. Of course, my brother had a different opinion. He was an excellent athlete and a bit of a daredevil. He was younger than me, but had always been supportive. As a kid, he would make jokes about my foot, saying things like, "Wow, what happened? Did you get that caught in a lawn mower?" We'd laugh. I think I was looking nervous because he looked over at me and said, "Hey, we can do this." And off he went. He thought I could do it, but I wasn't so sure.

I followed Eric and found my rhythm. My mind told my body what to do and it obliged. By accomplishing something I didn't think I was capable of doing, I was overcome with a feeling of bliss. It was so different from the helplessness I felt sitting on that bunk bed trying to move my foot up and down. Then I roared to a stop. The pitch had steepened and the run had become much narrower. Eric was below me and was looking up the steep slope wondering how I was doing. He encouraged me to go for it. This is where it always was hard for me. My right foot and leg turned more slowly than my left. Could I make the turn and continue down or not? Gut check. I'd already torn ligaments in my left knee while skiing. I had been in world-class condition at the time with my resting heart rate at thirty-six beats a minute and I still hurt myself. I was afraid. I hesitated, breathed, and went for it. Wow! The exhilaration!

That day skiing I was faced with a choice, one that I have encountered and continue to face every day of my life. Do I define myself by my limitations or not? Sometimes, this is a tremendous struggle. But I have my mom to thank for her encouragement, since she gave me the courage to try.

For years, Mom cried every time I said goodbye to her, whether on the phone or in person. I was always extremely uncomfortable with this, so one day when I was visiting her, I finally asked her why. What she said to me has stayed with me every day since. She said, "You are my little miracle." I finally understood. As she sobbed, I hugged her and said, "Mom, I'm okay; I made it. I made it."

Eliot Lowey is the President and Founder of Cascadia, People and Business Consultation, in Victoria, British Columbia. The Canadian Department of National Defense, the Province of British Columbia, and first nation's communities utilize seven Train-the-Trainer Programs developed by Cascadia in the areas of anger management, spousal assault, substance abuse, and violence prevention. Organizations utilize Cascadia programs and consultants in the areas of executive coaching, effective teams, leadership development, organizational culture transformation, and violence prevention in the workplace. Cascadia counselors provide services to Provincial Ministries, to Federal Government employees, and to adults and youth in Victoria. Visit www.cascadiaconsultation.com and contact Eliot at eliot@cascadiaconsultation.com

My Two Heart-Opening Moments

by Steven Svoboda

Both of the defining moments in my life confronted me with potentially life-transforming situations—a first meeting with a possible life partner and the danger of a stroke. Each challenged me to act differently to help promote a better life, both for others and myself. Let me start by going back a dozen years.

The year was 1999. The much-feared Y2K apocalyptic threat still lay months in the future. I was a thirty-nine-year-old single California guy who lived in a cooperative group house I had started a few years earlier. I also went to and performed in experimental theater. I was living on next to nothing while running an organization I had founded (and still operate) to stop male circumcision. Basically, I was pretty far out there.

Relationships had never been my strong point. I was so confused and fearful that I stayed a virgin until the age of twenty-six. I am an emotional guy who seeks personal growth concerning my own hang-ups and sensitive spots that sometimes explode into arguments. Until that point in 1999, I'd had only one relationship that lasted much longer than a year—a four-and-a-half-year-long, mostly live-in relationship that my girlfriend ended abruptly without much explanation. I did come to understand over the years that I had probably, unintentionally been a hard person with whom to share a life, somewhat of a piece of work.

I wanted to meet a woman who could become my partner and with whom I could have children. To this end, I engaged in Internet dating and placed personal ads in the newspaper but without much success. When I had an ad out, either in print or online, I would find myself obsessively checking the responses several times a day. This became counterproductive, so eventually I would go cold turkey on the ads, only to start up again when I got lonely.

My first defining moment arrived on July 4th (which my theater teacher liked to call "Interdependence Day"). I was scheduled to meet Marta (a pseudonym), a woman I met through an Internet ad. We had been corresponding and talking on the phone for a few months. She was in the Bay Area for a medical conference, seven thousand miles away from her island home. This would be the first time I had met someone from an ad in person.

Coming straight from a week with my nutty friends at dance camp, I drove directly to the beach. My car was a total mess and so was my appearance. I had on a grungy Elvis Costello t-shirt with the slogan, "The pretty girls look right through me"—and understandably so. Part of me was tempted to fix up my car and my appearance before meeting Marta, but I elected to just show up as I was and see what developed.

We met at a beachside café and it soon became obvious that we were both much more attracted to each other than we had expected from our emailed photographs. For me, the attraction was based to a large extent on what I knew about Marta and on the bond I already felt developing between us. We chatted for a while and shared some laughs. Things seemed to be going well and I asked her if she wanted to take a walk on the beach.

It was beautiful along the shore and I was feeling a mixture of happiness and desperation. Within minutes, Marta was leaning close to me, tacitly inviting me (or so I imagined) to kiss her. I felt it was way too soon. But before long, I impulsively pushed her down onto the sand and we were kissing passionately to the crash of the surf, excited by our mutual discovery of each other and, I suspect, rediscovery of ourselves. I had never before done anything like this and never expect to again. It was really a crazy thing to do and could have had a lot more downside than upside. I half expected her to get mad at my presumption and angrily walk away. But I felt we were connecting and I trusted it was right for me to take a chance and break through my inhibitions.

It worked. Marta seemed to like what I had done, and I understood the potential we had together. In what was basically a slow-motion continuation of my actions on that beach, I altered my plans for a six-week road trip, giving up tickets for eight Bruce Springsteen concerts, so we could spend more time together and cement our initial connection. We fit a lot of experiences into that time, even visiting my therapist, who after enduring years of hearing me complain about being single seemed delighted to be able to work with us now as a (potential) couple.

After a two-week trial run at her faraway island home, we connected to the extent that a few months later I took the leap and moved in with her. We lived together for four years before moving back to California.

If you fast-forward the tape, twelve years after our meeting on the beach, we have two wonderful children, a nine-year-old son and a six-year-old girl. We took them to the beach café on July 4, 2009, the ten-year anniversary of our meeting.

We definitely have our less than blissful moments. As I write this, the last few months have, in fact, been some of our toughest yet. But our shared commitment to honesty and personal growth has carried us through and helped us to create a mostly loving environment in which to raise our amazing kids. I have always felt happy about my whimsical decision to take a chance on that windy summer day on a San Francisco beach.

My second defining moment came as a total surprise in September 2006. One of Marta's best friends from medical school, and the godmother of our daughter, was visiting us. I was experiencing some puzzling severe headaches late at night and, since Marta wanted to stay with our kids, her friend kindly offered to take me to the emergency room. This led to my being diagnosed with an aneurysm and an arteriovenous malformation (AVM) in my head, which translated to my having a bloated blood vessel about to burst—a time bomb waiting to explode into a surely life-transforming stroke.

It's funny, the twists and turns life can take. Although AVMs cause headaches in the majority of folks who have them, tests eventually determined that my AVM was completely unrelated to the headaches, which were caused by a virus. It was my extremely good fortune to have the virally caused headaches since they led to the discovery of the AVM. Otherwise, I almost certainly would have had a stroke in the five years since then. I have always prided myself most on what I can do with my brain, so it would have been very challenging for me to recover from a stroke.

Around this time, I had left a job where I was somewhat underpaid but highly appreciated. Professionally, this proved a bad move. In my new position I had bosses who purposely devised projects at which I could not succeed, so that they could fire me for seemingly legitimate reasons. Ironically, this led to a fortunate change of insurance coverage that enabled me to have a very eminent brain surgeon from the University of California at San Francisco as my doctor. This young doctor performed successful brain surgery on a U.S. senator who had an AVM around the same time I did and has written many books.

I met an exceptional man in the hospital. He was a nurse from South America so we spoke Spanish together. He seemed to see straight into my soul with boundless compassion and love. He was so caring and loving in how he looked after me. I don't remember his name now but I will always be grateful to him for helping me with such grace and commitment.

The switch in insurance reminds me of the old stories where something seemingly unfortunate is later shown to be fortunate and vice versa. If I hadn't left a good job for a nightmarish one, I might have found myself forced to follow the recommendations of the doctor I'd seen first, who worked for Kaiser Permanente and is on the faculty of the prestigious Stanford Medical School. Marta and I were later told by other medical personnel that the treatment he suggested likely would not have prevented me from having a stroke.

Two chance events therefore may have saved my life. These things happened *to* me so I obviously can't in any way take credit for them. I was basically fortunate just to discover the AVM in the first place, and then to have the insurance change due to the job loss. Yet these incidents helped protect my family and me.

Brain surgery is of course a big deal, apparently second only to heart surgery in its challenging recovery process. In the aftermath of my surgery, I had several weeks of being so weak that I had to crawl to use the bathroom or to get a drink of water when no one was around to help. This amused me because my daughter was just learning to walk at that point. She'd be going in one direction while Dad went in the other direction.

However, in my weakened state, I had plenty of time to ponder my great fortune. My brush with mortality magnified my thankfulness for just being alive, and for my lovely children and wife. I remember taking a walk and feeling awed by the beauty of the trees and sky. The same trees and sky that were there weeks earlier but I had been too busy to appreciate them. Now, I swore I would never take them for granted again.

I can't say that since my survival of the AVM I haven't made mistakes or sometimes behaved in a less than fully present way; I have, more times than I care to admit. However, I do feel that my appreciation of this wonderful, all-too-fleeting gift of life has transformed my commitment to living my truth and to helping promote the higher good whenever I possibly can.

I believe that most of us do our best in life, including me. But all too often my limitations, issues, and other shortcomings keep me from activating the love and passion that I have available to me. I feel sad that so often many of us are less than we can be and that I can be petty, preoccupied, or oblivious to the feelings and beauty around me.

Yet what gives me hope are the moments when I see myself, my wife, or anyone transcending their limits and helping to co-create a better world. There are so many ways to do that. You can push an intriguing Internet woman you just met in person down on the beach and start kissing her. You can deeply celebrate when you get saved from a stroke due to pure luck, a great surgeon, and a loving nurse.

In the end, probably the greatest gifts I can give others are presence and love. I intend to work hard to continue learning from these defining moments in my life and to bring further truth and passion into my remaining years on this planet. I want to teach and learn from my children and my wife and continue to grow, scary though it often is. And most of all, I vow to keep my eyes and heart open. I'm sure I'll make many more mistakes, but I want to do what I now consider the most important thing in life—to live with love and to share love with the world.

J. Steven Svoboda considers his most important accomplishments to be his two children and his ten-year marriage with his wife. He is a proud graduate of the New Warrior Men's Training Weekend. After getting a master's degree in physics from UC Berkeley, he graduated from Harvard Law School and founded an anticircumcision organization, Attorneys for the Rights of the Child (ARC). He wrote the United Nations' first document focusing on circumcision and presented it in Geneva. He has co-authored a gender issues textbook and published nearly two hundred reviews of books about men and gender. In his day job, Steven practices patent law.

Part Seven: Divorce

Divorce Is Just the Beginning

by Brett Zachman

Impossible is just a big word thrown around by small men who find it easier to live in the world they've been given than to explore the power they have to change it. Impossible is not a fact. It's an opinion. Impossible is not a declaration. It's a dare. Impossible is potential. Impossible is temporary. Impossible is nothing!

—Anonymous

As the title suggests, this is a story of transformation. Let's begin with the end in mind; a story of who I am presently, followed by who I was previously ...

Presently, I'm "Zach" ... which is my nickname. It's a mispronunciation of my last name by elementary teachers. During high school and college, "Zack-man" rather than "Zoch-mann" became "Zach" because two syllables are one too many for football players when you're the quarterback. Present day, I'm creating a nonprofit for men and they start calling me "Zach." Odd, since they didn't know me when I played football. My friend says, "Names have meanings; look it up." Guess what? According to www.babynology.com, "Zach" means "pure; clean; innocent," shortened from the original Hebrew (Zachary/Zachariah/Zechariah), meaning "the Lord remembers."

I am a happily divorced father, raising two wonderful sons (ages 9 and 10½) via joint custody, and enjoying a budding friendship with my former wife. I'm an economics major from a liberal arts college, which means I like numbers, but I love to tell stories. I enjoy art, basketball, biking, drawing, hiking, movies, music, reading, running, and writing. After forty years of test-driving this thing called life, I finally know my purpose. I help people change their lives. I am clear, focused, peaceful, whole.

My personal and professional lives are congruent. My passion is wellness and I choose to work in two main areas I believe people experience hardship—finances and relationships. By day, I'm a Financial Wellness Coach teaching Americans how to refinance their finances, discover savings, and build wealth for retirement. By night, I'm building a nonprofit focused on male wellness and divorce prevention. My life goal is to positively impact a million people.

My story of transformation is not "one in a million" but "one of millions." I hope it inspires you and makes you uncomfortable enough so that you ask yourself a two-part question: What is my life passion? And how am I sharing it with myself, my loved ones, my community, and the world?

Validation

All men matter. You matter. I matter. It's the hardest thing in theology to believe.

–G. K. Chesterton

I believe life is not about pulling your fellow man down; it's about building him up and encouraging others. To have courage is to have heart; to encourage is to give heart.

I remember so many childhood playground contests about who could produce the best "cut-down." Those incisive remarks often left their mark, whether a bright red spot on the skin's surface or an emotional welt. Sometimes the effect was not felt or realized until much later in life. I am bothered that men are nurtured more for competition than for connection.

I champion a win-win world of abundance, rather than a "you win, I lose" world of scarcity. As the cliché goes, we attract more bees with honey than with vinegar. My focus is on affirming people's strengths and accomplishments, and on delivering positive energy—enthusiasm (Greek root: *enthousiasmos*, meaning "inspired by God").

Superheroes

One in three children are presently growing up without any involvement with their biological fathers, approximately 24 million children.

–National Fatherhood Initiative, August 2007

When I was three, my parents put me to bed during the winter in a one-piece, full-length, footy pajama with a zipper in front and a snap under my chin. Once closed, I was encased in 100 percent cotton from my ears to my toes, making it virtually impossible for me to pee in the toilet. Another genius maneuver was putting vinyl coating on the bottom of the feet. They were hard as a rock and textured to feel like one too. Thus, whenever I encountered a slick floor surface at any pace beyond a slow walk, I lost traction and was flung limb-from-limb à la Bambi's first skating expedition.

Sitting in my crib, I grabbed my blue, all-comforting blankey with football decorations printed all over it. Tying it around my neck like a cape, I felt like I could conquer the world. Then began my trek of scaling the inner wall of my crib, followed by an even faster descent of the outer wall. Arriving intact on the carpet, I would peek around the wall to scope out what was going on in the family room. Then, I crept up behind my dad and surprised him. After nearly having a coronary, he asked sternly, "Son, what are you doing out of bed?" I would then beg for our superhero routine. Since everything small is cute, adorable, and hard to deny, he would say yes. Then I would hustle back down the hallway as my father assumed his position—squatting down at the back door. Once I saw he was at the ready, I would take off like a bullet shot out of a gun, or like Bambi slip-sliding across ice. Navigating the hallway, I would eventually pick up speed (as long as I didn't career off the walls), and upon nearing my father (a presumably safe distance of twelve to eighteen inches) I would launch myself through the air before landing safe and sound against his chest.

You see, as a three-year-old, I *imagined* I was a superhero and I *believed* my father was a superhero. Later in life, I learned otherwise.

As an early-thirties man called Brett, I was married for seven years, with two sons, two dogs, two cars, and a corner house. I was earning $50K a year, was quick to anger, frequently frustrated, and often anxious. In our marriage, we had endured job changes and losses, infertility, an adoption, and the seemingly constant battle for "alpha." Our sex life had dwindled; we slept in different beds, so I turned to pornography. We verbally fought most of the time, and our home was no longer a sanctuary, but a minefield. From my perspective, life was consumed with house chores, trying to keep up with my obligations, and making my wife happy (I thought I had that power). In my drive to fix our broken marriage, I had foregone the things that once brought me joy. I let my friendships fade, no longer attended church, played sports rarely, visited the gym infrequently, and spent little time outdoors.

The End

Divorced and separated men are twice as likely to commit suicide as other men.
Per the study "Marital Status and Suicide in the National Longi-
tudinal Mortality Study" by Augustine J. Kposowa, Ph.D., at the
University of California at Riverside.

Where there is no vision, the people perish.

Proverbs 29:18

When was the end? Or better yet, the end of what? Well, it was the end of
my *machismo* journey. You see, I took the stereotypical male approach to separation and divorce. I call it the "Old Yeller." It goes something like this ... When
a wounded dog is sick, it limps into the woods and curls up under a tree. Then
one of two things happens: 1) the dog heals and comes back to the delight of
its master, or 2) the dog does not heal and dies. Now, men are not dogs, despite
what some ladies might think. Of course, we don't see men leaving their homes
and wandering into the woods like a scene from *The Twilight Zone*. However, the
life experience of divorce is figuratively and in some cases literally killing men.
For me, I became aloof and isolated. I did not seek counseling, nor did I ask for
support from friends or family. I did what men do best. I stuck it out alone to prove
to myself how strong I was by displaying fierce independence. Sound familiar?

My end occurred the first week of November 2004. On Monday, we filed our
divorce papers. On Thursday, my girlfriend ended our three-month, extremely
intense, physically romantic relationship. As I left her house, the pain of both
relationships crashed down on top of me. I experienced what I later understood
to be an anxiety or panic attack. It felt as if the grim reaper had arrived and the
hand of death reached up into my torso, underneath my rib cage, grabbed my
heart, and squeezed. The result was a literal pounding inside my chest as tears
streamed down my face. I thought I was having a heart attack. I was driving but
couldn't see the road. My motor skills felt like they were in slow motion, so I
pulled into a gas station. Emotion was wringing from me in waves. I remember
thinking, *What is wrong with me?* For the first time in my life, I felt terrified—pure
unadulterated fear.

I reached for my phone to call someone, anyone, but I could barely read the
numbers. I didn't know who I was going to call. Should I dial 911—no, that's just
melodrama ... my parents—no, that's weak ... my now ex-wife—certainly not ... my
male friends—how do I describe this? I'll sound like a scared little mama's boy—out of
the question! On and on I scrolled, until I found my sister's number. I hit the button.

Thank God I didn't have to dial, since my hands were shaking. When she answered, I croaked, "Hello." She asked, "Are you okay?" I couldn't speak.

The Decision
I guess there's just one thing to do then; get busy living or get busy dying!
–Tim Robbins in The Shawshank Redemption

In life, we can "choose" or "decide." Until recently, I thought the two were synonymous. However, a friend recently pointed out a clear distinction. To "choose" is "to select freely and after consideration" while to "decide" comes from it's Latin root, *caedo, caedere, caesum*, meaning "to cut, to cut down, to kill." I know the exact moment when my "decision" launched the journey that killed our marriage.

Our family was eating breakfast on Friday, July 4, 2003. It was Independence Day for the country and for me. I'd worked diligently the past four months to complete a business plan launching my first company and today was the big day. Within a few hours, my independence took a sordid turn. Our two-and-a-half-year-old was consuming cereal in his booster seat. The one-year-old was in the wooden high chair passed down through the family since I was a baby.

As usual, my wife and I began arguing over something insignificant, which was the space we lived in the last few years of our marriage. Her primary emotion was anger and I played a poor diplomat, constantly seeking peaceful resolution. Our disagreement escalated to the point of personal attacks, colorful metaphors, and yelling. When she called me a name in front of our children, I decided to take control of the situation. Notice I say "decided" and "control." My next comment was yelling something like, "Damn it! Shut up! One more name from you and I'm coming over there … !" My wife's response, "Bring it on. What are you going to do?"

You see, our battle was for "alpha." Who was going to be in control? So, I took a few steps toward her. In hindsight, I wasn't sure what I was going to do, since my father taught me, "Never touch a woman in anger." Thankfully, for some reason, I looked across the table at my two-and-a-half-year-old. For a brief moment, our eyes met; his were frozen in fear. He had stopped eating and was watching me intently with eyes the size of his cereal bowl. In that moment, the extreme rage bottled up inside of me drained out of my body. The anger simply flowed out of my feet as if a bucket of water had been spilled across the floor.

When I looked back at my wife, I was calm. In a defeated voice, I said, "I understand. It's okay. I'll move out. Give me a few weeks; I'll get my things together." Then, I quit. I literally walked out of the room and figuratively walked out of the family we had spent ten years creating.

The Breaking

The only devils in the world are those running around in our own hearts.
That is where the battle must be fought.

–Mahatma Gandhi

For me, the devil was divorce. Actually, the devil came before the divorce. It was a moment in time I call The Breaking, a personal epiphany of the dark side. It was the fall of 2002 and I was thirty-two years old. It was a full year before I would move out and begin the separation ending our eight-year marriage. As always before work, I had showered and was shaving, standing close to the mirror to avoid unnecessary cuts. Our cabinet was a three-part sectional, divided lengthwise, so it had three mirrors. On this morning, a question suddenly crossed my mind: *What am I doing with my life?* As that question lodged itself in the back of my cranium, one of the doors swung out. In doing so, it created ongoing images. As I noticed this, I stopped shaving. Then, I realized the question had grown more powerful. I began analyzing, as I often do, and questions started popping into my mind, seemingly one question for every mirror reflection: Am I pursuing a worthwhile career? Am I an adequate husband? Am I a good father? Am I a good friend? What am I doing with my life? Do I have a life purpose? Am I happy?

The answer was an emphatic *"No!"* to everything. I did not feel like a good brother, businessman, father, husband, friend, or son. I was not happy. At the end of my reflections, I concluded that I was miserable. I felt worthless. I felt as though I was wasting my life. I could not locate the dreams I had as a young college graduate in my early twenties.

I began questioning my life. I was ten years out of college. I'd been given every opportunity a middle-income, suburban American family could offer. I had not had a traumatic childhood: I was not physically or verbally abused; I went to church; and I was captain of the football team. Hell, I was the quarterback! I received a liberal arts education from one of the best colleges in the Western U.S. I found my partner, married, and bought a corner house. I had two dogs, two kids, and was working on my fourth job. We lived in an upcoming neighborhood in Northwest Denver; we had neighbors; I had family nearby; my friends (when we could get together—we were all busy building families) were terrific people. In essence, I followed the American Dream. Graduate, find a woman, get married, build a life together, and live happily ever after. Right? That's what Hollywood tells us to do. I'd been hearing it since I was a kid watching Disney characters kiss each other at the end of the movie.

So, what the hell was going on? Why was I so miserable? If I had it *all*; why did I feel like a piece of crap stuck to the bottom of somebody's shoe? One might flippantly say, "Well, Brett, you're just an overachiever and you've experienced a midlife crisis fifteen years early."

Call to Action

The problems of the world cannot possibly be solved by skeptics or cynics whose horizons are limited by the obvious realities. We need men and women who can dream of things that never were!

–John F. Kennedy

My challenges were numerous: altering our marriage, changing careers, moving my living space, etc. During the transition, I became my own best friend. It sounds soft, but I learned to love myself. In the journey, I required outside assistance, which I think is a sign of strength. Ultimately, I discovered the real solutions were not *outside* of me but *inside* of me. Everything I need to succeed, I already possess. The only requirement is faith—to believe in myself and God.

Brett Zachman's *passion is wellness. He chooses to work in the two areas where people experience the most hardship— finances and relationships. As a Financial Wellness Coach, he teaches Americans how to discover savings and build wealth for retirement (www.fiveringsfinancial.com). Zach's experiences with ReBuilding Seminars in 2005 led him to addressing divorce and its effects on men. His newest endeavor—BeMen (www.BeMen.org) is a call to action, an acronym for "The Brotherhood of Extraordinary Men," and a nonprofit organization focused on male wellness and divorce prevention. This chapter is an excerpt from Zach's book* Divorce Is Just the Beginning: Join the Brotherhood! *due to be released 12.12.12.*

Coming Back for Good

by Jay Heinlein

We live in challenging times, when even the most successful among us may occasionally become overwhelmed by problems relating to money, marriage, parenting, illness, stress, or any of the myriad challenges we all face from time to time

–John F. Groom, Author

This is a brief narrative about my own personal journey from success to divorce to near total ruin. My wish is that the reader will identify both with my negative experience in spiraling down, and with the ongoing redemptive and transformational recovery ... of coming back again ... for good.

Family Background

Overall, I am a wonderful freak. That is because I am the unusual combination of two parents from extraordinarily different backgrounds. *How* unusual would depend on whom I was speaking to and how well they know me.

When my parents met, Mom was a beautiful model living in New York City and Dad had just returned from the Second World War. They were both Catholic. Perfect match. They got married.

Dad's family: efficient German and proper English descendants, highly educated, overachieving, reserved Northeasterners.

Mom's family: artistic French and bold Spanish descendants, fun, loud, and food-loving, hardworking, Louisiana-Cajun Southerners.

They loved each other, and they loved my brother and me very much. They made good lives for us. We went to great schools, were very involved and successful in sports, and enjoyed growing up on the Columbia River in Washington State. For all of their cultural differences, my parents went the distance. Their marriage was a good model. They were married more than forty years, which is a triumph by any standard these days.

About My Getting Married

I met my daughters' mother in Dallas, Texas, at a small "hippie bible college" while pursuing a personal objective to "find and differentiate myself" spiritually and career-path-wise. I was nineteen; she was eighteen. The girls' mother was from a broken marriage and remarriages. She had a bright, pretty smile. She wasn't Catholic. Perfect match. We got married and remained married for almost twenty years.

I Got Married to Stay Married

And if real life was like the movies, I should have lived happily ever after.
                                                                    –Piper Laurie

We got married because we were in love. Like most people, we wanted to grow old together, to have children along the way, to live the fairytale. For several years, we *were* happy, passionate, and enjoying our active lives together.

Along the way, three beautiful girls were born. We were very involved in church; made good friends; lived in beautiful homes; and adopted beloved family pets, including a cherished Crabbett Arabian horse. We enjoyed hiking and camping, Tae Kwon Do, and many other fun family activities and trips. We looked like a "perfect little family." In fact, after joining the corporate world, I suspect that our lovely family image strongly influenced some of the promotions I received.

The "Perfect Storm" and the Demise of Our Marriage

A "perfect storm" is a confluence of events that drastically aggravates a situation.

                                                            –www.wikipedia.org

We had the usual ups and downs, but we were still mostly happy. Things continued to move along well for us. And then suddenly came "the perfect storm." What had always seemed so clear and bright became blurry.

As a family, we moved several times on my way up the corporate ladder, which was difficult for everyone, especially the kids. My job as a sales executive was demanding and included an aggressive travel schedule. Our company, like many at the time, became involved in what turned out to be a rather hostile and conflicted merger, then a move to the "big show"—the New York Stock

Exchange, followed by a series of acquisitions. My job wasn't fun anymore. Among the people I worked with at a prominent Christian publisher in Nashville, including co-workers and high-profile best-selling Christian authors, were pretentiously pious, smarmy hypocrites with a lot of dark secrets and behaviors. I wanted very badly to bail from what was by outward appearances a very good job.

The girls' mother went back to college and became a dental hygienist. She was skillful and natural at her profession. Her father and brother both run successful dental lab businesses. But she worked a lot and it was stressful for her. And she was still a full-time mother of three girls. We were both working very hard in our family and careers.

After a series of lengthy illnesses, my father died. Then suddenly and unexpectedly, just one and a half years later, my mother died. My father had appointed me as executor of his will, and I had followed his wishes to the letter. When mother passed, my brother and his wife initiated a bitter, expensive estate battle. Around the same time, a respected mentor and several other friends and business associates died. Some of their deaths, I am certain, were directly related to the unusual stress of their jobs. Even our beloved family horse contracted a rare skin cancer, and we had to put him down.

It was dizzying and bizarre. The fog of emotional pain and draining distractions became mind-numbing. I felt like Lt. Dan in *Forrest Gump*, clinging to the boat mast in the midst of a hurricane while helplessly bobbing in an angry, swirling ocean. What else could happen! It was an overwhelming and tragic absurdity. I was reeling and suddenly, nothing mattered. I lost my focus, my idealism, and resolve.

Ultimately, I failed to be faithful to my marriage and family—a common descent. I felt and rationalized that I deserved the attention, sympathy, compassion, and support that I wasn't receiving at home. I justified being disappointingly human and weak. My wife was hurt and mad as hell. She wasn't loyal either, and told me so to my face.

In the throes of serious marital problems, we made a few attempts at counseling, which proved a fiasco. But I still never thought we would be divorced, since I had never consciously considered divorce to be a possibility. Suddenly we were there. We had a family meeting with the children in the living room; it was beyond devastating for everybody.

About Fairness ... or Rather the Glaring Unfairness of the Divorce Court System

My divorce was long and bitter, and the divorce decree, when it finally came, was a farce.

–Terry T, www.mybrandnewlook.com

We intended an amicable breakup, and for a while we succeeded. We even sat together at some of the girls' school functions and athletic events. However, it didn't end up amiable. Greedy lawyers became involved and ultimately, I was slaughtered financially in divorce court—a common experience for many divorced fathers these days. It's hard, to nearly impossible, to explain to someone who hasn't lived it. You really never get to tell your story or to have it understood. Even well-meaning friends often said, "Why don't you just get over it?" like it was some goofy *Dr. Phil* show where everything gets solved in an hour.

The resulting financial devastation for me felt like getting my legs blown off, and then being blamed for not being able to grow them back. I didn't get to start again at zero. Instead I went into a deep hole financially. Worse, the divorce court system requires no accountability on the part of the ex-spouse as to how child support money is actually spent. Because of the excessive obligations, and with my having no say in the process, I felt degraded, hindered, and marginalized in my role as a father. My ability to provide for and to protect my children was greatly diminished.

And my part was that I gave in when I should have fought back fiercely on behalf of myself and, ultimately, my children. Later, when I went to seek legal advice to try and undo some of the damage, I literally got screamed at by a lawyer. He called me a "stupid dumbass" for succumbing to such a bad deal. That was humiliating beyond words.

My Journey Back ... Coping and Recovering from the Tragedy of Divorce

Don't allow your wounds to transform you into someone you are not.

–Paulo Coehlo, Author

My internal frustrations grew into bitterness and despair. Nightly, my sleep became interrupted by the grinding of my teeth. My jaw would often hurt when I woke up. The internalized, burning anger never cooled. I didn't experience any peace or the ability to attain it. Out of desperation I finally called a former colleague who had become involved in drug and alcohol addiction counseling, primarily for Nashville music artists and related executives. I told him I wanted him to be my sponsor. He said, "Jay, if you have an addiction, you sure hide it well." I told him that I was indeed hiding it well, but it wasn't the kind of chemical grip that attaches itself to most of the people he was working with. I was pissed. Deeply suppressed resentment was ruining all attempts at moving on.

Together, my sponsor and I created a modified and unorthodox version of the Alcoholics Anonymous (AA) Twelve Step program, with the first "A" standing for *Anger*. The Twelve Steps gave me a framework for emotional healing and personal improvement. Since then, I have discovered that there is actually a version of the Twelve Steps called Emotions Anonymous (EA).

> A twelve-step program is a set of guiding principles outlining a course of action for recovery from addiction, compulsion, or other behavioral [struggles and challenges].
>
> –www.the12steps.com

Enlisting the help of a trusted sponsor was like having a personal trainer. It gave me someone to be accountable to, on the road to becoming whole again. As with any ambitious exercise program, my process was excruciating but well worth the effort.

> Pain is temporary. It may last a minute, or an hour, or a day, or a year, but eventually it will subside and something else will take its place.
>
> –Lance Armstrong, Cancer Survivor,
> Seven-Time Winner of the Tour de France

The most difficult thing to deal with might be having to accept that my ex-spouse may never acknowledge her part in the breakup, nor the pain and misery that she inflicted on me and her own children after the divorce through the court system.

Recovery is all about facing one's own shortcomings and dealing with the choices that we can actually manage—our own. I had to acknowledge and relinquish the things over which I realized I had no control.

> He who has been forgiven much—and knows it, loves much, but he who has been forgiven little, loves little.
>
> –Jesus

Today I am back for good. Today I am surrendered spiritually. I am at peace. Today I am back for good. Consistent with the original Twelve Steps, I will always be in a program of personal improvement and transformation.

I am so very proud of my girls. I love them more than anything in the world. The oldest is married and she and her husband work for influential nonprofits in New York. The second is a traveling nurse who works in the labor and delivery area of hospitals. And the youngest is finishing college, enjoying her life, and working. I have a good relationship with two of my daughters. I look forward to full reconciliation one day with the other.

I enjoy an active Colorado lifestyle and am very involved in volunteer and local community service. I have a fulfilling job and continue to work on special projects in the publishing industry, which is my passion.

I envision sharing the remaining quality moments of my life with a special person, as a healthy and whole person myself. I look forward to falling in love and to being in love again. I can't wait to meet her.

Jay Heinlein describes himself as a proud father, publishing and marketing professional, social media enthusiast, and midlife adventurist. He enjoys "all things Colorado," which includes hiking, skiing, biking, and eating trout. Jay is deeply involved in volunteer and local community service. His driving passion is to influence and impact the world for good—to leave a mark. Jay's blog musings regarding publishing, writing, education, and social and cultural happenings can be found at www.heinleingroup.com.

Part Eight: Identity and Perceptions

Three Identities

by Robert White

> **i·den·ti·ty** —*noun, plural -ties. The condition of being oneself or itself, and not another; condition or character as to who a person or what a thing is; the sense of self, providing sameness and continuity in personality over time and sometimes disturbed in mental illnesses, as schizophrenia.*

Hmmmm … schizophrenia … While I don't choose to identify myself as mentally ill, I do confess to at least three very distinct identities during my adult life to date, each with its own strengths, weaknesses, and growth possibilities. It occurs to me that sharing my journey might be of value to others.

Let's begin with my "learner, humble student, there's something I can learn from everyone" identity. I adopted this one unconsciously in early childhood and kept it through success in radio, launching several entrepreneurial ventures and moves from Wisconsin to New York to California to Japan. It served me well. I learned, I grew personally and professionally, and it allowed me to operate somewhat behind the scenes and shine the spotlight on others—friends, spouses, and colleagues.

Identity No. 1 took me from a wrong-side-of-the-tracks poverty to wealth I had barely imagined: semi-retirement at age forty-six in a 15,500 square foot home in Aspen with five vehicles and a private jet, a gorgeous wife, raising four great children, skiing eighty days a year, service on six nonprofit boards, trips around the world … a bucket-list cross-off exercise on steroids.

It also included a gradual and again unconscious migration to a new identity where I essentially stopped learning and decided there were few people from whom I could learn. The new identity was … drumroll, please … "successful rich guy in Aspen." Be clear: I'm not making Identity No. 2 wrong. It was a lot of fun, plus it opened many doors where I could leverage my ability and money into significant contributions and accomplishments. Also, I felt I had earned it with a lifetime of hard work, ethical business practices, and a commitment to serving others.

But truly, pride goeth before a fall. Business failure, an unwanted and savage divorce process, and health problems combined to serve as a major interruption to my ten years of blissful vacation. In the midst of the painful meltdown— several friends referred to it as the "divorce from hell"—I woke up a little, not a lot at first, but it was the beginning of a life-changing shift in awareness and a transformational experience.

I initially felt alone, betrayed, hurt, angry, confused, and disappointed. This was the family of my dreams, and the dream was shattered abruptly and, in my opinion at the time, unnecessarily. For the first time in my life I was adrift and essentially unable to function normally. Looking back I now realize it wasn't just the marriage, family, and business success terminations; it was the shattering of my identity.

Longtime friend, the late John Denver, was going through a similar unwanted and unexpected divorce experience. One weekend we went to the vapor caves and hot springs pool in Glenwood Springs, Colorado, to escape our crazy lives, relax, and see if we could support each other through the turmoil we were going through. Those two days were an amazing experience on many levels.

While sitting in the sulfuric steam we opened our bodies, hearts, and minds. We decided that anything this painful must have some value imbedded within it or God would not have allowed its creation. We pledged to each other that we would work to go beyond the mess in front of us; we'd put aside our hurt, sadness, disappointment, and anger as much as possible; and we would seek to learn what we needed to learn from the experience. A mutual friend, who knew of our jour- ney, sent us a message that we spoke aloud to each other through some tears: "You are loved, guided, and protected."

Our motivations were identical and clear: continue to be great fathers and discover whatever learning the mostly painful situation was calling forth. Each in our own ways, we embarked on a midlife reinvention process. It's not appropriate for me to share John's choices. I will observe that those next five years, the last five years of his life, included an experience of personal joy and satisfaction he had long sought. Plus, he wrote and sang some truly great music.

I learned that the research was overwhelmingly clear: Young daughters of divorce often grow up with eating disorders, academic failure, drug abuse, and inappropriate promiscuity. I loved my girls and those outcomes were unacceptable. The only known preventive measure was an effective co-parenting relationship. Putting aside my anger with my former wife, her lawyer boyfriend, and the many legal attacks, I committed to creating a positive relationship and began acting as if it was already a reality.

I attended the Sterling Men's Weekend; I saw a Chinese medicine practitioner; I put myself into intensive therapy; I became more fit than I had been since age eighteen; I read Carl Jung and A *Course in Miracles*; I sat for hours with skilled coaches; I journaled; and I prayed daily. Perhaps most impactful was attending the Wright Leadership Men's Weekend where I received an in-depth experience of the power of accessing and communicating my feelings openly and honestly—a first in my life.

One result was Identity No. 3: "I am a trustworthy resource; a bearer of wisdom and truth; an interruption that serves and contributes to people and organizations."

That might sound more than a little grandiose; however, it is true for me and it was arrived at after significant conscious effort and reflection. That "conscious" part is, of course, a first in my lifetime of dealing with my own identity. I also have an awareness that my identity is subject to future edits, revisions, even total change.

I've learned that my three identities all served me. In fact, if they hadn't served me at some level I would have become aware and adopted new ones. I've also learned that the first two identities limited me in terms of full self-expression and accomplishment.

Identity No. 1 (the learner) brought growth, accomplishment, and wealth. Its limits included my staying behind the scenes in my family and in my business life, even when it was inappropriate and where 100 percent participation was wanted and needed. Humility was a plus in many ways; however, when I carried it too far, it became a handicap.

Identity No. 2 (rich guy) included gaining a level of self-confidence I had lacked all my life. It empowered me to fully participate and play a much bigger game personally and professionally. The limitation was it encouraged me to focus on things and events—not continued personal growth and my purpose in living.

The jury is out on Identity No. 3. What I am presently aware of is how good it feels to have consciously chosen my identity and how it feels just right to live it "out loud."

What I am most proud of in my life is creating the effective co-parenting relationship with my former wife in service to our children. They are healthy, well functioning, loving, and caring young adults. I know our mutual commitment has contributed to their well-being. I absolutely know that this commitment and all of the joy and satisfaction came as a result of my own journey of increased awareness, taking personal responsibility for a vision that mattered to me, and acting in alignment with an evolving, freely chosen, and positive identity.

I am so very grateful to the many dear friends, coaches, and teachers who supported me on this journey, and to myself for having the courage to dive into it.

Robert White *was President of training industry pioneer Mind Dynamics and founder of Lifespring Inc. and ARC International Ltd., companies that graduated more than one million people from high-impact personal development seminars. He's a Fellow of the World Business Academy, a Baden Powell Fellow of the World Scout Foundation, a Board Member of the Desmond Tutu Peace Foundation and Plant-It 2020, co-author of the photo essay,* One World, One People, *and author of* Living an Extraordinary Life. *Developing extraordinary leadership effectiveness in others is Robert's personal mission. He's a powerful public speaker and an experienced executive coach. You can receive tips for being more personally and professionally effective by subscribing to Robert's free weekly ezine,* An Extraordinary Minute, *at www.ExtraordinaryPeople.com.*

Seeing the Light

A Story of Life, Illumination, and Discovery

by M. Stuart Tessler

There was a *flash!*

Not a lightning bolt, per se, more like drawing back the curtains on a bright summer morning. But a thunderbolt, in effect. Suddenly the room was brighter; there was a clarity. Something new, something exhilarating had happened. Something had changed. That something was me.

Let me take you back. I was on the train called "career." After years of schooling, years of building a practice and reputation, I'd made it to the crest of the hill. I was my mother's "son, the eye doctor" and, in my late forties, primed, over the next decade or so, to coast into retirement.

The view from the crest, however, was not an entirely pleasant one—not nearly. Never married, I was still recovering from a traumatic relationship. The chemistry we'd shared had been hard to avoid. We danced around the obvious attraction, but neither could deny it. We even tried to avoid each other. After all, she was engaged to be married. It was the better part of a year before we agreed to have lunch, just a simple innocent lunch. We both knew better. That's how it all started.

We took things slowly; it was a very romantic six months. But what followed, I wouldn't wish on my worst enemy. How I survived is still a mystery.

What had blossomed so romantically had also created a loving, nurturing "safe place," as the therapists would later surmise, for her deeply-hidden abusive childhood to spontaneously come bubbling to the surface. An accomplished pharmacist and pilot, suddenly her legs would unexpectedly collapse beneath her at work—or she'd wake gasping for air with her heart beating, as we'd later learn, over 200 beats per minute. In far too many trips to ERs, we met far too many doctors with far too little understanding of what was going on. Lots of scares, lots of concern, and the doctor in me, the loving partner in me, said we'll solve this thing, together.

Not long after, everything changed.

What had been manifesting physically, just as suddenly turned emotional. Over many intense months of ugly heinous memories, tears, and rage, we sought therapists … specialists … diagnoses … *help!* Finally the consensus was MPD, Multiple Personality Disorder, which we soon found out nobody really had a clue how to treat, though plenty of therapists, clearly in over their heads, were willing to try.

It wasn't pretty. We were no longer alone. Ultimately, there were something like fifty-six distinct personalities, or group personalities, who could appear at any given moment. Mostly females, of all ages, they each had different names and widely varying dispositions. They looked different, sounded different, even sometimes smelled different, and each had its own take on whatever was going on at the moment. There were several groups, like "the kids" or "the girls," and a few guys thrown in, for good measure. Some loved and protected me: They saw me as a friend, helper, lover, or even savior. Others hated me. After all, I was a threat to their existence, their dissociative status quo, for it was that dissociation that saved her when she was being raped by the uncles, priests, and nuns, from the time before she could talk until she was thirteen. Altogether, they were "the committee" and if "Rachel" was around, you'd best be on good behavior and ready to duck. Oh, I could tell you stories.

This, too, was my life: scary, painful, sometimes bloody, sometimes fascinating, but never fun, and always overwhelmingly exhausting. For over two years I was on call and on guard 24/7. But even so, if I could get out of the house without being attacked, choked, bitten, or having to peel "someone" off the windshield or hood of my car ("Don't leave us!"), I typically made it to work each day, saw my patients, collapsed against a wall to catch my breath, and headed home to see what today's disaster might be.

For all my loyalty and devotion, I stayed too long. Much too long, if you ask the few people who knew what I was going through. Ultimately, I lost my strength and my health. I'll never forget a particular moment's respite from the drama inside.

I was sitting on the front porch, shirtless and exhausted, when I happened to glance down to find a little tuft of lint snuggled into my navel. It woke me to the agonizing realization that I was giving so much and receiving so little, I didn't even have the time, much less the energy, to clean the lint out of my own navel. For the first time on this hellish ride, I could no longer play the hero. I sat there and openly wept.

Soon after, I crashed from the exhaustion. My reservoirs were dry, I had nothing left to give. By necessity, we parted, and today, seventeen years later, my nagging fatigue makes it clear I still haven't fully recovered.

So, why am I telling you this story? Actually, I haven't shared with you the half of it. But this was my life outside of my work, which basically meant that although I was getting to work each day to see my patients, I was completely unavailable to help manage the daily business side of the practice. My business partner at the time, who never saw an aspect of the practice she didn't want to control, was there to be sure everything ran smoothly. But in her so doing, over time *our* practice took on *her* personality, and the next thing I knew, I found myself in an environment that didn't feel like me anymore.

I'd built something that felt so right, yet suddenly it felt alien and uncomfortable. I'd lost my romance; I'd lost my health; and now I'd lost my practice, or at least that was how it felt. I was unhappy and, frankly, too exhausted and too weak to do anything about it. Coasting into retirement was now a distant dream. If anything, I wanted to escape.

Then it happened. One day, there was that *flash!*

It was a perfectly ordinary moment. I was walking across my exam room, doing my best to never let my discontent affect my work, taking it one day at a time. I don't quite remember what happened next. Maybe my patient said something, or maybe I heard something down the hall through the door that was now closed to keep all that negative energy out. Inside, this was still my room, my energy, and my practice.

Or, maybe it really was a lightning bolt with my name on it, though frankly, nobody else seemed to notice. In an instant the room lit up, it was brighter, the colors more vivid. It was like an awakening, exhilarating, illuminating, and it brought with it a thought, a thought that was until that very moment, unthinkable.

Oh sure, my career train was going over a rough stretch of track, but for all intents and purposes, at this stage of life, it was the only track. So many years spent "finding myself," so many years of schooling and building a practice, so much of me invested in reaching that "crest of the hill." The next few years should have been a breeze, but now I couldn't stomach even thinking about it.

What stars aligned? What butterfly flapped its iridescent wings? The flash, the thought, appeared from nowhere, "You know, Stuart, you don't have to wake up tomorrow being an eye doctor." I was stunned. It stopped me dead in my tracks.

This previously unthinkable thought had never crossed my mind. But, in a flash, it did, bringing with it new awareness that changed my life instantaneously.

Suddenly, options appeared that I hadn't seen before. All it took was a change in perspective. Within a year, I'd sold my practice and was off on a new adventure, one of healing and discovery. The healing came slowly, but the discoveries came at the speed of light. Those discoveries were about how a life can change by a mere shift in perspective.

Change can sometimes seem so difficult, yet when I was at my lowest, that thunderbolt brought perspective that almost effortlessly changed everything. I started noticing and appreciating how even subtle shifts in perspective brought change—a friend's opinion instantly flavoring my own, or an insight allowing new understanding. A new book afforded new sympathies, or a new person inspired new empathy. Heck, even new seats at the ballgame brought new appreciation for the subtleties of a game I thought I already knew. Each time, I was changed by the experience.

It made sense to me that perspective is a product of life experience, which, being different for each of us, leaves us oblivious to the ways it *limits* us. This seemed especially true when it came to deeply-held beliefs, patterns, and emotions, particularly self-defeating ones. Looking back at my ordeal, I could see where I resisted insight, understanding, or even safety, simply because it challenged my self-image or sense of purpose as a devoted partner. However honorable, in the midst of the fury, I couldn't see the bigger picture until it almost destroyed me. No wonder a major change, as in one's professional identity, requires catharsis, catastrophe, thunderbolts, and the like, just to get our attention.

If only there were an easier way to gain new perspective, to see with more objectivity, to see ourselves with fresh eyes. If only we could take a "perspective pill" before bedtime, waking to a bright new, sunny beginning. As it turns out, there may be.

For several years I had been experimenting with an esoteric form of light therapy used to treat vision problems. As this work developed over time, not only were my patients' vision problems improving, but to my surprise, many of them were reporting that their lives were changing.

No talk therapy, no behavior modification, no self-help books or enlightened texts. Yet, they reported being more relaxed, less stressed, more open and capable of change. They were seeing things with a whole new perspective, often with a new sense of who they were in the world. It was really quite amazing.

I discovered that, not only does perspective expand with life experience, but it can also constrict as a consequence of stress, especially chronic stress. Ironically, in my work, this was something I was already measuring as part of our basic human survival mechanism: the fight-or-flight response. But it's our fight-or-flight response gone awry that causes many problems.

In the face of an immediate threat, stress, or challenge, we instinctively narrow our focus, creating a sort of visual and mental tunnel vision zeroed in on our survival. We've all experienced how small our world gets when we're stressed, scared, or angry. Though our daily stressors are rarely life threatening, they can be unrelenting: work, family, health, finances, traffic, pollution, etc. Over time, it's no wonder we can actually get stuck in fight-or-flight mode, and its narrowed perspective along with it.

To my amazement, the light therapy was shifting my patients' nervous systems out of fight-or-flight, and *voilà*, their lives were changing, seemingly without effort. They were becoming more relaxed, less stressed, and often happier. They were seeing themselves and their lives with new perspective. Suddenly there were more options and opportunities available to them. From that work, a new modality, Fight or Flight Therapy, and a new career were born.

Funny how life works. In the midst of our struggles, clarity can seem so painfully elusive. From the depths of my drama, it took a crash and a flash for me to see the light. I'd found my new perspective the hard way, but along with it came new direction and passion. New perspective was the key. How comforting it is to know there are easier ways to find it. How ironic, and incredibly gratifying, that now in my work I'm in a position to help others find theirs.

Dr. M. Stuart Tessler grew up in Buffalo, New York, received his BS from SUNY/Buffalo, and his doctorate from Pennsylvania College of Optometry. He built a successful practice in Denver, Colorado, and in 1990 was introduced to a little-known esoteric light therapy. As his work with light progressed, it became clear that people's lives were changing. That work evolved into Fight or Flight Therapy. Dr. Tessler is currently having excellent success treating stress- and trauma-related conditions, including stress, anxiety, PTSD, head injuries, and more. He lives in Denver with his wife, Mira, and cat, Pounce. Learn more or contact him at www.FightorFlightTherapy.com.

Life through the Lens

by Michael Sharon

Sweating. Shaking. Pulsating.

I sit in the small playground tunnel. Alone. I am cocooned within the crazy world around me. It's the only place I feel safe as I wait for my mom to come take me home from preschool. Paralyzed with fear that she will leave me at school, nervous energy cascades through my body. All I can think about is being abandoned—a deep feeling of being unwanted, as if my mom had given up on me. Finally, after an eternity, the clock strikes noon. My mom comes through the doors and I bolt toward her with relief.

This anxious, warped mentality lasted for much of my school career as a child.

Screaming. Kicking. Fighting.

My school persona seemed to be caused by my home life. Similarly, I was the quiet observer at home, as the family seemed to be spiraling out of control on many nights. My younger sister's strident tantrums screeched through the house. My parents ran low on patience after so many sleepless nights. Doors slammed. The ceiling shook. I felt helpless and scared. Were my parents going to just leave? Would they abandon my sister and me because it was too much to handle? What if I became an orphan? What if I never saw my parents again? *What if*—That phrase consumed me at a young age. Habitually, I would leave my room in the middle of the night to check that both cars were in the garage. I could not sleep unless I knew they were still there. But I didn't want anyone to know how I truly felt. I was the strong, capable, "perfect" son. I took on such a burden trying to appear secure and unfazed by the commotion. Not one person knew the extent of my anxiety.

One night, my sister and I constructed a fort out of sheets in our playroom downstairs. We thought it'd be fun to spend the night there. As it grew late and I settled into my sleeping bag, I heard the cars start in the garage. A tremendous jolt coursed through my body. Beads of sweat instantly appeared on my palms.

They are going to leave, I'm sure of it. I tossed my sleeping bag off and rushed to the playroom door.

"Where are you going?" my sister questioned.

"Mom and Dad are leaving!" I exclaimed frantically, racing out of the room. Running up to the garage door, I peered out to see my parents jumping a dead car battery. They weren't leaving. They were still there. *Relief.* Regardless, the visceral response this fear evoked was draining. I always had the urgent need to know I was safe, yet maintain my façade as the strong, good child. I knew my sister was a lot to handle, so I buried all the feelings deep down inside. No one had to know how I truly felt; I would just appear perfect. It was better that way—or so I thought.

What is a lens? For many, it's a mere piece of glass. To me, it's the most mirac-ulous device—one that can change not just the appearance of something, but can alter an entire perspective. Ever try to walk around with someone else's heavy prescription eyeglasses for a whole day? Everything appears hazy, unclear, and it's impossible to decipher the way the world really looks. As a kid, and still today to some extent, I had the "wrong lens" over my eyes, which clouded my vision. Similar to having the wrong eyeglasses, often perceiving something the wrong way is exhausting. I have been battling distorted viewpoints my whole life.

The metaphor of the lens became literal the day I picked up a video camera and made my first movie. The idea of holding a device that could alter reality was enthralling. Much like an eyeglass lens, a camera lens in itself can change the image to the extent of bringing an entirely different perspective to the story. At age thirteen, when I first saw the power of the camera, my passion was sparked. The family was borrowing a friend's camcorder and I burst with excitement. I couldn't believe I was on the brink of making a real movie.

"Well, what should we make the movie about?" my sister asked, getting out a notepad.

What's something we were never able to do as a play? Something that has a lot of action and fun gadgets? I pondered. My eyes widened. "Let's make a spy movie where we are undercover!" That moment my first movie, *Spyz,* was born. We came up with the premise that I would be recruited by a female bank employee when I find out she is a spy. The only way to protect her identity was to bring me on board with the spy agency. The crazy part about this was we had developed only those two basic ideas when we rolled the camera. Everything was improvised.

Characters, events, lines were all made up on the spot while the camera rolled. It was just my sister and I making a movie at my house while my parents moved my older sister into her new home. We had our own little movie studio.

I began to see the house in a whole different light. Certain areas would work as parts of the set. The deck became a coffee shop; the office became a bank; and my bedroom evolved into spy headquarters. It was literally a brand-new perspective on the environment I grew up in, because I was enveloped in a story through the lens. The movie ended up shooting for almost a month and included my dad and an array of family friends joining the cast. I filled up the entire fifty-minute tape, filming the entire story sequentially. It was nothing short of magical. A story unfolded in front of my eyes, with fresh ingredients continually being added. It was a breathing entity that could be changed anytime.

Anticipating. Excited. Bursting.

After completing filming, a large group of family and friends came to the big screening—that is, the screening on the 32-inch tube television in our friend's living room. The experience of making this movie was a blast, but looking around at everyone beaming, laughing, and enjoying my hard work was simply invaluable. For fifty minutes, I brought joy to the people I care about through film. Chills ran down my spine. A broad smile formed on my face. My heart skipped beats. I suddenly knew this was what I wanted to do as my life's work. To me, there is nothing better than eating popcorn and enjoying a movie with my friends and family. The fact that I was able to deliver that satisfaction through my first movie brought a joy that I had never felt before.

Making *Spyz* really helped me to look back on the hardships of my childhood. I was too busy picking up the pieces of my shaky family dynamic to really look inside of myself. I believed that if I took the time to examine my own wounds, instead of consuming myself with the lives of others, I would be considered weak. I was petrified of showing vulnerability because it was my duty to be strong in the midst of the familial storm. I had put myself on an illusory pedestal, attempting to project an image that I could never really live up to.

Brewing. Festering. Overflowing.

Shortly after showing *Spyz*, I developed frequent stomach pains and became extremely sick. The gut-wrenching illness impaired me to the point of having to complete eighth grade through homeschooling. The cause and diagnosis of my illness continue to be a mystery. I underwent procedures such as a colonoscopy and acupuncture, and even had to choke down both celery and sauerkraut juice daily. Following all of the Eastern and Western forms of tests and treatment, all we could conclude was that excessive stress was the cause. Looking back, I believe that all of the childhood trauma that I stuffed down had finally surfaced. Filmmaking was quite possibly the catalyst for it to all come to a head. It was as if a giant balloon of pain, weakness, and fear had been inflating to the brink of popping, and finally burst. The ailment erupted like poison seeping through my body carrying all the issues I never had the courage to face.

In January 2003, as a new home-schooled student, I dove headfirst into my next exciting spy-related script—*Undercover Secret*. This time, I was equipped with my own camera, editing software, and an eager cast of family and friends. The realization that I no longer had to shoot in a linear fashion, and that I now had computer effects at my fingertips was exhilarating. I could feel myself slowly cracking through my shell as I organized shooting dates, constructed props, and orchestrated actors. This was my element. I found my passion. *Sheer excitement. Pure glee.*

Six amazing months later, *Undercover Secret* was completed. My Russian neighbor, as the undercover KGB, brought authenticity to the story; the high-speed car chase through the neighborhood zipped across the screen; my grandma even got to try on her acting chops. The movie may not have been a piece of art or the spitting image of professional, but it was mine. It was something I researched, wrote, shot, edited, directed, and starred in. *Undercover Secret* showed me what it was like to make a full-length movie and how the process can bring together so many people to create one product. To my amazement, my older sister graciously used her connections to get me on local TV news channels and even arranged a screening at a theater in downtown Denver. I was fourteen and had my movie on the silver screen, with my movie title on the marquee. *"Elated" even falls short of describing the sensation.* I felt a deep sense of purpose and my stomach pains had noticeably subsided. The power to communicate my story had a profound impact on my healing.

Secure. Safe. Confident.

The sense of being a lonely and scared child has steadily faded after I began attending a great alternative high school, continuing to find my voice through participating in video production classes at Cherry Creek High School, then honing my various filmmaking skills at Colorado Film School.

Today, I have a very close group of friends, both in and out of film. My cocooned childhood self and my current, young-adult self seem miles apart. The frightened inner child seems to be a completely different entity from who I am right now. However, that inner child still comes out in times of vulnerability and I continue working on being a stronger person. Without film, I doubt that I'd have my present perspective. Film has reshaped the lens I look through, which is not nearly as warped anymore. Although I still have my fearful times, I am now generally focused and am filled with drive and raw passion to get my voice out in the world. To me, life always occurs through some sort of lens; it's just a matter of what lens I choose to look through and if it's right for me. Subjectivity is a gift, because everyone has his or her own unique perspective. My goal is to present my spin on the world, my lens, to large audiences and to share my story of who I am, inside and out.

Michael D. Sharon, *an award-winning filmmaker, is a senior majoring in cinematography at Colorado Film School in conjunction with Regis University. Michael has been making films since age fourteen and working with professional production companies since 2005. He was the recipient of the Fine Arts Scholarship for his video production in high school and won first place two consecutive years at the Scholastic Art Awards. A diverse filmmaker, Michael excels in narrative pieces, documentaries, and commercial work. Writing has always been a hobby for him; he loves portraying story through words. Filmmaking has always been his ultimate life passion and he is committed to making his pieces unique, effective, and visually stunning. Born and raised in Denver, Colorado, Michael currently lives with his girlfriend Dana and enjoys cooking, hiking, camping, and playing football and basketball. Professionally, Michael is doing various videography and editing jobs for clients who are making a difference in the world by increasing awareness about the environment and economic development. Michael may be reached at filmboi123@yahoo.com*

Optical Illusion

by Gregory Boyer

I went to bed and woke up blind;
The world I knew I couldn't find.
For it was just there yesterday;
Now—somehow it had gone.

You'd think my eyes would be the blame
To all the things appearing changed.
The smiles and angry faces shown
Are still there from those I have known.

The ways of love and pain and sin
Remain the way they've always been,
And yet the world that I once knew
Is different in this wakened view.

Should I be shook or alarmed
To see the world I knew as harmed?
The answer to this mystery
Is simply how I choose to see.

To take the usual, typical day
And look at it another way.
Though I have vision in both eyes,
It's not where I see truth or lies.

And neither can I always see
How God sees you or He sees me.
But I have learned to look both ways
And use my heart in every gaze.

To learn this lesson took some time
In knowing I was never blind.
You see, this world was never gone;
I just woke up with glasses on.

–Gregory Boyer

The eye is the lamp of the body.
So, if your eye is healthy
Your whole body will be full of light.

–Matthew 6:22

In this verse from the Bible, Jesus is trying to teach us about having "spiritual vision." Our upbringing, culture, spiritual beliefs, experiences, and self-esteem can "cloud" our ability to see who we really are and to see the world as it really is. I'm constantly trying to be aware of this world of "optical illusions" to perceive the truth of who I am, who others are, and how we all fit in it together. By doing so, I feel I can contribute the greatness in me to make a difference in this world. At the same time, when "wearing my glasses," I am able to enjoy and receive the greatness of others. I believe that everyone has a great story to tell and an amazing journey to be shared.

I want to share three short stories that changed me, and in the process, changed how I saw myself and those around me, altering my vision of the world.

When I was born, the doctor told my parents I was going to die. I was born weighing about three and a half pounds and was losing weight. For whatever reason, I wouldn't eat anything that was given to me. My parents refused to simply sit back and watch me die because the doctor or the hospital staff couldn't figure out how to save my life. So they took me home and tried to feed me the food they regularly ate, which seemed to them to be an obvious medical solution. My mom took the broth from some collard greens, turned it into a paste using cornbread, and noticed my tiny mouth moving to enjoy it. I don't know why my body wouldn't accept breast milk or formula from the hospital, but since I had dropped weight at the hospital, from three and a half pounds to two pounds, my parents felt they had to think outside the box for me to survive. My parents never completed junior high school, but figured out a problem the doctors and medical staff weren't able to solve. They couldn't accept the hopelessness that the staff saw in the situation. Thank God they saw other possibilities.

I grew up healthy and normal. I was a picky eater and very slim, but I was rarely sick. I grew up hearing this story, which taught me to see there can be more than one solution to a problem. I learned that no matter what your educational background, you are likely to be smarter than you regard yourself to be. Also, I saw how special I was and that my life had great value.

At the age of nine, I remember playing hide-and-seek behind my grandmother's house. As one of my friends covered her face and counted to one hundred, the rest of us ran to our best hiding places. While my friends hid behind the usual spots and obvious hiding places, I decided to hide where I thought nobody would consider looking—right in the open! While my friend was counting, I ran and sat down in the middle of a nearby open field of tall wild-growing wheat. Waiting quietly, I watched her find everyone else but me. As I expected, she looked in all the customary hiding places.

As I sat and waited for her to count to one hundred (which seemed like forever), I could hear the wind blowing over the wheat grain. I could see the tips of the grain swaying side to side as if they were dancing to music. Before long, I wasn't paying attention to her counting, but noticing how quiet the world became. I also observed how much bluer the sky appeared, how white the clouds were, and how great the sun felt against my skin. I became overwhelmed with what I keenly noticed and gave in to the urge to stand up, close my eyes, lean my head back, raise my arms to the sky, and exclaim, "This is the best time of my life!"

After pausing for a moment to soak in the warmth of the sun, I squatted down again in my little hiding spot. A second thought then came to me: "I am such a weird kid." But it wasn't a negative thought. I had the biggest smile on my face, because I realized at nine years of age that life is beautiful when you can see how wonderful simple moments can be. I sat there long enough to reflect some more about this *aha* moment and thought, "I want to keep this feeling for the rest of my life. To do that I must enjoy the simple things in life, look for the beauty in my everyday life." Again, I was only nine years old; I knew nothing about philosophy. I wasn't spiritual, nor was I a poet. Heck, I didn't even get good grades in school. But that day changed me forever. I would continue playing with my school friends and look at them, or whatever activities we were doing, and be amazed at what I had never previously considered: how beautiful life could be once you choose to see it differently. My friends looked different. My world looked different. I began to look and act differently. And I took it as a compliment whenever someone said to me, "Greg, you are so weird."

The last vignette magnifies the other two stories. The "glasses" I put on back in 1976 opened my eyes to literally hearing the voice of God. I had quit college because I got a job as a fashion designer before anyone else in my class. I was always considered very good at art and often received compliments on my looks. I was easily liked, had many friends, including girlfriends, and my new jobs paid me well. I have always had a great feeling about life and felt like there was nothing but good things in store for me. However, despite all of my positivity, I would often lay my head on my pillow at night and feel very sad. It didn't make sense to me, but suddenly life appeared so empty. Something was missing.

I grew up not believing in spiritual things. I never told my family or friends that I didn't believe in God, because I had done well with seeing life the way I did. I was a very happy and contented person. It didn't take much to make me feel that way. I was okay with being an atheist. But I also accepted other people believing in God or having a spiritual lifestyle. It never bothered me and I never saw it as a crazy way to live; I just couldn't relate to that area of life. As time passed, I got more and more confused about why I wasn't happy, when I had every reason to be happy. As a result, I thought I needed to seek out God. It seemed like a good idea at the time. So, I went to church, tried to read and make sense of the Bible, and waited to connect to something greater than myself or others. Nothing was working.

Two people consistently stood on a corner in downtown Los Angeles handing out Christian literature. I would pass them every day on my way to work and avoid them. One time I decided to listen to them share their story. They invited me to go to church with them, and I accepted. That night at their church, people stood up and shared their testimony of how they had found God, how He saved them from drugs, suicide, or prostitution. Well, I got the idea in my head that, "I guess you really have to be a bad person before you can have an experience with God." At the end of the service, I was asked if I wanted to ask to have a relationship with God. I said, "Sure." But secretly, I just wanted to get out of there because I thought I didn't qualify for a relationship with God, who only seemed to care about those with messed-up lives.

Even so, I closed my eyes and proceeded to repeat a prayer that I was asked to say to confirm and seal this new relationship with God. I had made up my mind that I would just repeat the words and not mean them, and just continue my search for spiritual relief and purpose. As I started to say the words, my tongue suddenly felt swollen and I couldn't speak. I started to become afraid because I knew something beyond logic was happening to me. I was experiencing something spiritual, but not in a way that was comfortable or inviting. I finally ended up praying inside my head, "If there is a God out there and you were to let me know you exist, I will spend the rest of my life being the person you want me to be and loving you with all my heart." Right after offering that silent prayer, I heard a voice as clear as day say, "Greg, I am here." Immediately I started to cry. I didn't know why I was crying until later that night. I became overwhelmed with emotion realizing that God had allowed me to live according to how I saw things in life, never acknowledging His existence. And yet, He had protected me and kept me safe during times when I could have been harmed, or died (perhaps during birth).

After making a decision to follow Jesus and worship the Living God, my eyes were truly opened. I now understood the verse that said, "One thing I do know. I was blind but now I see!" (John 9:26). The way I saw the world the very next day was amazing. I had already been living a life looking past the optical illusion of how the world looked. But connecting to God elevated my eyesight to a higher level that I could never have attained on my own.

These stories I have shared are just a part of many life-changing moments that tell me, "My journey has been amazing." And this new insight has me believing that everyone else also has had an amazing journey, though not necessarily one that Hollywood would want to make into a movie. But I'm sure that each person's journey is just as powerful as any other's. If you can't see that, try putting on your glasses.

I want to drive vigorously down life's superhighway. What a journey! Let's take a ride together, my friend.

Gregory Boyer, *a certified life coach and behavioral health professional, works with students who attend Arizona colleges from all over the world. He also serves young adults as a full-time employee of a mental health agency. Gregory especially loves mentoring youths to discover how amazing they are as unique individuals, and to follow their own inner purpose. He is also an artist and a motivational speaker. Visit his website at www.beachbodycoach.com/gregoryboyer and contact him at boyercollection@gmail.com.*

Talk to the Hand

by Les Jensen

It seemed simple enough. Too simple, really. His hand seemed to levitate in the silence of the room—kind of a surreal moment. I didn't know what was about to happen. All he wanted was for me to push on his hand. "Show me your anger," he kept saying. I put my hand on his and pushed. As I pushed, I just sank further into the overstuffed couch, one I had sat on for nearly two years. My psychiatrist and I had worked on "me" for what seemed to be ages. Sure there were moments when I felt I had come a long way. But that night just seemed out of place. Why was he pressing me so hard to show my anger? I really thought it would prove to be a gigantic waste of time. My boss was angry, but I didn't have an ounce of anger in my everyday life. I was a lighthearted, easygoing kind of guy. I never showed anger. I just didn't have any issues with anger. No shouting or yelling. No temper tantrums. Nothing to raise a flag. And yet he persisted.

Looking back, I could see the signs. They were there. Quite distinct really, when I knew what to look for. One subtle sign involved wanting to just sit on the couch and crash, channel surfing for an hour or so every night when I got home from work. More notably, I ignored upsets in my relationships, not wanting to push anything that might lead to an argument. I would concede my points of view to make sure that I didn't rock the boat, avoiding any kind of heated conflict with anyone. I simply did not express anger. Yet, my body, fully engaged in resisting this silent condition, was sending me signals. For example, I gnashed my teeth in my sleep. I also experienced continuous upheaval and duress in my digestive tract for over a decade; ulcer symptoms were beginning to show themselves. Perhaps the biggest sign was my "wake." That is to say, if I considered my life as a boat going through the water, my wake was straight as an arrow. I had become a master at keeping my life safe and predictable. I subconsciously and automatically monitored my environment, making sure of the outcome of every choice before I actually made any choices. You could transplant me to another country, and I would quickly find a safe routine to get me through my days. No dreaming; no creative adventures; no risks; no big rewards—just "safety."

I now don't know how I could have been in such a silent "prison" with invisible bars for so long. So much of my life occurred below my radar screen, limiting me in a profound way. Every moment of every day, my unexpressed anger was making a lot of my choices, effectively shutting down whole arenas of life possibilities. That kept my deeply-suppressed anger from surfacing. I was very guarded with my every move.

Extending his hand once again, my psychiatrist told me quite bluntly, "Look Les, I give you permission to show me your anger. I want to see it. It's okay for you to show your anger now. *Now, show me your anger!*" Geez, he could just chill a bit. Why did he persist with such a meaningless point? What does he think he will find--something in me of which I am not aware? Eventually, I came to realize that what I didn't know about myself was much bigger than anything I did know about myself.

I finally put my hand against his hand again, but then something happened that I didn't anticipate—something that would change my life forever. A whole new life path was about to be born, yet I knew nothing of it in that moment. And what I felt changed how I thought about myself and my life. When I pressed against the doctor's hand again, something deep inside of me, some magical valve or gate opened, for the first time in my life! I pushed his hand again; an absolutely huge wave of energy came flowing out of me. I instantly knew that I was releasing pure anger. The funny thing was that I did not feel scared or overwhelmed. The energy felt impersonal; I watched with detachment as it gushed out of me. I remember thinking how odd it was to feel such intense energy and not be at all concerned about it. After several extended waves, it subsided. In that moment, my life changed.

I remember driving home thinking, "What the hell was that? Where did all that energy come from? Why didn't I know about it before? Why did it feel so impersonal?"

I had been working with energy in my job, as a television-broadcast engineer, creating vast electrical power through television transmitters. Television transmitters are "big beasts," that silently create the signals that provide TV programs. To broadcast those programs, we would generate up to a million watts of power. Get it right, and everyone is watching the game; get it wrong, and the power would easily leave the transmitter in a molten puddle on the ground. I had contemplated the nature of

pure energy. Working with the high power levels that television transmitters generated, I had to be careful that I understood the nature of the undetectable energy with
which I was working. I compared the transmitter energy with the huge amount of
energy I had jut released from within my own being.

I started watching people around me to sense if they were living with unre-
solved "stuff" that they were protecting. What surprised me was suddenly realizing that my angry boss was just as afraid of anger as I had been, except he chose a
different way to master it. His tactic seemed to be to keep everyone else in check,
so that he could feel safe. His anger appeared to be a defense against a much
deeper feeling, one of fear. My frustration towards my boss quickly shifted to
compassion, once sensing that he was "scared to death." I also noticed anew that
almost everyone I knew had boundaries of which they were not cognizant.

When I viewed my early family life, I saw that anger was prominent. My dad
was a World War II vet. When he became angry, everyone in my family would try
to become invisible. As a very young child, I learned to avoid showing any anger
that might trigger my father's anger. So, I did the best thing I could do at the time
to keep my environment safe. As a reflexive survival tactic, I suppressed my anger
before becoming conscious of it. As that young boy, I felt very afraid when my
whole family would react to Dad's anger. I wasn't about to do anything to induce
that reaction to myself or to my family members. My posturing with anger began
with those subconscious childhood decisions.

As I watched myself, I started noticing other arenas of posturing. I observed
my tendency to favor pleasant experiences, while avoiding painful ones. In the
process of doing so, I found that I compromised a lot of my power.

My job as a chief engineer at a television station required a lot of techni-
cal knowledge and consistently knowing what to do. Although, of course, I was
expected to be competent, it was curious and bothersome to me that I was so
vested in being right all of the time.

I decided that I must be losing some power by acting like I was constantly
right. So, I deliberately allowed myself to be viewed as wrong. While it took a lot
of nerve for me to do so, during a department meeting that I was leading I told
the staff I had made a mistake in my planning and that what we were working
on was taking us in the wrong direction. I remember the staff reacting as though
I had completely lost my mind. But I stuck with it. Several times over the next
few weeks, I openly admitted to being wrong. Curiously, when I made it okay for
me to be wrong, I created permission for staff members to be wrong, too. Yikes.

What had I done? Did I just unravel the power of the group? Had I just thrown the character of our whole department "under the bus?"

A most curious thing happened. In the past, when I would ask for ideas, only a few employees would respond. The seasoned guys would contribute suggestions with how they would do it and a big part of the staff would remain quiet. But when I made it acceptable to be wrong, I started getting ideas from people who would have never chimed in before. Besides receiving more ideas, those who started contributing felt a sense of ownership and connection with the direction and intention of the department. They felt more empowered. The department's morale and productivity increased dramatically, reaching an all-time high! I would hear people discussing how new opportunities were available to them. People became excited to come to work and were actively engaged in improving the department. Talk about better management ... Wow! My single mindset shift led to much-enhanced management and a breakthrough in team attitude.

As I revealed my subconscious programming and claimed my power, I opened to life again in a way I never had before. I felt a sense of fulfillment and joy in my everyday life. I no longer wanted to avoid any of my feelings. I didn't want any of my power to go untapped. I developed a desire to help others discover a greater experience of true freedom in their lives.

Feeling empowered, I now live life wide-open. I have a deep sense of inner peace. My current ideal is learning how to bring my full potential into play in every aspect of my life. And boy, do I love it! I love showing up for myself and for others, opening to possibilities everywhere. I never considered myself as an author, but I overcame that limited self-perception. The satisfaction and joy of helping others is priceless. I am glad I found the writer in me. What else is seeking expression from deep within me? I am eager to be totally free to be the best me.

Les Jensen is an advocate for healthy men. Les is a published author, speaker, radio show host and visionary. Les is founder of the Authentic Man Men's Group in Boulder, Colorado and of the Authentic Man radio show. Through immense struggles, Les has learned the hidden reasons why we can want change, yet not be able to actually bring it into our own experience. Les brings new insights and perspectives on how we can all live healthy, prosperous and just plain fun lives. Visit his website, www.lesjensen.com.

Plastic Glasses

Learning to Love on the Rims of Culture

by Brian Rants

Breathlessly, I ran through the cemetery overlooking the lush green valley near our Kent, Washington home. My brain misfired at machine-gun pace as I tried to wrap my 18-year-old mind around this brutal fact: my family was falling apart. Not just any family, but a pastor's family. Clergy. There were secrets and lies going back to my childhood that seemed too large to be hidden in my fishbowl life.

This was not the first time, but the most acute to date, where I struggled with my chosen path in life. I had taken Goody Two-shoes to a whole new level as a child: student of the year in five out of my six senior year classes; never missed a day of school from second to twelfth grade; leader in my church youth group. Yet I never felt like I fit in.

Each rim of my childhood glasses was the size of an apple, and the color of the plastic was applesauce. Sweet, gentle, and silly by nature, I had a fuzzy head that every adult seemed to rub for good luck. To say I was sort of conscientious would be akin to saying the Pope is kind of Catholic. When I returned home from school I would unburden my soul by telling my mother the sins of the day: calling a kid "dumb," talking in class, thinking bad thoughts of another—really seedy stuff.

The tenderness of my heart was fertile ground for a deep and abiding love of others. It was also unfortunately very receptive to the pressures, spoken or unspoken, of being a pastor's kid. As a PK (as we of this "club" call it), I felt expected to be the pride of my family, my school, my church, and my community. I tried not to let anyone down, and was valedictorian, senior class president, and a thousand other titillating titles.

As I ran to the edge of the manicured lawn on that beautiful July day, a small seed was planted in my racing mind. Were all my efforts to live an exemplary life built around a sham? Had I been bamboozled into running an imaginary race?

Growing into manhood, I began to shed many of the exterior trappings of the Evangelical American Christian culture. I figured that listening to the band U2 was a safe place to start; got my ears pierced; and (Lord have mercy) realized that Ben Franklin was spot on when he said, "Beer is living proof that God loves us and wants us to be happy."

I became ashamed of my Biblical Studies degree and stopped listening to Christian music. I expanded my vocabulary to four-letter words and decided God just might not care all that much if I sped a little on my way to work. Oh, and I started wearing contacts. *That's me in the corner. That's me in the spotlight. Losing my religion.*

Something quite unexpected and beautiful happened. As I unfolded my identity from the religious wrappings, I found myself even more profoundly drawn to God. Rather than coming to Jesus to exceed my community's expectations, I came to Him to learn to live like He lived: to forgive my enemies, to defend the powerless, to join others in their place of pain and walk with them to a place of healing.

I also began to believe a very consequential little proposition: that I was loved by God not for what I do, but for who I am. And as in the movie *Inception*, that paradigm shift changed my faith from self-improvement to the source of my engagement with a suffering world.

> *God is love. When we take up permanent residence in a life of love, we live in God and God lives in us. This way, love has the run of the house, becomes at home and mature in us, so that we're free of worry on Judgment Day—our standing in the world is identical with Christ's. There is no room in love for fear. Well-formed love banishes fear. Since fear is crippling, a fearful life—fear of death, fear of judgment—is one not yet fully formed in love. We, though, are going to love—love and be loved. First we were loved, now we love. He loved us first.*
>
> —1 John 4:17–19

In his letter (epistle), the Apostle John gives a little opus on God's love. This was no intellectual exercise as revealed in his Gospel of John, his account of Christ's love. When he appears in the story, as he does often, he refers to himself as "the one Jesus loved" (John 20:2). His identity was found in God's love for him, so much so that it became his name in the grand drama of Jesus' life on earth.

As I stare at the computer screen and will my fingers to tap out something inspiring, I look through thick black plastic glasses. I've also increasingly found my identity as "the one Jesus loves." Freed from the fear of not fitting in, I can embrace the fact that I'm damned good at school, I love the Bible like a friend, and I'll probably never get in trouble. I am also free to be a Democrat, love beer like a friend, speak out about the injustice done to our Native Americans, and work in Africa (as I do) to end poverty.

I am not limited by the Evangelical culture of my youth, but I am proud to be a follower of Christ. And I can see how my upbringing was instrumental in making me the man I am today. I learned that people are more important than prestige; character trumps cash; being understanding of others overrides being upwardly mobile. I learned that the opinions of others are passing, but the love of God is eternal.

I also learned that everyone is human, and that my family's shortcomings in no way diminish the beauty of each of us. In fact, it provides the bridge to connecting with everyone we meet: "Be kind, for everyone you meet is fighting a hard battle."

So it is that I've come to believe: I'm okay with living on the rims of culture, as long as I'm smack in the middle of love.

Brian Rants *loves life in Denver with his (incredibly smart and beautiful) wife, two purse dogs, and a baby on the way. Now a Creative Director at Blue Riot Labs, he wrote this article during a life-changing stint as Executive Director of The 1010 Project, which does business development in Kenya. He enjoys soccer, songwriting, and urban farming.*

Part Nine: Reform

The Cure is Curiosity

by Lloyd Barde

A day that might have been fraught with trepidation, concerns regarding safety and a gnawing inner sense of inadequacy was poised to show itself. It was the middle of summer 2003, and we were going to San Mateo, California to spend a day with the inmates of the Choices Program at the county jail/correctional facility. Michael had invited three of us—Vinny, John, and myself—to come along for his program called "Incarceration of the Mind." I had been looking for opportunities to present some of my newly discovered personal wisdoms and was seeking new forums in which to speak, hear my voice, be of service, and navigate the chasms of separation that showed themselves in my daily life. As I was about to find out, this was the way and today was the day.

What I knew going in was that Michael had done this numerous times during the past six years; that he was well received in this jail; and that he was given a fair amount of leeway, while still operating within the guidelines and rules of the institution.

Michael is my closest male friend. We had spent many hours going deeply into vulnerable spaces, discussing fears, relationships, patterns, and degrees of freedom. He is a powerful African-American man with a strong presence, robust energy, distinct courage, and a soft, emotionally engaging manner. Not long after his father died, we were sitting in a hot tub late one night, and he inspired my resolve to speak at the memorial service of my own father, who was dying of cancer at the time. Years before, another friend and fellow single parent had encouraged me to have my nine-year-old son move in with me full-time, and I might not have done so without carefully taking in my friend's experience. Those were both defining moments in my life.

I had met Vinny a couple times before and had lasting impressions of him during a powerful weekend workshop that we shared with seventy-five others. His background was striking. He had grown up in the mean streets of New Haven, an ex-con whose father was an ex-con, and whose mother had died in a very impactful way during a time of great influence. Vinny had emerged from this with greater compassion, a giant heart, and a dedication to Buddhist practices like mindfulness and meditation, skills he incorporated into his own work in the correctional system.

I had met John a couple of times, noting his kind manner and how he spoke from a place of truth and receptivity.

I had been a lifelong student of personal disarmament, and had participated in and led groups to explore communication, relationships, and gender roles, along with aspects of shame and hope. My creative expression came through my love of music, dance and movement, hiking, tennis, entrepreneurship, and developing lasting friendships along the way.

During the hour-long drive, Michael asked if we had any questions. Curiously, there were none. Then he gave a brief overview of the day: introductions, check-ins, short meditation, open the circle for sharing during the morning, then determine the structure for the afternoon based on the energy of the group. There were six floors, with two PODs (or units) per floor, and this particular one had been receptive in the past. He made the cryptic comment, "There is no hugging allowed in this POD, but I assure you, there will be lots of hugging taking place." The remainder of the ride was mostly in silence, each of us in our own thoughts.

Upon arrival, we grabbed our lunches and entered the building. After the requisite red tape, some quick handshaking, standard orientation, signing in, and showing I.D.'s, we were permitted to enter the jail. With that, the door closed … Clank! We were now in jail, and if there were a lockdown we would be in it, right along with the criminal offenders serving life sentences. I had never been in a jail before. Getting locked in was a moment I will never forget.

We walked down the corridor and were led into the space where we would spend the day, the Choices POD. My first observation was of ninety-six men all dressed in orange jumpsuits, of widely varying ages, physical stature and build, and presence. My response could have been that these were scary people who could be easily stereotyped and held as different from us. I was aware of my own prejudices and judgments, products of my sheltered upbringing.

I was also aware that all personal situations were immediately equalized. There we were, the greater "we," and there were no differences in our fears, the soft spaces of kindness inside, or the desire for connection, shattered over the years as it may have been. As I scanned the high-tech circular room, I noticed an upstairs space with a narrow balcony encircling half the room, and small, two-person rooms. Two armed guards were present the entire time. There was total visibility from every angle—a very small, enclosed space with outdoor exposure in which to exercise and some chairs. Certain men stood out: some boyish in appearance, wise elders with pockmarked faces, scrawny men, and those who were imposing. Some men were potential felony offenders, while others were serving sentences of twenty-five-years-to-life for non-violent felonies. My overall impression was one of lives well-worn and filled with shadows. Some met my gaze; others moved around, muttering incessantly or keeping up chatter between established cliques and buddies. One particularly imposing man might have had his picture in my own dictionary next to the word "scary." He reminded me of wrestlers like Shag Thomas, who I watched on TV as a kid. They appeared to have no neck whatsoever and could seemingly break your spine just by thinking about it. I wasn't going to get anywhere near this guy.

Michael, our fearless (and peerless) leader, had been to this POD previously, so there was a mutual familiarity, especially with those who were still in this particular program. He made introductions and spoke of our intention, which was open-ended: to speak about "the work" and how to make the time (as in "doing time") matter. We each participated in a brief check-in, followed by a short meditation. We were given a chance to perceive the space, get a feel for each other, and become attuned in our own ways to the day about to unfold. My perspective broadened, so that I was able to take in more details, and not allow fear to limit my own awareness and receptivity.

Members of the group voiced grievances and concerns, as some eagerly seized the chance to clear the air. High fives, shout-outs, and backtalk were immediate forms of acknowledgment. Others spoke of their lack of interest in participating or applying themselves to the task at hand: getting real and speaking out. For example, one inmate said, "I'm not into any of this crap. I signed up for this on the chance it just might get me the hell outta here even a few days earlier. So leave me alone!" I could tell he meant it. However, in the midst of ninety-six orange-suited inmates in such close quarters, it's pretty hard to be left alone. In order to stay in the Choices Program, one had to participate and do his work, with the possibility of moving into a residential facility such as Delancey Street or Walden House in San Francisco.

From life experiences and adverse programming translated into hopelessness, it took a lot of courage for the inmates to speak. Whether oriented toward the positive or negative, comments had meaning. They were long overdue—and pent up in some cases. In both far-reaching and seemingly insignificant ways, I was shown that my life experience had been quite different from those of the men around me. Who was I to speak, to suggest, to invite, or even open my mouth? Yet, once I started speaking, and from listening to Vinny and John, I realized the only requirement was to do whatever I could to match the heart, courage, and authenticity of those I was speaking to. I could share my perspective, experience, and viewpoint as an offering.

Right before lunch, the energy began to wane, even as the connections expanded, and I was moved to speak again. I motioned to Michael that I had something to say. I said to the group "After lunch I will let you all in on the cure … (long pause) … the way to make each moment of your life meaningful. Please enjoy your lunch; I know I will enjoy mine." We were not permitted to mingle with the inmates during lunch, so we four visitors sat together off to the side. Right away Michael eagerly said, "Man, I can't wait to hear what the cure is." I replied, "Me, too!"

After we regrouped, Michael couldn't wait to have me return to where I had left off. I spoke with the confidence that comes from not knowing, trusting in letting go, recognizing the equality, and the lack of separation between myself and anyone and everyone. I was hearing my voice anew. "The cure is curiosity," I said. The thought spilled like water and now spread around the men. I talked about supposing one didn't know what might happen, being open and interested in finding out, as life unfolded. The men's comments supported beliefs about returning to their outside lives but still being at the mercy of old habits, patterns, and addictions—a setup for failure and a likely return to imprisonment. I invited them to wonder what might happen, taking conscious steps to turn "live and don't learn" into receiving the lessons of life and all that it presents. And I spoke about each of us having choices in these matters. I said, "Believe in your experience, and take the needs and views of others into account. Be open to life being different." There's a wise adage that says, "If you keep heading in the same direction, you'll get where you've always gotten." Having gradually learned from my own experience, I suggested that if you ask questions from your heart, your will, and your deepest wish, it may take time and practice to let the old tapes run off the spool, but it will unwind the momentum that has taken you down particular chosen roads in the past. When inner change occurs, outer experience is perceived differently. Being curious opens this possibility and allows for one to stay present to what is. For years I had been tied to patterns of thought and behavior that blocked this natural flow. But I had come to realize there is a natural rhythm to life, a continual moving back and forth between being open and closed, like the waves of the ocean.

Michael laid out the afternoon plan. We each had another chance to address the group and exchange our thoughts. From the discussion and questions based on "why it couldn't work," I could sense varying levels of shame, guilt, and people having painted themselves into a corner. At one point, after hearing facets of fear expressed about backsliding, or reverting to past destructive ways of living, I was moved to ask, "How many of you have kids?" This opened space for reflection, inviting the men to consider the outside world and their deepest connections to it. There were no children present, but suddenly I could feel the spirit of youth and practically hear young voices. It is helpful to get outside of ourselves to reconnect on the inside.

Vinny shared his story in greater detail, and his path from a destructive, violent upbringing to a life of service—quite a dramatic and jaw-dropping narrative. He then had everyone form circles of six men each. The men were asked to take turns speaking, using the model, "If you really knew me, you'd know ...," with each completing that sentence several times in different ways. Soon the men in each group had locked arms and were frequently reaching for the box of tissues strategically located in each circle. There was some serious sharing and getting real, although beyond earshot.

After the circles had run their course and we had regrouped, only a couple hours remained in the program. By now, everyone was sitting casually together. Gradually the acknowledgments turned into hugs, including for us the four visitors. As the conversations deepened emotionally, tender layers were revealed and the hugs expanded in feeling and frequency. I could barely believe my eyes, ears, and my own words. A genuine authenticity was becoming apparent, without opposition or competitive inclinations. Men were connecting with their hearts, beyond any sense of "them" and "us." Billy, who had spoken in the morning with such a strong warning to be left alone, ended up at the very center of a ninety-six-man group hug and cracked open like an egg. Tears were now flowing, and several of the men, including our team of four, were sitting with our arms around each other's shoulders. The man who had scared me the most was seated right next to me. He had a heart of gold, a kind and gentle manner, and spoke with a soft Southern drawl. I found myself deeply loving this man, and we ended the day with our arms around each other, looking into one another's eyes. We exchanged many long good-byes, as if we had been at the most fun party ever and no one wanted to leave. I was extremely touched by the process of the day, the miracle of opening and connection that was occurring throughout Choices POD. As if beyond time, the outside world seemed to disappear, and the faces of the men, vivid in their oneness, blended with a vulnerable softening.

On the ride home, Michael, Vinny, John, and I exchanged heartfelt appreciation, and commented on how we felt toward each other, what we had noticed, and our personal impressions of this extraordinary day. There was both exhilaration and silent reflection. Each of us holds the keys to our self-made prison, and Michael's theme, "Incarceration of the Mind," had newfound and literal meaning. We had also found and nurtured the ability to work together. This was a defining moment in my life, as I was able to hear my own voice, recognize commonality and equanimity at a new level, and further dissolve the separation between others and myself. Whether relinquishing the keys, the paintbrush, or our binding beliefs, when we open ourselves to embracing curiosity, the walls soon come down.

Lloyd Barde *has an instinctive gift for producing music for creative movement, yoga classes, meditation, and healing, and has been an inspired source of sound advice for almost forty years. Lloyd's musical path has allowed him to journey through the entire musical spectrum as: record buyer, store owner, wholesale distributor, record label president, and mail-order entrepreneur. He now offers his expertise in several areas, including journalism (Music Editor for Common Ground magazine), artist representation and management, producing two prestigious monthly concert series in the Bay Area, and creating dance events as DJ Heartbeat. Each year he also serves on the Grammy Awards selection committee for New Age Music.*

The Ultimate Measure of a Man

by Harold Oberlander

The early seventies were an exciting time in the Catholic Church. With the Vatican II reforms being implemented, my wife Vaud and I had new hope for the church. As a convert I had finally found reasons to feel more comfortable in my chosen religion.

This all changed one day when Father Brown, the assistant priest in our parish, came to me as I was playing cards with some of my buddies in the office of our confinement hog barn on the edge of our small town. Since he was fairly new in town, I thought maybe he'd come for a tour of the barn, which at that time featured a new concept in feeding hogs. He asked to talk to me in private, and as we walked out of the office, I was shocked, though not terribly surprised, as he told me that he had heard nasty rumors about Father Smith, our pastor, and had set out to dispel those rumors.

Much to his dismay, Father Brown found that everything he had heard and even more was true. He had obtained numerous signed affidavits from people who testified to the damage Father Smith had done by sexually abusing them. This included young boys and girls, as well as several vulnerable women in our parish with whom he had had affairs. Because we lived in a small town, we knew many of these people. So when our priest friend asked for our support to get our pastor psychological help or, failing that, to get him dismissed from the priesthood, I replied that there was no way I could deny him support in a situation as bad as this. When I told Vaud about this awful turn of events, she was in entire agreement with me that we would do everything we could to change the situation.

In the ensuing days and weeks, I tried to enlist the support of other parishioners, a difficult task, but I did manage to get about twenty people out of two parishes, numbering two hundred plus families, who were willing to stand up for what was right. With assurance of the support of these few people, Father Brown called a meeting of the Parish Council members, the school principal, the bishop, and our pastor. At that meeting the bishop asked our pastor, Father Smith, if the rumors were true and amazingly, he admitted that all these rumors and more were true. We were sure this would be the end of the problem, but as time passed it became apparent that the bishop was not going to do anything about the situation. Father Brown and several nuns who were teaching in the school resigned from their jobs in protest. Despite this, few people were willing to face the reality of what was happening, preferring to live in denial.

Our pastor, Father Smith, helped this situation along by using the bulletin and other means to convince most of the parishioners that we and our group of supporters, whom he called rebels, were trying to destroy the church and the school. He actually encouraged people to run us out of town. In the March 7, 1971 bulletin he wrote:

> The parish and school are being done untold harm by these trouble-makers in the parish … I have held my supporters back because I did not want a parish civil war and have the school destroyed in the process—but my supporters' patience is getting thin and if the troublemakers continue I think they will have greater problems. I have not wanted the school and the parish destroyed. Is that what the rest of you people want? Is that what you want them to do?

After that letter, one of the prominent men in our parish told me that what the Protestants couldn't get done, we were trying to accomplish. I told him that, as painful as it was, I would surely do it again to stop this so-called holy man from doing more damage to people. Despite the growing anger against us, I knew that I had to stand up for what I strongly believed was right and do all I could to stop the hurt and pain our pastor was causing to so many innocent victims.

We had formed a prayer group with the few people who felt the same as we did. We gained courage from them to continue our fight to get our pastor help, or failing that, to get him dismissed from the priesthood. Vaud and I, as part of our protest, took our children out of the Catholic school and began to attend church in a neighboring town twenty-five miles away. The parents in our prayer group also took their children out of the school. Certainly, we would not continue to allow our children to attend a school where such a sick man was pastor and superintendent.

Our main strategy was to continue pressuring the bishop about the immoral things Father Smith had done, so we met with the bishop several times. At one point we took the police chief of our town along. He testified that our pastor had been picked up by the narcotics division in Albuquerque, New Mexico, during one of his frequent absences from the parish. Rolls of cash with consecutive serial numbers had been found in the trunk of his car. When the police learned he was a priest he was let go.

Eventually, we discovered that our pastor had used parish funds to invest in the stock market and had made huge profits, amounting to so much money that he became something of a real estate tycoon. He built one of the first motels at Disneyland in California and owned numerous motels throughout the western United States. These were places where he could take unsuspecting people for "vacations." Money gives power, and we suspected that part of the reason for the bishop's reluctance to right this horrible situation was that he was bribed by Father Smith, who was contributing substantial sums of money to the parish and diocese.

As a year went by and we continued our protests, my wife and I lost twin sons in a stillbirth. Our pastor, who never quit slandering us, had told Vaud's sister's religion class that there was a young couple in town who were cursed, and the proof was that they had lost twin sons. In a small town, there was no question whom he was talking about. We were devastated—talk about being kicked when we were down. When I made an appointment with Father Smith to buy a burial plot, he told me our babies would have to be buried by the fence, out of the consecrated part of the cemetery, because they had not been baptized. My first angry reaction was to say, "In that case, what is wrong with abortion?" His stance on the burial place for unbaptized babies was the last straw. I told him if he would not sell us a plot, I would take the babies to the Lutheran cemetery where my parents were buried. Apparently that would have been too much for him so he conceded to sell us the plot. The morning the funeral director buried our babies, Father Smith was nowhere to be found. He would not allow our assistant pastor to attend either, so the only other people present were two of my dear sisters-in-law.

One day Vaud got an unbelievably horrible letter in the mail. In part it read: "You are from the devil himself. How can you expect God to help and bless you when you are doing such devilish things? … You are really possessed by the devil … You should be run out of town." We had the letter examined by a hand-writing expert who concluded that in all probability it had been written by Father Smith. Father was a very powerful and controlling person. He ran the church and school with an iron fist. People did what he said when he said it. At that time many Catholics still saw the priest as second only to God.

Despite continuing harassment, we were determined to continue to "fight the good fight" for the sake of all those who had been abused and for those who might be abused in the future. I felt that the reason people didn't respond to

Father Smith's plea for help to run us out of town was because deep inside many of them knew the truth about him. But he had totally controlled them for eighteen years, and they were either afraid or didn't know how to respond.

After approximately three years, the situation was finally resolved when the pastor of another area church, who was sympathetic to our cause, drove to Montana where he knew four of the abused victims were living. He obtained written affidavits that were so compelling, the bishop finally decided Father Smith's tenure as pastor of the Catholic church in our town should end. At this point our pastor "threw in the towel" and left the church. In his farewell church bulletin, he managed to throw a few final salvos against the "rebels" when he detailed the amount of money they had cost the church by encouraging the resignation of several teachers and the assistant pastor. He gave detailed financial information and ended by writing: "You see now why I stayed when the rebels tried to chase me out. At the time of the rebellion you did not have ... " Then he listed all the wonderful things he had done for the parish. The last line was written in capital letters: "THE DEVIL VERSUS CHRIST IS ALWAYS THE BATTLE."

Our long, painful journey to get this man the kind of help he needed to overcome his sexual addictions did not have a happy ending because as far as we knew he never got the help he needed. We did see to it that he would never be the pastor of a parish again. To his credit, when he died he left a large sum of money to the school, to Mother Theresa, and to family members, as well as to a priest and several charitable foundations. Unfortunately, little of this money found its way into the hands of the people who needed it because the IRS and lawyers got most of it. He had used church money to make his fortune and the people running his trust were not very capable of retaining the money for its intended use by the church. The bishop continued to ignore the situation and didn't bother to say anything to the parishioners when Father Smith left, so we were never exonerated of the supposed evil we had tried to do to the parish. To this day, there are people who are still convinced we tried to destroy the parish and school.

We moved on ten years later to buy land in South Dakota, where we have had a successful farming operation for many years. We are happy parishioners in a wonderful Episcopal church, where we are loved and respected.

In the midst of all our turmoil, Father Brown had written to us: "We are sharing in the terrible hurt, frustration, and anger that many have suffered over the years in your town. It takes great faith to change any situation. Where there is that great of a faith, there must of necessity be great love." We kept the faith and we surely found the joy of great love in the people who supported us throughout this terrible time. Although none of the victims ever thanked us, we know they couldn't help but be grateful for the knowledge that a sick man would never again be in a position of power where he could harm people. We found that we were not disillusioned by this difficult experience, but were stronger for having "stuck to our guns."

A quote from Martin Luther King, Jr., given to us by Father Brown at that time still means a lot to me: "The ultimate measure of a man is not where he stands in moments of comfort and convenience, but where he stands at times of challenge and controversy."

Harold "Obie" Oberlander, born in 1931, is the thirteenth child of a German-Russian couple who homesteaded in North Dakota. He attended grade school in a one-room country school and graduated from high school in New England, North Dakota. He served four years in the U.S. Air Force, two of them in Germany. A lifelong grain farmer in both Dakotas, he built the first confinement hog barn in North Dakota. Harold is married, is the father of five children, and has fourteen grandchildren. He is active in the Episcopal Church, having served three terms on the vestry. He has been a hospice volunteer since 1984 and since retiring from farming, he visits the housebound and helps his sons on Oberlander Farms.

From the Ashes of This Culture

by Jordan Brody

I guess I have a curse. Stained perhaps from birth with an ability to see the tears that stain the streets that surround my suburban island. Sometimes when I am driving down a road like any other, the loud monotony of traffic, interfering with the natural flow of my thoughts, seeing lifeless bank after lifeless shopping mall, I imagine everything I see vanishing, dissolving, ceasing to be. Not the people—of course not the children, still adorned with the wings of their yet uncrushed hearts. I wish the façade would fade, because of the uncrushed hearts, and too, the crushed hearts that could still recover. And so I could breathe fully, the wind could flow freely, and the stars could be more than a respite from a chaos-driven nightmare.

How did I come to feel others' pain acutely? The past is both a window into my mental evolution and a window into the yet uncertain. So as we walk this twisted cobblestone path, enhanced by the backdrop of an electric sky, a possible future emerges—not just my future, but also that of a more humane world. This is not the 1960s, and I won't naively carve a sculpture adorned with flowers and fairytales—forging this new world will require struggle and incalculable tragedy. Since I feel that much of our current world could aptly be described as a perpetual war on humanity itself, the aforementioned tragedy appears a relatively small price to pay.

From the initial moments of my first grade year, my inherent shyness sketched a silhouette of a less-than-friendly world. Soon after entering the classroom, two students made it their mission to make me feel insecure and inadequate, extending this taunting throughout the year. My well-maintained façade of outgoingness and disruption for disruption's sake masked my underlying insecurity. This experience, while not overly traumatic, perhaps sowed the initial seeds of my difficulty relating and connecting to others, and my consequent lack of identification with mass society. My shyness, melded with a difficult early school experience, made it easier to accept harsh injustices that would later shatter my innocence.

I'm at a dinner party tarnished by awkward, trivial interactions and disembodied laughter. Inane commentary from the "idiot box" insulates the innocence from intellect and from humanity. I don't know what everyone else is chattering on about, and nor do I care. *Echoes prodding me into conformity: If only I would try harder to be sociable...* A distant voice mentions that the new gym is incredibly beautiful. How is it that we can "appreciate beauty" in a metal cage lined with workout *machines*, yet we cannot appreciate beauty in a bird or a sunset? To reaffirm their humanity, these people need to fiercely attack the conditions that have stifled them. Perhaps they can draw inspiration from the occasions when the veneer is peeled away from the façade of order, as chaos demonstrates briefly that *it* could be the new, healthier order, if only given its time to blossom from the ashes of this crazy culture.

At age fifteen, I found myself poring over articles about atrocities perpetrated by the Israeli government. Confronting my family with my newly formed views was initially met with considerable hostility—the inevitable consequence of expressing unpopular perspectives. At least family members and friends showed interest. The rest of society seemed immersed in an illusory world where consumer products were deified and reality was repressed to prevent it from surfacing. So be it. I would carve my world on the borderlines, and whoever propelled me into their grand delusion would be met with my wrath. It sounds romantic, but for me, it has proven extremely difficult, as conformity and familiarity are often as addicting as they are paralyzing. Ultimately, it took more than a negative first grade experience and some Internet research to spur me away from the dominant culture.

"They murdered my uncle"—the words of a seventeen-year-old Palestinian sharing her pain with her enemies. As I listened attentively, heart palpitating rapidly, I knew unquestioningly that she had every justification for devoting her life to the cessation of the underlying conditions that had rendered her uncle lifeless; for a healthy world is a pipedream without a consciousness that infuses compassion with rage, the yin and yang of our beingness. Rana has a smile that conveys a love of life woven through the sorrow of a birthright denied. I wondered how much pain one can endure and still maintain a radiant smile, and then, whether the cries of every child forced to incinerate his dreams to complete the bloodstained jigsaw of Western industrial society, and every Afghan child crippled by U.S. sanctions and slaughter, could use her pain as a conduit for aggressively reclaiming their humanity.

My experience with a program called Building Bridges for Peace strengthened my opposition to injustice by bringing a human dimension to my research. However, I took issue with the program's chief doctrine: that we should empathize *equally* with the Israelis and Palestinians, attempting to find "common ground," overlooking the underlying governmental power dynamic. Ironically, the experience affirmed my developing ethos that meaningful resistance is necessary and just.

Staring deeply into Rana's eyes, I wondered how someone—*anyone*—from the United States of America could possess the degree of disassociation from physical reality, the moral-pedestal-climbing egotism, to tell her that she did not have a right to dedicate every fiber of her being to resisting the murderous governmental apparatus that had caused her, her family, and her people, so much needless suffering. It seems that most American liberals exhibit fake neutrality and peace advocacy by saying that they condemn acts of violence on *both* sides. In a single month, fourteen hundred Gazans were massacred by Israel. To attempt to find "common ground" with the "other side" through shrill screams as white phosphorous burns, let alone enact meaningful societal change, is futile. As the roof caves in, lives are lost; all that remains are the tearful memories of families under siege.

I left the Building Bridges for Peace experience with friendships gained, and returned home to the stark reality that the sugar-coated side of the mainstream political spectrum offered little more for my conception of the world than did the neoconservative fanaticism I so despised. A further shattering of ties to the dominant paradigm, laying the bricks for a foray into resistance.

Sparked by separation from mass society, fueled by indignation, I waded into resistance's waters. "May I see your ID?" Waiting to enter the airport security checkpoint, I responded factually, "I can't find my ID." I soon found it, but clearly I was "testing the system," so I was asked to submit to additional screening. Already enraged by the recent, highly degrading "security enhancements," I refused, noting that as an allegedly free human being, this was a clear violation of my rights. "A violation of your rights?" a TSA official responded in considerable disgust, a tacit admission of the dissolution of our freedoms. A policeman searched me and I was denied access to the flight.

The two-day train ride back provided the picturesque antithesis of the airport experience. Peering out at the vast expanses of still-undeveloped wilderness, I became infused with the awareness that freedom still exists. I feel in my primordial depths the felling of trees for profit—my stifled cries. If your inner flame were being extinguished, what would you *want* to do? What would you *really* do, given this system's legal confines? There's a reason why rape victims sometimes kill their rapists despite the legal and emotional deterrents: resisting oppression is natural and cathartic. The airport experience demonstrated that while people are being starved and murdered from Gaza to Iraq, people are also having their dignity denied here at home, allowing me to internalize the pervasiveness of injustice in our world. Fully aware that my recalcitrance wouldn't undermine the TSA's unjust policies, I practiced noncompliance to resist oppression and to reaffirm my dignity.

In the wake of the TSA interaction, I began pondering my leukemia diagnosis of a year prior. In March 2009, I found its ethereal echo reverberating through some facet of my being. Four days later I was out of the hospital and taking a daily medication, but I was plagued with debilitating side effects for the next few months, before my body adjusted to the change. Through this process, I learned that sometimes surrender is necessary. It would do no good to combat conditions beyond my control. Consequently, I broadened my exploration of resistance by pondering the surrender/resistance dichotomy as it pertains to our reactions to crises. Our medical industry spends an exorbitant sum of money to prolong life, to subjugate the natural process of aging to its clinical control.

Yet we make little effort to control the fullness and richness of our existences. We seldom even meaningfully resist the instruments of domination in our own neighborhoods—the cops that murder with impunity, the surveillance cameras that increasingly transform the landscape into a large, open prison, or the decimation of the environment that sustains us, for corporate profit. We are distracted with control over trivialities, while we choose to not attempt to control what we *must*: that which is causing incalculable misery.

When confronted with injustice, one is seldom encouraged to resist. Far too often, we succumb to those who seek to obliterate our birthright to be valued members of healthy communities. Individuals are too often blamed for the emotional traumas that beset them. For my part, I reject the attempts of the formal channels to implicate me in my enslavement, and intend not to succumb to the doctrine of moderation and management. I recognize that passion, compassion, rage, and whatever other unsanctioned emotion I feel, is my natural reaction to conditions that I have been subjugated under without being afforded the opportunity to participate actively in the elaboration of my life. I intend to lash out against the institutional forces that have stolen from me my birthright, perhaps amassing strength enough to pierce the false prisms that have been constructed as the arbiters of our very consciousness.

Behind every manicured suburban lawn, and apparent in every bullet-hole-ridden ghetto, are souls denied the chance to float free in a world of their own making. Maybe you were raped, or beaten … Maybe you lost a friend to suicide. Maybe you blamed yourself for your parents' divorce; maybe you never could relate to others; maybe your anxiety crippled you. Maybe you dealt with cancer. Now realize that there are two million prisoners in America, most locked away on nonviolent offenses, many drug-related. Psychologist Carl Rogers said, "Behind everyone's darkest secret is a universal story." Have you ever smoked a joint? Wished you could lash out against your boss? What would it take to regain some sliver of your youthful innocence? If you have been beaten, would you like to prevent others from being beaten? If you are a rape victim, imagine your struggle being generalized—imagine no rape victims. As sadism has been institutional-ized, to impart hope would be self-defeating—too many have hoped, and conse-quently, haven't tried.

I guess I have a strength. Blessed perhaps from birth with an ability to see the tears that stain the streets that surround my suburban island. I know not whether the cracks can be leveraged to unearth the beauty buried deep underneath this culture's grand tragedy. I do know that the "peace and love" approach has been rendered futile by the power of insanity. And I know that we must try. I cannot embark on this journey alone. Our world is being murdered by depraved men and women who care only for the perpetuation of the death that is a reflection of their brokenness, and as much as I'd like to fight without reservation for the dawn-ing of a world where laughter is not confined, I am scared. Scared for what this world will be when all the wilderness is gone. Scared for what this world will be when the surveillance state extinguishes the last slivers of privacy, freedom, and humanity—or when our chains further tighten. And I am scared to fight back, knowing that anyone who meaningfully resists the status quo may face the wrath of a State that prioritizes self-perpetuation *far* above justice.

So I implore you: Join me in the formation of a viable movement of struggle. Imagine your loved ones in chains; then realize that they already are. Recover your imagination and your dreams from their ashes. One million dead Iraqis— police murdering Blacks with impunity—*this is not normalcy*. Realize that violence defined as the antithesis of and the combating of a system that is fundamentally rotten at its core is in fact compassion, a love indescribable that could spread throughout the world if only we realized that we have nothing to lose and a healthy world to gain, a world without countless needless deaths from "workplace accidents," a world without empire and so much unnecessary misery.

Close your eyes. Return to your youthful innocence, before the scars and glass slits embedded themselves within your heart. Imagine what it would take to realize a healthy world.

Let me illustrate my deepest yearnings. A falcon sweeps through fertile lands; waves collapse rhythmically on shores; birdsongs radiate into night skies, piercing through the bark of trees into their existential cores; the snow blankets industrial civilization, briefly muting the insanity—the merest sampling of the natural, cathartic, wild, undomesticated, crystalline, existent still in this late hour; masses passionately battle the Illegitimate Police Force of the State; salons like those of old, featuring geopolitical and sociological discussions in dimly lit attics; printing self-published zines, keeping literacy and sustained concentration alive at least in the underground, if it is elsewhere extinguished; climbing a large oak tree, staying there day and night to prevent another corporation from destroying another piece of the Earth for profit; overlooking an animal research/torture facility, ready to destroy their sadistic research; playing on the piano a spontaneously composed ode to innocence that reflects and enhances the inner workings of your palpitating heart and soul; displaying art on urban streets; growing trees, fruit, roots, seeds ... Hopping a train en route to the Transcendental Forever with nary a thought save the repeated mutterings of a homeless man under a bridge you pitied when you should have heeded his wisdom. He said: *"The dominant culture must be fully destroyed for beauty to flourish."* And he meant it.

Jordan Brody was born on September 11, 1991. Having long recognized the insanity of modern society, he has decided to blend his interest in politics with his personal experiences, to spark the hearts and minds of those who are towing the line between accepting and rejecting the perspectives perpetuated by the dominant culture. Aside from his desire to witness a return to humanness on a societal and global scale, Jordan loves animals and enjoys spending time with his two dogs.

The Impact of My Near-Death Experience

by Rev. Rudi Gelsey

Some may wonder, perhaps even you do, whether near-death experiences really exist. According to a recent Gallup Poll, 5 percent of the U.S. population—or one out of twenty people—claim to have had a near-death experience. The figure surprised me. My guess would have been that I was more special.

At age eight a transformative experience occurred in my life. At midnight my mother Erika drove me to a hospital a hundred miles away on the recommendation of the local village doctor in Zalaber, Hungary. A student intern examined me and told Mother I needed an operation for osteomyelitis, a critical bone infection. Erika asked whether the hospital's surgeon could be called to perform the procedure. The student replied it would take the surgeon at least half an hour to get to the hospital and by then I would be dead. Meanwhile, in the receiving room, I had a near-death out-of-body experience. Deceased ancestors and angels greeted me, although I could not identify the ancestors nor did I see any wings on the angels. They appeared transparent and clad in white feminine garb.

Though I did not question myself at the time, in hindsight I am surprised I did not meet a holy figure like Jesus or Mary. Such an encounter might have been natural in a 96 percent Roman Catholic country such as Austria, my birthplace. In my case, perhaps the message suggests that God is spirit and therefore invisible. A very pleasant feeling replaced the anxiety and confusion. Suddenly the vision stopped when, on the operating table, the intern used his craftsmanship to remove the pus from a bone in my upper arm.

When I told my mother about the near-death experience, she dismissed my vision as a hallucination. Mom indicated that high fever causes such a condition. She tried to convince me that the nature of the phenomenon consisted of a bodily reaction accompanied by the transition from life to death. As an eight-year-old, that explanation struck me as a lot of gobbledygook.

After returning to Vienna, Austria, I related my experience to my father's butler, Martinek. Good-humored and down-to-earth, he offered me a different perspective. "You might as well be grateful that you survived." Then, with a big smile, he added, "In gratitude, you and I should do what we can to make this a better world." His invitation has resonated in my heart ever since. A short sentence, but with huge impact.

The osteomyelitis turned out to be recalcitrant. The staphylococcus traveled through my body like commuters, causing recurrent episodes and prolonged absences from school. It occurred to me that if I wanted to "make this a better world," I had to prepare myself well. Over time, I availed myself of my parents' library, which filled the walls of a large room. My efforts led me to German classics like Goethe, Schiller, and Hesse. Books by Goethe particularly struck me, especially one about a young man committing suicide. This work led many contemporary youths to follow the character's example. Not me, however, for that would bring the seed of my mission to a premature inglorious end.

Another Goethe theme attracted me, that of a young man who sold his soul to the devil. Just as Satan in the Bible tempts Jesus, Mephistopheles offers Faust anything he desires provided that at Faust's death the devil can take his soul. The story frightened me and made me decide not to follow Faust's example.

On the positive side, I loved Schiller's plays exhorting freedom and justice. At age fourteen, a performance of *Wilhelm Tell* by local farmers near Lucerne, Switzerland, made a big impression on me. Hermann Hesse in his book *Siddhartha* introduced me to the life and compassion of Buddha. Being repeatedly bedridden, where a good library was at my bidding, had the unintended consequence of starting me on the path suggested by Martinek.

These early experiences started to manifest while in college in Geneva, Switzerland, where I became a strong advocate for a European Union and even a democratic world federation. My professors in political science convinced me these would be the best ways to ensure permanent peace. Unfortunately, the beginning of the cold war between the West and the former Soviet Union prevented my dream from becoming a reality.

In despair I left for Montreal, Canada. In a new country and on a different continent, my interest and ability to function in the political realm abated. My life centered around getting married at age twenty-four. My wife's serious illness four winters later was followed by a tragic parting of the ways as my partner returned to Europe. I drove my wife Aggie and our child Florence to the boat and parked at the quay of the Montreal-St. Lawrence Port. After a tearful farewell, I sat in the car for five minutes debating with myself. *Should I step on the gas and plunge forward into the icy river or back up and give life another chance?* During that pivotal and painful decision-making process, the words of Martinek jumped into my mind: "In gratitude, you and I should do what we can to make this a better world." And so my story continues.

My Montreal years were not consumed by tragedy. I found inspiration to change my religious affiliation from Catholic to Unitarian. Six years after becoming a member of the Church of the Messiah, my life moved in a new direction. I enrolled at the University of Chicago Divinity School, a prelude to my forty-one years of Unitarian ministry.

Quickly, my new vocation merged with history in the making. During the spring of 1965, I responded to a "call and challenge" presented by Rev. Martin Luther King, Jr. In support of his civil rights campaign for the right of black citizens to vote, I flew to Selma, Alabama. I joined the Southern Christian Leadership Conference walk from our church headquarters to city hall to pray for two people who had recently been killed. One victim, a black teenager, had thrown himself upon his grandmother to protect her from being shot by a trigger-happy police officer in their home. While exiting a local diner, the second victim, a Unitarian colleague, had received a deadly blow to his skull from an angry resident violently opposed to integration. That minister had spoken at my church in Philadelphia the Sunday after the assassination of John F. Kennedy.

When city hall in Selma denied permission for the walk permit, we heard through loudspeakers that we would march nonetheless. The organizers asked the ministers to lead up front. Fear flowed through my veins. I went into a corner of the AME church and debated with myself. With a wife at home, should I go to the front of the line, or remain mixed in with the crowd where I might be safer? I decided to join the front ranks. My initiation into civil disobedience for a better world felt like a baptism by fire.

My next civil disobedience experience occurred six years later, when a media source publicized the secret bombing of Cambodia during the Vietnam War, ultimately landing me in the "clink." As co-chair of Clergy and Laity Concerned about Vietnam in Westchester County, New York, my desire to make a difference swung once more into concrete action. A group of us from all across the nation attended the U.S. Senate hearings, where legislators discussed the dangerous escalation of the war. The Senate adjourned without declaring the secret Cambodian bombings illegal. In protest, we moved from the gallery to the Russell Senate Office Building Rotunda, where we sat, legs crossed, on the cold, hard floor. Five minutes before closing, marshals warned us to leave the grounds by 5:30 p.m. We did not budge. Unceremoniously, the officers carried us to buses waiting outside.

Humiliation gripped me as the officers booked and fingerprinted me. I wanted to let my wife know I would not come home that night. The officers bluntly refused my request for a telephone call, violating my rights. After some of us had been processed, we heard a piercing scream—a woman's voice. Later we learned that one of the protestors refused fingerprinting. Thereupon, two marshals held her down while another grabbed her by the throat and choked her unconscious. The woman's offense consisted of her plea, "I'm not a criminal." The next morning, while awaiting our hearing, we learned the women's toilets were in full view of male guards. The guards directed catcalls at them, such as "I like your butt." Our entire group was appalled by these tactics.

In the male quarters, each cell contained one bunk for eight people, requiring us to take turns lying down throughout the bleak night. To keep our spirits high, we sang freedom songs for a couple of hours. I slept on the bunk all of half an hour. By the time of our hearing, we looked bleary-eyed. Most of our crew chose to plead guilty to the charge of disobeying the marshal's instructions, paying the fifty-dollar fine. Out of a hundred and fifty activists, only nine of us pleaded "not guilty." We considered standing up for justice in a society acting in unjust ways our moral obligation as citizens.

In retrospect, our decision seems foolhardy. At the time, we did not know that our penalty, if we were convicted, could have been up to a year in prison. As we waited for weeks to appear before the judge, I became concerned how a prison sentence might affect my ministry and livelihood. My anxiety increased when receiving the summons: "We the people of the United States of America against Rudi Gelsey and others … " How could I stand up against a whole nation?

In my hometown of Vienna, in front of city hall, stands a majestic statue of the victorious Greek goddess of justice, Athena. In her right arm she carries a spear as an expression of her fight for justice. On our "judgment day," we were happy to report that *Pallas Athena* (the divine power of Athena) was with us. The judge declared us "not guilty."

Along with my lifelong desire for a better world, another curious element surfaced. Besides butler Martinek's recommendation and the Gallup Poll's findings, extensive research has been published on how near-death experiences impact the survivors. The most common consequence appears as an enhanced interest in and practice of spirituality. Accordingly, I studied Silva Mind Control, a method of healing by creating states of altered consciousness. Furthermore, Dr. Carl Jung's psychology fascinated me. Today, I am still inspired and enlivened by almost thirty years of Sufi meditation practices. The Buddhist worldview attracts me and the mythology of the world's religions captivates me. In that spirit, I authored a self-published book, *Conversation with Sacred Masters: Bringing the World Together.*

Enough reporting about my various experiences. Despite having worked as a civil rights, environmental protection, and antiwar advocate, I still had lingering doubts whether I had done enough to fulfill Martinek's invitation to work for a better world. In civil rights, we sometimes take two steps forward, only to retreat again. Unnecessary wars continue raging. We are far from having succeeded in creating a sustainable planet with peace, liberty, and justice. The encouragement of Martinek still resonates in my mind and heart and guides me, as an octogenarian, to leave a legacy of how perpetual peace can be ours. In that regard, I am currently, at age eighty-five, writing a book called *Perpetual Peace: Pipe Dream or Possibility?*

Rev. Rudi C. Gelsey, *a native of Vienna, Austria, received a Master's Degree in Political Science, from the University of Geneva, in Switzerland, and a Bachelor of Divinity from the University of Chicago. During his retirement in Williamsburg, Virginia, he taught "Human Civilization, from the Renaissance to the Present Day," at Hampton University. He was a member of the Swiss Alpine Club. At his alma mater, he was tennis champion for two years. At age 75, he swam across the James River, in Virginia. He is the author of* Perpetual Peace, Pipedream or Possibility? *Rudi can be contacted at: rudigelsey@eathlink.net.*

Afterword

All of the stories you have read in this anthology were submitted by men wanting to touch or benefit you in some special way through sharing their own life experiences. Please let us know how you were moved, inspired, or empowered by our personal essays.

We invite you to regularly read our blogs, and to share your comments and your own experiences with our ever-growing community of men aspiring toward the ideal of wholeness, at www.mensanthology.com.

You may be interested in purchasing multiple copies of *Ordinary Men, Extraordinary Lives: Defining Moments* for your family and friends, network, community, business, or clients. You may also want to recommend this anthology for high school or college classes or for men's groups. To receive a volume discount, excellent service, and direct shipping, please write docjimsharon@yahoo.com or visit our website, www.mensanthology.com.

We encourage you to avail yourself of the services offered by many of our contributing authors, such as coaching, consulting, and speaking. Please directly contact the specific authors of interest to you via the contact information provided in the biographies at the end of each story.

Jim Sharon, Ed.D., and his select team of speakers are available to present or facilitate seminars and programs on topics related to themes in this book. Please contact Jim at docjimsharon@yahoo.com to arrange a presentation.

For information about bringing Whole Man Expo to your city, or to coordinate that event in a large city in the United States or abroad, please contact Whole Man Expo founder Jim Sharon at docjimsharon@yahoo.com.

About the Editor

Jim Sharon, Ed.D., has served as a pioneer in the contemporary movements involving men's development, wellness, and conflict resolution. He began his professional career as a mental health center psychologist in Harrisburg, Pennsylvania, and in Norfolk, Virginia, from 1970 to 1973. After completing his doctoral degree in counseling psychology at the University of Northern Colorado in Greeley in 1977, he remained in Colorado to work as a counselor in private practice, as a consultant, and as a part-time college and continuing education instructor.

With his wife Ruth, Dr. Sharon founded and co-directed Greeley Center for Human Development, which offered a wide variety of wellness and personal growth programs and integrative health services, from 1976 to 1980. During 1977, he began his private practice as a psychotherapist with an established Greeley counseling group. Jim and Ruth joined Carl Kuhlman, Ph.D. and Associates in Denver in 1984, and since becoming licensed as a psychologist in 1989, Jim has had his own counseling practice with Ruth in Centennial, Colorado: The AFDA Group, Inc. The business name was derived from the extensive consultation and training the Sharons led, beginning in 1989, based on an original model of conflict resolution developed by Ruth.

Having a special interest in wellness, Dr. Sharon has published *Holistic Health Inventory* and articles in professional journals on stress management and burnout.

A member of Psi Chi, a national psychology honor society, and Kappa Delta Pi, a national honor society in education, Dr. Sharon has been listed in *Who's Who in Human Services*.

After participating in a couple of peer groups with men friends at the onset of the men's movement in the late 1970s, Dr. Sharon began co-facilitating therapy groups and weekend retreats for men. He later became involved in several other leaderless men's groups. He has also worked extensively with men and their partners/wives in couple's counseling, and with Ruth has taught seminars and led retreats titled Secrets of a Soulful Marriage.

In addition to compiling and editing *Ordinary Men, Extraordinary Lives: Defining Moments*, Jim is founder/coordinator of Whole Man Expo, presented by the Sharons' relatively recent wellness-centered subsidiary, Energy for Life. This men's anthology will be launched September 10, 2011, at Whole Man Expo at the Sheraton Denver Tech Center Hotel, Greenwood Village, Colorado. Jim's vision is to expand Whole Man Expo in the Denver area and to introduce it in other large cities in the United States and abroad.

Jim has been married to Ruth Sharon since 1970 and is the father of three adult children; he also has a granddaughter. In his spare time, he enjoys spiritual development, reading, various ball sports, swimming, hiking, movies, and classic board and card games.